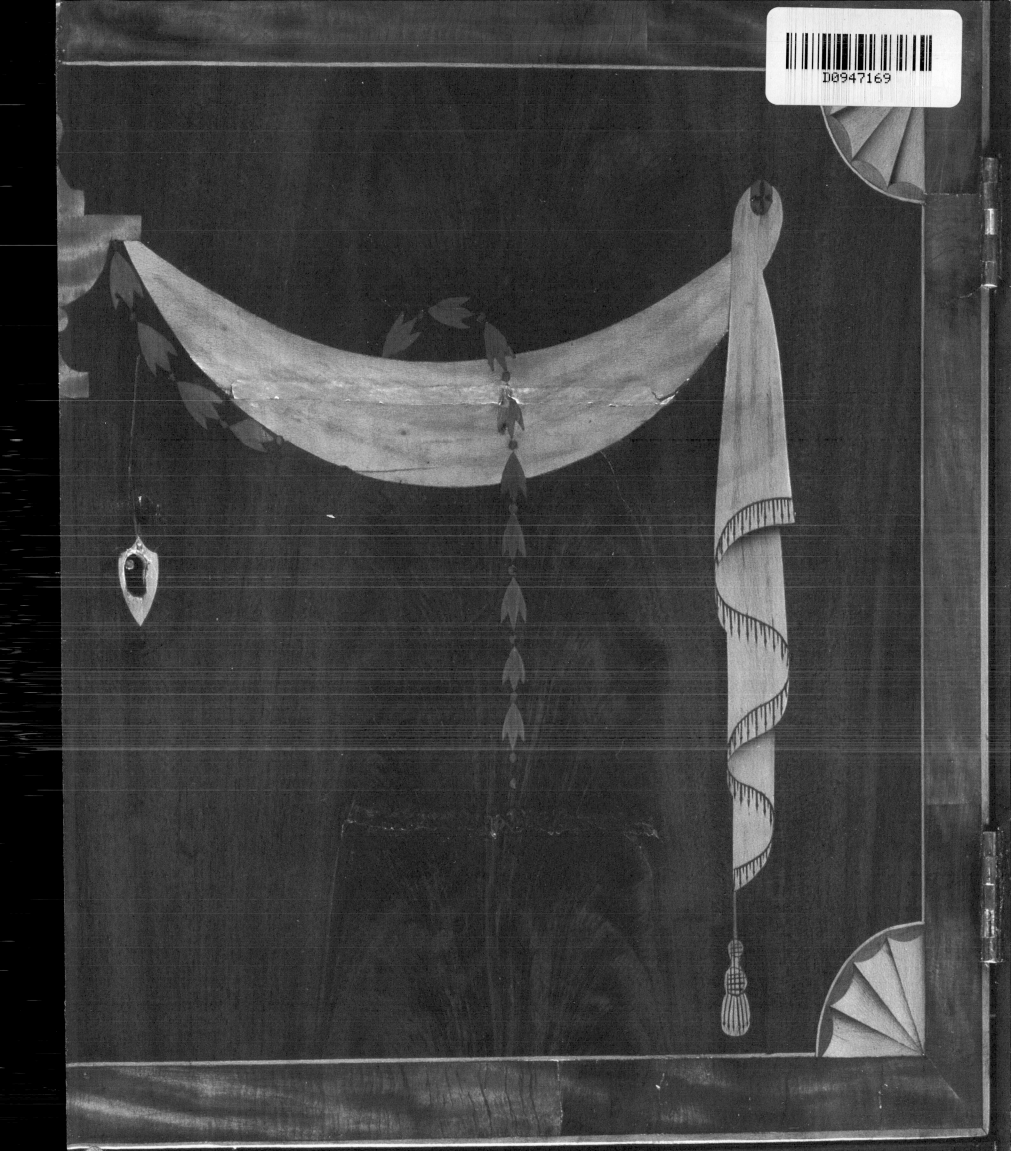

American Furniture
from the Kaufman Collection

0010457

American Furniture
from the Kaufman Collection

J. Michael Flanigan

INTRODUCTORY ESSAYS

Wendy A. Cooper
Morrison H. Heckscher
Gregory R. Weidman

National Gallery of Art, Washington

DISTRIBUTED BY
Harry N. Abrams, Inc., New York

Selections from the Collection of
George M. and Linda H. Kaufman
and the Kaufman Americana Foundation

Photographs by Dirk Bakker

Edited by Judith Rice Millon
Typeset in Sabon and Snell Roundhand
by Composition Systems Incorporated, Falls Church, Virginia
Printed by Princeton Polychrome Press, Princeton, New Jersey
on Potlach Quintessence paper
Designed by Frances P. Smyth

Library of Congress Cataloging-in-Publication Data

Flanigan, J. Michael.
American furniture from the Kaufman collection.

Bibliography: p.
Includes index.
1. Furniture, Colonial—United States—Exhibitions.
2. Furniture—United States—History—18th century—
Exhibitions. 3. Furniture—United States—History—
19th century—Exhibitions. 4. Kaufman, George M.—
Art collections—Exhibitions. 5. Kaufman, Linda—
Art collections—Exhibitions. 6. Furniture—Private collections—
United States—Exhibitions. I. National
Gallery of Art (U.S.) II. Title.
NK2406.F58 1986   749.214'074'0153   86-21844
ISBN 0-89468-099-4   ISBN 0-8109-1864-1 (Abrams)

Contents

Foreword

One of America's first great art forms was furniture. Like our early great buildings in the Georgian manner, and later in the Federal and neoclassical styles, many of the decorative arts crafted for interior use blended aesthetics with practicality. It has been a particularly native and democratic impulse in American culture to seek both refinement of form and usefulness of purpose.

Over the century from the period just before the American Revolution to the full flourishing of the Republic in the decades before the Civil War, American architecture and furniture alike demonstrate the importation, adaptation, and transformation of inherited European forms.

Aside from being one of the largest and most refined collections of early American furniture in private hands, the works in this exhibition lent by George and Linda Kaufman exemplify American craftsmanship at its highest quality and offer vivid lessons in the evolution of national and regional tastes during this highly productive period of our nation's development. It begins with impressive examples of the Dutch style known as William and Mary, at the beginning of the eighteenth century. Among its later glories are elegant pieces in the American Queen Anne and rococo style. The collection is rounded off with the imposing presence of objects made in the Federal and Empire phases of neoclassicism during the first half of the nineteenth century. Their bold shapes and ornamentation reflect the exuberant self-confidence of the established American nation.

In addition, the Kaufman collection offers a marvelous opportunity for comparing the different tastes and achievements developed in the great regional centers of production, such as Boston, Newport, Philadelphia, and New York. Even more, we have the chance to savor the particular refinements of design and execution attributable to the most celebrated individual craftsmen of the colonies and early republic, including John Townsend, John and Thomas Seymour, and Duncan Phyfe.

Excepting the furniture assembled for the Diplomatic Reception Rooms of the State Department, there are no permanent collections or surveys of American furniture in Washington's museums. As with other fields in which the National Gallery does not actively collect, we take the opportunity to show them through our exhibition program. Thus we are especially pleased to be able to present to a wide audience examples of American furniture at its best and seldom seen by our public.

This undertaking has been coordinated on behalf of the Gallery by J. Michael Flanigan, administrator of the Kaufman Collection. His kindness and hard work have been welcomed by all the members of our own staff, and he has served as an able intermediary with Wendy Cooper, Morrison Heckscher, Gregory Weidman and our colleagues elsewhere.

This exhibition follows in the spirit of *In Praise of America: American Decorative Arts, 1650–1830*, which was seen at the Gallery in 1980 and included distinguished loans from the Kaufman collection. Indeed, the Kaufmans have been notably generous to many institutions, not just in lending objects but in helping to fund catalogues of museum collections and sponsor scholarly research in the field. The Gallery is pleased to acknowledge their generous friendship, as donors to its Patrons Permanent Fund and members of our Collectors Committee. On this occasion we gratefully welcome their loans of American furniture and the chance to share temporarily these treasures with our many visitors.

J. Carter Brown
Director

cat. no. 36, detail

Acknowledgments

I am first and foremost indebted to George and Linda Kaufman for giving me the opportunity to publish their collection. This catalogue is only the latest in their continuing efforts to ensure that the finest examples of American furniture are available to the public through books. They have allowed me to crawl under, upend, and disassemble the furniture with which they live. They have also been taskmasters, demanding accuracy and honesty in the examination and publication of all that can be learned of the furniture in the time devoted to this project.

The essayists, who also functioned as advisors—Morrison Heckscher, Wendy Cooper, and Gregory Weidman—have helped guide a novice through the terrors of a first effort. Most notably I thank Morrie Heckscher, whose reassurance and counsel were much appreciated. Also, my wife, Gregory, who has shown great forbearance for the project through both our wedding and the birth of our first child.

The broadness of the collection has brought me in contact with scholars throughout the field. Their insights and expertise are, I hope, evident in the entries. Their quick and thorough responses to my inquiries were a great help, especially in the early stages of the project. Among them are Jayne Stokes, Baltimore Museum of Art; Ronald Hurst, Colonial Williamsburg; Dean Lahikainen, Essex Institute; Lynn Hastings, Hampton National Historic Site; Philip Zea, Historic Deerfield; Margaret Stearns, Museum of the City of New York; Luke Beckerdite and Bradford Rauschenberg, Museum of Early Southern Decorative Arts; Jonathan Fairbanks, Museum of Fine Arts, Boston; Jean Burks and Beatrice Garvan, Philadelphia Museum of Art; Christopher Monkhouse, Rhode Island School of Design; Brock Jobe and Robert Mussey, Society for the Preservation of New England Antiquities; Donald Fennimore and Nancy Richards, Winterthur Museum; Charles Venable, Winterthur Program in Early American Culture; Jenine Sherry, Yale Art Gallery; Phillip Zimmerman, York County Historical Society; and Page Talbott.

Other professionals have also helped provide information on the history of various pieces in the collection and closely related objects. Among these are Sue St. Amant, Robert Lee Gill, Sylvia Tearston, Joseph K. Ott, Jeanne Vibert, Arthur and Zeke Liverant, Bernard Levy, Nancy Skinner, Donald Webster, Thomas Schwenke, Robert T. Trump, Stuart Feld, Joe Lionetti, the late John Walton, Charles Dorman, Susan Detweiller, and Jan Herda. Harold and Albert Sack deserve a special note. Their knowledge, and willingness to share it, proved almost as valuable as the objects they discovered.

Special thanks go out to Georgeann Linthicum who sifted through the entire run of *The Magazine Antiques*, and to Brad Rauschenberg of MESDA who did the microanalysis of wood samples.

The excellent photographs are the work of Dirk Bakker of the Detroit Institute of Arts and his assistant, Steve Yungquist. The photo session that produced them required the coordinated efforts of a number of people including Jeff and Jim Aldrich, Jack Brown, Robert Brown, Daniel Hall, and especially Walter Raynes.

The preparation of the manuscript, organization of the files, and my numerous inquiries were handled with aplomb by Jodi Mullins, Jean Frantz, and Rosalynne Dillon who also compiled the indices.

The staff of the National Gallery of Art provided both expert guidance and inspiration throughout the project. Designers Gill Ravenel and Mark Leithauser and editors Frances Smyth and Judith Millon gave form to the exhibition and focus to the catalogue.

The responsibility for any errors that may have survived the contributions of all these people is entirely my own. I wish to thank those whose support and encouragement predate this project: my family, especially Margaret R. Donahue and the late Raymond J. Donahue; also W. Lee Beck, Harry D. Berry, Jr., Stiles T. Colwill, Frederick S. Koontz, and William Weaver.

J. Michael Flanigan
August 1986

cat. no. 91

Note to the Reader

The heading for each entry follows these general rules: The name for an object is that, which when known, is the one most probably used at the time of manufacture. The dates give the widest time period possible. The regions are based on the idea of a style center and not geographic boundaries. The materials do not list inlays or veneers but are limited to primary and structural elements. Those woods identified by microanalysis are marked by an asterisk. All other identifications have been by eye or by a ten-power hand lens. Veneers are cited in the *Construction and condition* notes. The dimensions are taken at the widest point in each direction. They may be thought of as describing the smallest box into which the piece would fit. The dimensions are given for each object as seen in the photograph (i.e., table leaves are up).

The nomenclature of periods and styles has been vexing scholars for decades. It is a question far beyond the scope of this book. This collection is composed of pieces from the urban style centers and thus avoids entirely questions concerning Windsor, folk, and other styles. This catalogue follows the format based loosely on the English two part system of period by monarch, and style by the designer or idea most influential in the production of a piece. For the purposes of this catalogue, periods are defined as: Colonial: up to 1785; Federal: 1785–1815; and Empire: 1815–1840. Styles are defined as William and Mary, Queen Anne, baroque, rococo, Federal, neoclassical, and Empire. Designers such as Chippendale, Hepplewhite, or Sheraton are cited when they are thought to have had a direct infuence on an object.

Most of the eighteenth- and nineteenth-century provenances cited are based on information supplied by the seller. Unsubstantiated histories are cited, in the hope that they may elicit more accurate information even if only by rebuttal. The dates of each owner have not been included except for the original owner when known.

The *literature* citations include all books and catalogues and all major periodicals, but no advertisements. For chairs and tables, publications related to mates and others from the same set are cited. Exhibitions and loans of the objects before they entered the collection are cited when known.

The information in the *Construction and condition* section is not intended to be inclusive; rather it is intended to give an overview of how a particular piece is constructed, noting elements not visible in the illustrations and techniques that differ from the common practice. These notes are also intended to aid in the examination of similar pieces to determine if the similarity extends beyond form and decoration. I have also attempted, when possible, to show how certain construction techniques affected design decisions, or vice versa.

A familiarity with the basic construction techniques employed by eighteenth- and nineteenth-century cabinetmakers is helpful when using the notes. Certain techniques are so common that their use is not always noted. For example, unless note is made to the contrary, drawers are always dovetailed together; the mortise-and-tenon joint is standard for all frame constructions; all drop leaves rotate on rule joints except where noted.

All the woods in the original construction are noted; woods and fasteners used in repairs are not. The various types of hinges are not cited because the card tables, leaf tables, and doors use the standard type for their function. The antiquity of the hinges is accepted unless otherwise noted. Locks have not been cited either. Beyond differentiating between nails and screws, no attempt has been made to remove them to assure their age or originality. Brasses, unless otherwise noted, are original. Since all the pieces are illustrated in color, there has been no attempt to describe patina.

None of the upholstery pictured is original nor are the brass nail patterns based on original evidence, except where noted. Evidence of original upholstery, upholstery substructure, and brass nail patterns are cited when known. Replacement parts, major repairs, and the addition of material to support repairs or weak joints have been noted, but veneer patches, breaks, and the wear and tear of two hundred years have not. I have avoided classifying certain techniques and decorations such as dovetails, carving, or inlay. Judgments on these are difficult to convey in a few words and are highly subjective.

A truly thorough and inclusive report on any piece in this catalogue would have taken more space than the entire entry and photograph. It is my hope that these notes will act as a guide and general overview to the pieces.

J.M.F.

American Furniture Styles in the Colonial Era

Morrison H. Heckscher

Almost from the earliest years of settlement, furniture-making was an important industry in colonial America. The cost of importing English or European pieces was so great that only the very wealthy could do so, and frequently even they chose locally made pieces. There was a limitless supply of local raw materials, including many woods that had no exact parallel in England: northeastern white pine and cherry from New England; tulip and American black walnut from New York and Pennsylvania; yellow pine and cypress from the south. There were also large numbers of furniture craftsmen. Joiners, turners, and japanners, cabinetmakers, carvers, and upholsterers —all emigrated in large numbers to the land of opportunity. In New England alone some 150 first generation emigrant makers are known. They came from widely diverse parts of England, bringing with them regional styles they already knew. In other words they transplanted English regional styles to America, styles that tell more about the background of the joiner than of colonial tastes. But these transplanted styles rapidly became local American preferences, and this is the overriding feature of American colonial furniture: there are a number of distinct regional style centers rather than any one American style.

The earliest American furniture was made in what, for want of a more descriptive title, is called the seventeenth-century style. It is heavy furniture, four-square or rectilinear, and often ponderous in form. The visual effect is produced by extensive surface ornamentation. Case furniture, that is chests and cupboards, usually made of oak, was the work of joiners. Joiners were craftsmen who specialized in panel-and-frame construction, heavy mortise-and-tenon frames into which thin panel boards are fitted. The surfaces of both frames and panels were often richly ornamented with low-relief carving, moldings,

and applied turnings or painted decoration. Seating furniture, as well as most tables, was the province of wood turners. The craftsmen turned the framing members on a lathe, in combinations of rings and urns, and then mortise-and-tenoned them together. This style predominated in the seventeenth-century settlements of Massachusetts, Connecticut, and Pennsylvania.

The decade of the 1690s witnessed a dramatic change in taste with the introduction of furniture in the William and Mary style, named after William of Orange, ruler of Holland, and Mary Stuart, who assumed the British throne in 1688. The luxurious and elegant new style, which had originated on the Continent, primarily in Holland, became fashionable in England during the 1660s, after the restoration of the monarchy. Its introduction into the colonies may have coincided with the installation of a Royal Governor during the mid-1680s, in which case the style may be seen as a visual symbol of the shift of power from the Bay Colony's old Puritan oligarchy to Anglicans and merchants with closer ties to England.

Furniture in this new style is lighter in scale, taller and more vertical in form, and exhibits more movement in design (greater contrasts of thick and thin, for example), than furniture in the seventeenth-century manner. A variety of new furniture forms were introduced—among them easy chairs, dressing tables, and fall-front desks—and regional styles began to emerge.

Seating furniture still consisted primarily of turners' work, but was now characterized by vasiform posts and bold bulbous stretchers. Fashionable chairs often have high narrow backs with richly carved crests, small seats, and splayed Spanish feet; the seats and backs are caned or leather-covered. On cheaper examples the seats are rushed and the backs have split spindles. Couches, what we call daybeds, were introduced as were fully upholstered easy chairs, our wing chairs. There was an altogether new interest in comfort.

Case furniture was now the work of cabinetmakers rather than joiners. The boards forming the top, bottom, and sides of chests or desks are dovetailed together; so are the pieces forming the sides of drawers. Moldings, particularly those of cornices, adopt shapes found in classical architectural details. Walnut and maple supplant oak as the favored furniture material. Many pieces have applied surface decoration—either burl walnut veneers framed with herringbone-pattern edges, or painted decoration in imitation of oriental lacquerwork. A high chest and a dressing table, both japanned (cat. nos. 17, 18), are two remarkably preserved examples of the latter type. This collection, however, really only begins with furniture in the Queen Anne style.

It was about 1730 that American furniture design changed course and embraced what is now called the Queen Anne style. The essence of the style in America is form—curvilinear, self-contained, and graceful. The preferred wood is native black walnut. Chairs provide the purest examples of the style. Their primary component is the S-curve—what Hogarth was to call "the Line of Beauty"—found in the rounded back and seat, the baluster splat, and, most of all, the gracefully curved cabriole leg with its projecting knee, narrow ankle, and pad foot. For the most part carving was of little importance. Shells, while often executed in low relief to accent crest rail and knees, do not affect the outline or shape.

Case furniture, particularly high chests and secretary desks, is now embellished with architectural features—bonnet tops or scroll pediments, molded cornices and fluted pilasters—details also found on the houses of a new generation of leaders, men like John Hancock in Boston and James Logan in Philadelphia. In addition to modernizing case furniture and altering the form of chairs, craftsmen in the Queen Anne style introduced new types of tables to accommodate changing social patterns—marble-slab serving tables, folding-top card tables, and circular tilt-top tea tables.

The Chippendale style, the name now popularly given to American furniture showing rococo influence, made its appearance in the mid-1750s and was dominant until just after the Revolution. Its primary features include: architectural forms for case pieces; complex, even jagged, forms for chairs and tables; elaborate naturalistic carving, and cabriole legs with claw-and-ball feet. It is, in good part, a carver's style: the carving often determines the shape or outline of various parts of a piece. Mahogany, ideally suited to the chisel, is the preferred wood. Although chairs, now with eared crest rails and square seats, are drastically different from the Queen Anne, the form of case furniture remained basically unchanged. Indeed, it is not always possible to distinguish between these two styles. On the other hand, during the late colonial period when the Queen Anne and Chippendale styles were dominant, regional styles became so pronounced that each furniture-making center must be looked at independently.

Boston was the leading urban center in New England during the seventeenth and eighteenth centuries, and the type of Queen Anne style furniture introduced there in the early 1730s influenced furniture design throughout the region. Stylistically, the earliest example in the Kaufman collection is a walnut-veneered, flat-top high chest (cat. no. 19) that differs little from William and Mary examples except in its legs. Four cabriole legs supplant six turned ones; in the three-part skirt are pendant drops, vestigial remains of the two inside turned legs. A second walnut-veneered high chest (cat. no. 20) represents the fullest development of the Queen Anne form, with broken-arch bonnet top, carved and gilt shell drawers, and inlaid stars—all features in vogue by 1733. Chests and desks, on the other hand, very often had facades of solid wood shaped in block, bombé, or serpentine form. The block front, with sides projecting and center receding, is a form known as early as 1738. However, veneered blocking is unusual, and a veneered blockfront dressing table (cat. no. 21) is a decided rarity.

As early as the 1740s Boston's economy and population had begun a gradual decline. Her craftsmen, mostly descended from long-established furniture-making families, refused to allow outsiders to infiltrate their domain. Inevitably this bred a conservative approach to design, which may explain why the straight-front high chest of drawers and blockfront pieces remained a staple of New England cabinetwork well into the 1770s. It also helps explain why the style of Thomas Chippendale's *The Gentleman and Cabinet-Maker's Director*, published in 1754 and again in 1762, was not embraced by New Englanders with the same enthusiasm that had received the Queen Anne style. While a few copies of the *Director* were owned in New England, its designs had no influence on local furniture style. Most case furniture remained Queen Anne in form, but the best examples of the sixties and seventies often exhibit—through serpentine fronts and the delicate proportions and profiles of certain details—a lightness and playfulness that is rococo in spirit (cat. no. 23). The same can be said of seating furniture. On a celebrated Masonic Master's chair (cat. no. 4), for example, the traditional form—smooth rounded arm supports and turned stretchers—is brought up to date with flat, leaf-carved knees and raked-back talon-claw feet.

Newport began its rise to commercial prominence in the 1740s, just as Boston's growth had peaked. Newport had a close-knit group of Quaker craftsmen who took the Boston Queen Anne style and brilliantly transformed it. The result was what is often considered the most uniquely American, as well as among the best crafted, of all American furniture. Among the leading practitioners were members of the Townsend and Goddard families, two intermarried dynasties of Quaker cabinetmakers. During the late forties and fifties Newport craftsmen produced an elegant, angular version of Massachusetts Queen Anne high chests and tea tables, with distinctively pointed pad feet. Then, about 1760, they adopted the blockfront form; by the addition of boldly lobed shells they transformed it into the famous block and shell pattern that continued in fashion, virtually unchanged, over a thirty-year period until the early nineties.

A number of important examples of the style are included here: a chest-on-chest and a "kneehole" chest, or bureau table, each with four shells (cat. nos. 25, 26), and a three-shell, three-drawer chest bearing inscriptions by members of the Goddard family (cat. no. 24). We know that John Goddard (1723–1786) owned a copy of Chippendale's *Director*, but it had no impact on this piece, much less on Rhode Island taste in general. In addition to the block and shell, Newport cabinetmakers devised cabriole legs with intaglio-carved knee ornaments and claw feet with open talons for use on tables and high chests (cat. no. 27). A square tea table (cat. no. 12), one that can safely be ascribed to John Townsend (1732–1809), the doyen of Newport makers, is in the collection. So also is a firescreen (cat. no. 33), part of a group of tripod-pedestal furniture with diminutive cat's-paw feet.

New York City had, during the late colonial period, a furniture-making industry that approximated that of Newport in size. The city's great growth came only after the Revolution. While some models of Queen Anne chairs made in the two cities were so alike as to be today indistinguishable, generally speaking the furniture was totally different. Whereas Newport developed a unique and distinctive style, New York faithfully followed English practice. The city's population was heavy with Loyalists who wanted English furniture—whether made here or there was immaterial. Thus, not surprisingly, New York furniture appears in familiar English forms and has the broad and heavy proportions of the imported English examples that it copies. It was good, middle-class furniture that New York makers copied, not the fanciful rococo imaginings of the *Director*. A chest, cat. no. 28, has these qualities, with characteristic New York fret pattern, chamfered corners, gadrooned skirt, and square claw feet.

Philadelphia began a meteoric growth in the 1730s; by 1740 she was second only to Boston in size; by 1765 she was half again as big. The 1740s was the golden age of Philadelphia chairmaking. To compete successfully against the flood of

cat. no. 20

14

seating furniture imported from Boston, the local makers produced chairs that are a perfect manifestation of the Queen Anne style. The stiles and crest rail form an unbroken curve; the balloon seat is boldly rounded. Cat. nos. 2 and 3 are examples from two different sets of such chairs in this collection. The other Philadelphia Queen Anne furniture form that survives in particularly large numbers is the drop-leaf dining table, illustrated here by one that is notable for its twelve-sided top (cat. no. 11).

The style associated with Chippendale in Philadelphia actually had its beginnings just prior to the publication of the *Director* in 1754. By this time Philadelphia cabinetwork had begun to assume a new importance. A mahogany bonnet-top high chest with shell drawers, acanthus-leaf knees, and claw feet, now at Colonial Williamsburg, is dated 1753. A high chest and its matching dressing table (cat. nos. 29, 30) also exemplify the early phase. The skirts, in the William and Mary manner, rise in a high central arch. Centered above the arch is an applied shell that is identical to one found on the seat rail of a chair (cat. no. 6) which, by virtue of the heaviness of its parts, may be assigned a similar date.

The most popular pierced splat pattern for Philadelphia Chippendale chairs is the strapwork splat type. In addition to cat. no. 6 there is one from the elaborate set once owned by the Lambert family (cat. no. 5), also of relatively early date, and two examples that must have been made in the mid-sixties or later. On these latter (cat. nos. 7, 8), the framing members are thinner, the carving is freer, and in places actually defines the chair outline. The ogival, Gothic-type splat, another popular local pattern, is also represented (cat. no. 9).

But the fullest development of the carved chair in Philadelphia is found in the set made about 1770 as part of a suite of furniture for General John Cadwalader's opulent town house. In addition to a pair of chairs from this set (cat. no. 10) there is a richly carved firescreen (cat. no. 32) that can also be associated with the Cadwalader suite. These pieces are in the late phase of Philadelphia Chippendale—after the publication in 1762 of the greatly enlarged third edition of the *Director* and after the nonimportation agreements of the sixties had rendered inadvisable the importation of English furniture. Thus the London-trained cabinetmaker, Thomas Affleck, came to Philadelphia in 1763, *Director* in hand, and found a willing public. On a monumental desk and bookcase, whose upper case unit is in the Palladian style of the 1740s, the lower case is taken directly from Chippendale's first edition (cat. no. 31). The Chippendale style in America followed a progression that can be clearly seen in cat. nos. 14, 15, and 16 from the rococo through Chinese and Gothic variations to the Marlborough style. This last offered an alternative to the cabriole leg and was a harbinger of the neoclassical style which was to eclipse the rococo by the end of the eighties.

1
Side Chair
1730–1760
Newport
Walnut; maple slip seat
39¾ x 21¾ x 20¾ in.
ACC. NO. 83.2

The refinement of the Queen Anne chair in New England reached its apogee with this form. The gentle curves of the back, seat, and legs have a flowing naturalistic quality different from the robust, almost electric, quality of Philadelphia examples seen in cat. nos. 2 and 3. These chairs are often referred to as compass chairs for the shaping of the seat. In the eighteenth century they were also called "Indian" chairs in reference to their oriental derivation. The attenuation of the back is marked by a flawless transition of the fully molded stiles to the shallow, arched crest. The gentle curved vasiform splat with its high volutes supports this effect. The shell resting on a reverse C-scroll caps the design.

Conventional interpretation states that the turned stretchers of New England's Queen Anne and rococo chairs are a vestige of the William and Mary period that reflects Yankee conservatism and detracts from the form. In fact they are a holdover, but the chairs have been designed around them. Without the stretchers the delicately wrought back would seem overwrought; high and narrow, with a rectangular silhouette, the back would seem out of place with the broad compass seat and cabriole legs. The stretchers help bring the seat and legs into balance with the back.

A number of chairs are similar in form and decoration but differ slightly in dimensions and execution. They are all attributed to Newport. A set of four chairs owned by Moses Brown and thought to have been made by John Goddard on the basis of correspondence between them are the best documented (Carpenter 1954, no. 11). Another set of six (Jobe and Kay 1984, no. 91), of which four remain, are thought to have been owned, along with two other sets of Newport chairs, by Charles Barrett, Sr., a New Ipswich, New Hampshire, merchant. A pair, along with a matching slipper chair (I. Sack n.d.–1979, 3:745) and a single chair (Greenlaw 1974, no. 51), are part of this group, but have no eighteenth-century history.

Provenance: Dr. and Mrs. Joseph Kreiselman Collection, Washington; Bernard and S. Dean Levy, Inc., New York

Construction and condition: The chair frame is constructed entirely of walnut. The rails are tenoned and pinned to the legs and stiles. They are shaped on one side only. This makes the inside of the seat trapezoidal in cross section. The returns in the rails are cut from the solid. The side and front rails are rabbeted to accept the slip seat. The front rail is marked IIII in the rabbet. The rear rail is thinner than the stiles. Modern blocks support all the leg joints. The side stretchers are tenoned to the legs and the cross stretchers are doweled in place. The knee-blocks are glued and nailed. The slip seat is maple. It is mortise-and-tenoned together. Its members are shaped on one side only.

The shoe is separate from the rear rail. The splat is chamfered along its edge and seats directly in the shoe. The stiles are tenoned and pinned to the crest rail. The stiles in cross section are more of a rectangle with rounded corners than an oval or ellipse. The crest-rail shell is carved from the solid.

2
Side Chair
(one of a set of five)
1735–1760
Philadelphia
Walnut; white cedar slip seat
41⅞ x 20¼ x 21 in.
ACC. NO. 78.6 a–e

All the elements that define Philadelphia's Queen Anne chair style can be found in this set. There is a strong vertical emphasis delineated by a fully curvilinear design. The compass seat is deeply curved as well. The highly articulated baluster splat, stockinged trifid feet, delicate shells with deep scrolls, and fully rounded stiles are hallmarks of its fullest development.

Philadelphia chairs achieve this light vertical quality by eliminating stretchers and thinning the seat rails. The technical basis for this is that the seat rails are very deep and shaped on only one side to accommodate the deep curves. The rails are tenoned through the stiles. This reduces the rack and twist that stretchers and wider rails can eliminate.

The legs of these five chairs show the same styling as Heckscher 1985, nos. 38–41 and Fitzgerald 1982, fig. III–30. The distinguishing features of this style leg are widely spaced toes, a ridge along the outside edge, and the thick pad of the foot. None of these chairs share enough other quantifiable details to establish that they were produced in the same shop. The legs may be the work of an independent craftsman who supplied them to various shops.

The set of five chairs was purchased along with a similar sixth chair. The five are numbered II, III, IIII, V, VII. The slip seats are numbered II, III, V, VI, VII. A chair illustrated in Rodriguez-Roque 1984, no. 48, appears to be from this set and is marked with the number VI. The sixth similar chair in the Kaufman Collection matches one in Kirk 1972, no. 54.

Provenance: Florence Traemmer, Point Pleasant, Pennsylvania; Israel Sack, Inc., New York; John Schapiro Collection, Baltimore; Israel Sack, Inc., New York

Construction and condition: These chairs, like cat. no. 3, employ the standard techniques of Philadelphia Queen Anne chair construction. The chair frame is made entirely of walnut. The front legs are doweled through the rails and supported by knee-blocks which are glued and nailed in place. The side rails are horizontally tenoned to the front rails and vertically tenoned through the stiles. These joints are secured by modern pins. The returns are applied and are also tenoned through the stiles. The rear rail is thinner than the stiles and is

tenoned to them. These joints are secured by two pins in each stile. Returns in the rear rail are cut from the solid. The rounded lip enclosing the slip seat is cut from the solid in the front rail and applied on the side rails. The slip seats are made of white cedar. Although a few of the rear rails are replacements, the rails are shaped on one side only, mortise-and-tenoned together and pinned at the front.

The shoe is a separate piece and the splat is seated directly in it. The splat is solid crotch walnut, chamfered along its edges. Both the inner and outer curves of the stiles are finished by applied pieces. All the carving of the crest rail is cut from the solid.

Literature: P-B 1955, no. 320; I. Sack n.d.–1979, 6:40–41, 1530–1531

Exhibitions: New York, P-B Galleries 1955 (Art Treasures Exhibition); Norfolk, Virginia, Chrysler Museum 1979–1980

3
Pair of Side Chairs
1735–1760
Philadelphia
Walnut
41⅝ x 20¾ x 21 in.
ACC. NO. 78.9 a, b

These chairs are the summit of American Queen Anne chair-making. They represent the height of curvilinear design. Like cat. no. 12, they are among the finest pieces of American eighteenth-century sculpture. The only right angles visible are at the joint of the rear rail to the stiles. There are other chairs that have more carving, ball-and-claw feet, or pierced strap-work splats, embellishments that shift the emphasis of the chair from line and form to decoration. Here, in cat. no. 3, the shells, leafwork, and scrolls enhance without dominating the form. The refinement of the rounded stiles and broken-front compass seat with molded edge stress the curvilinear design of the chairs. The production of chairs of this kind, also represented by cat. no 2, required larger amounts of expensive woods than any other chairs of the Colonial or Federal periods. Most significantly, the splats are made of solid crotch walnut. They are S-shaped in cross section, consuming even more wood. The deep curves of the compass seats are made from rails shaped on only one side, and the molded edge of the front rail is cut from the solid.

At least five of these chairs are known: this pair, a pair shown in Kirk 1972, no. 56, and a single chair shown in I. Sack n.d.–1979, 5:1218. Both pairs have histories of descent from the Coates family of Philadelphia.

Provenance: Descended in the Coates family of Philadelphia and New York; Elsie C. White, New York; Christie's, sale "Phyfe," 21 October 1978, lot 290; Israel Sack, Inc., New York

Construction and condition: These chairs, like those in cat. no. 2, employ the standard techniques of Philadelphia Queen Anne chair construction. The frame is constructed entirely of walnut. The front legs are doweled through the rails and supported by knee-blocks, which are glued and nailed in place. The side rails are horizontally tenoned to the front rails and vertically tenoned through the stiles. These joints are held by modern pins. The returns are applied and are also tenoned through the stiles. The rear rail is thinner than the stiles, and tenoned to them. Two pins in each stile secure this joint. The molded lip containing the slip seat is cut from the solid in the front rail and applied on the side rails. Both slip seats are modern replacements. The shell of the front rail is made in two sections; the upper half is carved from the solid and the lower half is applied.

The shoe is a separate piece and the splat is seated directly in it. The splat is solid crotch walnut, chamfered along its edges. Both the inner and outer curves of the stile are finished by applied pieces. All the carving in the crest is cut from the solid.

Literature: Chairs from this set are illustrated in Hornor 1935, pl. 82; Kirk 1972, pl. 56; I. Sack n.d.–1979, 5:1218–1219

4
Masonic Armchair
1765–1790
Massachusetts, probably Boston
Mahogany; maple
50½ x 28 x 24¾ in.
ACC. NO. KAF 79.6

The "art and mystery" of cabinetmaking is herein joined to the symbols and traditions of freemasonry to produce one of the finest Massachusetts chairs of the period. Exactly for whom it was made or by whom are not known, but its Massachusetts origins and masonic connection are clear. The use of finely turned stretchers, the sharp line of the knee, and the thin raked talons grasping the ball all point to the best in Massachusetts cabinetry and to Boston in particular. Further refinements are found in the chamfering of the rear legs and the shaping of the arms, which combine a smooth inner curve with a hard bottom edge and a fine line along the outside.

The masonic symbols and their meanings are these: the fluted columns of the stiles, the pillars of Solomon's temple; the brickwork crest, the arch of heaven; the compass and square, faith and reason; the mason's level, equality; the serpent swallowing its tail, rebirth; the trowel, the cement of brotherly love; the mallet, untimely death. Below the mallet are the pick and spade needed in the search for truth. The sprig of acacias represents immortality; the panel enclosed by the serpent containing the sun and crescent moon, vigilance; two globes on turned columns, the universality of freemasonry; the pattern of white and black, good and evil; the mosaic floor, the floor of Solomon's temple.

Masonic symbolism and its arrangement was not standardized in the eighteenth century and therefore the overall purpose and importance of each element in the splat is uncertain. The cabinetmaker did, however, use the well-known C-scroll, with two long C-scrolls rising from the base to support the serpent, and a group of three C-scrolls to tie the serpent to the crest, which unites the various elements into an artistic if not mystical whole.

Provenance: The chair was acquired by Israel Sack who included it in the sale of the George S. Palmer collection (Anderson Galleries, sale 2280, 18–20 October 1928, lot 209). The catalogue entry states: "Known to have been made to the order of a New Hampshire lodge of Free Masons," but provides no other documentation. The chair was bought by Joe Kindig, Jr.; Joe Kindig, Jr. and Son Antiques, York, Pennsylvania.

Construction and condition: The ceremonial function of this chair may have played a part in its survival in so pristine a condition that the finish and upholstery appear to have been untouched since the end of the eighteenth century. Tool marks left by the carver, usually obliterated by refinishing, are still visible on the knees and splat. The original cover of striped black horsehair remains intact as does the hair stuffing, canvas platform, and linen webbing. The original brass nails have been removed but their shadow, in the form of four swags, remains. The webbing is pulled over the rail and nailed to the front edge, and the horsehair is pulled over with no padding. (Today webbing is often nailed to the top of the rail and the front edge is padded.) A second covering of plain black horsehair and nails was probably put on in 1790.

The date 1790 is written in gilt on the back of the central tablet of the splat. A second coat of gilding, sloppily applied, may have been added at this time to the crest and parts of the splat. The gilding of the balls of the feet and the splat is more carefully applied, as is a white composition material that may be contemporary with the manufacture of the chair.

The front and side rails are maple. The rear rail is mahogany. It is tenoned and pinned to the stiles and is stepped to accommodate the upholstery. There are no blocks supporting the joints of the rails and legs. The knee-blocks are glued in place. The shaped brackets applied at the rear legs appear to be later. The side stretchers are tenoned to the legs and the cross stretchers are doweled. The arm supports are tenoned to and lapped over the rails. They are tenoned to the arms which are notched and tenoned to the stiles. The splat is sawed and carved from a single board. It is tenoned to the crest and rear rail. The shoe is a replacement. The stiles are tenoned to the crest rail and have broken through. The crest rail is rounded on top and flat on the back. The upholstery shown here displays the original nail pattern.

Literature: Nutting 1928–1933, 2: no. 2212; Randall 1966, 286–287; Fales 1972, pl. 132; Fairbanks 1975, no. 335; Cooper 1980, fig. 123; Heckscher 1985, no. 12

Exhibitions: Boston, MFA 1975 (Paul Revere's Boston); New York, MMA 1978–1986

5
Side Chair

1755–1770
Philadelphia
Mahogany; white cedar, oak slip seat, mahogany blocks
41⅝ x 24¾ x 22⅛ in.
ACC. NO. 79.1

The beauty of this highly carved Philadelphia chair lies not merely in the profusion of carving, but in the integration of the carved elements into a chair style found plentifully in plainer form; plainer versions can be seen (Hornor 1935, pl. 77; I. Sack n.d.–1979, 3:115; Fitzgerald 1982, fig. N–18). To insure that the decoration does not appear pasted on, the cabinetmaker-carver altered a number of elements to achieve a naturalistic flow of carving that distinguishes the masterpieces of the Philadelphia rococo school. In using a softer knee, the leg is shaped differently than the standard. The carved plinth and the knee flow into each other and help carry the line of the carving from the front rail. The forethought given to this can be seen by a close examination of the joints, which reveals that the pieces were carved before assembly, for the carving does not actually flow across either the plinth or the knee blocks.

This balance of carving and design is seen within the front rail. The edge is a cutout of a pair of cyma around a C-scroll that mimics the legs, while the carving is a slightly asymmetrical combination of leaf and vine over shell work and C-scrolls.

The problems posed by the back are solved in the reverse of the legs and skirt. The carving actually does flow across the joints of the crest rail, stiles, and splat. The carved spiral ears of the crest help maintain the carving in the same plane. The effect of the back as a single carved and cutout panel is thus achieved.

The integration of the carving into the design has created a sculptured form rarely achieved. This chair originally came from a set comprising twelve pieces of which nine are known, including this one and an unpublished example at Colonial Williamsburg. A closely related example (Bishop 1972, fig. 152) has only slightly less carving, but with less integration into the overall design.

Provenance: The chair is from a set thought to have been made for the Lambert family of New Jersey. This history was first noted when one was sold at the Reifsnyder sale in 1929; George Cluett Collection, Williamstown, Massachusetts; Israel Sack, Inc., New York

Construction and condition: The side and front rails are tenoned to the front legs. The side rails are tenoned through the stiles. The front rail uses one and a quarter inch stock, thicker than the standard three-quarters inch, to accommodate the carving which is cut from the solid. The horizontal shaping of the side rails is also cut from the solid. A rabbet is cut in the front and side rails for the slip seat. The rear rail is straight across with no shaping. It is thinner than the stiles, tenoned to them with two pins in each to secure the joint. Fillets of mahogany are glued to the rear rail to support the vertically grained glue-blocks. Two-part vertically grained mahogany blocks support the front leg joints. The knee-blocks are glued in place. The slip seat is mortise-and-tenoned together with white cedar rear and side rails, with an oak front rail.

Literature: Chairs from this set are illustrated in Hornor 1935, pl. 336 (one of a pair now at the PMA, acc. nos. 40-16-5, 40-16-6); Downs 1952, no. 128; Rodriguez-Roque 1984, no. 62; Heckscher 1985, no. 51; Rollins 1984, 1117, pl. 20; *Antiques,* November 1985, 800; I. Sack n.d.–1979, 6:1677 (cat. no. 5)

6
Side Chair
1755–1770
Philadelphia
Mahogany; poplar slip seat
41⅜ x 23½ x 22½ in.
ACC. NO. 72.6

This chair is a bold and exuberant expression of Philadelphia's rococo taste. The high back and broad crest rail dominate, while the deep knee and convex shell add to the overall effect. This is one of five chairs said to have been part of the furnishings of the president's house in Philadelphia (Hummel 1976, fig. 65). An armchair without such a history is thought to be from the set (Hummel 1976, fig. 41). This chair is numbered IIII on the front rail and slip seat. A pair of chairs (I. Sack n.d.–1979, 1: 571) differ only in the carving of the applied shell.

The splat of stylized strapwork was very popular in Philadelphia; cat. nos. 5, 7, and 8 represent three variations. No exact design source has been discovered. Robert Manwaring, in *The Cabinet and Chair Maker's Real Friend and Companion*, published in 1765, shows a number of closely related splats, though a more likely and probably earlier source is some unrecorded imported example. The few known English examples indicate that this design found greater favor in the colonies than in England (Kirk 1982, nos. 878, 879).

These chairs were once thought to be from Maryland or Chester County, Pennsylvania (attributions based on a version of the "Connecticut theory" of origins which stated that anything definitely New England but quirky must be from Connecticut). Whatever did not conform to the accepted canons of the Philadelphia aesthetic, but was clearly of the Philadelphia school, was said to be rural or Maryland (see Downs 1952, nos. 37, 38). George Washington may not have sat in these chairs, but their history of use and ownership in Philadelphia at least historically denies a Maryland or rural origin. Aesthetically, the masterful handling of the crest and high quality of the carving, especially of the shell, which is similar to shells on cat. nos. 29 and 30, show the hand of a highly trained and skilled craftsman successfully interpreting a popular Philadelphia pattern.

Provenance: The chair is one of five that are said to have been used in the presidential house in Philadelphia; Col. Frank Etting Collection, Philadelphia; Joe Kindig, Jr. Antiques, York, Pennsylvania; Winterthur Museum, Winterthur, Delaware; John Walton, Inc., New York; Albert Smiley Collection, Warwick, Rhode Island; P-B, sale 3393, 23 June 1972, lot 231

Construction and condition: The front and side rails are tenoned to the front legs and secured by two pins each. The side rails are tenoned through the stiles and secured by two modern pins each. The horizontal shaping of the front and side rails is cut from the solid. A rabbet is cut in the side and front rails for the slip seat. The rear rail is straight across with no shaping. It is thinner than the stiles, tenoned to them with two pins to secure each joint. The glue-blocks supporting the leg and stile joints appear to be replacements. The knee-blocks are glued but not nailed. The shell of the front rail is applied. The rail is cut out in a conforming pattern to support the shell. The slip seat is poplar.

The shoe is separate and the splat is seated directly in it. A horizontally grained mahogany strip supports the splat as it joins the crest. The splat is chamfered along its edges. The crest rail is carved from the solid and is brought to a point in back, with a flat section behind the shell.

Literature: Chairs from this set are illustrated in Decatur 1941, 8–11; A. Sack 1950, 35; Hummel 1976, 65; *Antiques,* May 1985, 949

Exhibition: Winterthur, Delaware, Winterthur Museum 1951–1961

26

7
Side Chair
(one of a pair)
1755–1780
Philadelphia
Mahogany; white cedar slip seat, *red cedar blocks
41⅜ x 23¾ x 23 in.
ACC. NO. 71.7. a, b

These are among the most highly evolved examples of this early form of Philadelphia rococo chair. The eared crest rail, stylized shells, and strapwork splat were among the first decorations for the new rococo style chair, though their presence here does not imply an early date of manufacture. Another pair in this pattern, by a different hand, are shown in cat. no. 8.

Each element in the overall form is distinct, with little attempt at integration. The stop-fluted stiles act as columns framing the splat and supporting the bowed crest rail, where acanthus fronds flow beautifully from the shell to the stylized ears. Leafage decorates the scrolls of the splat, while the carved tassel fills the central void. Gadrooning covers the shoe. The shell of the front rail reflects the shell of the crest.

Three sets of chairs from the same shop exist in this pattern, varying primarily in the height of the back. This variation within a single design is achieved by elongation of the splat at its base. The same effect is seen in cat. no. 6. This chair is from the tallest set; others are shown in Montgomery and Kane 1972, 155, Comstock 1962, no. 263, and Hipkiss 1941, no. 86. The shortest set is seen in Hipkiss 1941, no. 85 and Downs 1952, no. 125. (The shells of the front rail have only five lobes instead of the seven in the other sets.) Heckscher 1985, no. 50 and Kindig 1978, no. 44, among others, represent the middle-height version.

Provenance: Israel Sack, Inc., New York; Cornelius C. Moore Collection, Newport, Rhode Island; P-B, sale 3259, 30 October 1971, lot 124

Construction and condition: The side and front rails are tenoned to the legs and the joints secured by pins. The side rails are tenoned through the stiles and each rail secured by two pins. The horizontal shaping of the rails is cut from the solid. A rabbet is cut in the front and side rails for the slip seat. The rear rail is thinner than the stiles. Two pins in each stile secure the rail. Returns in the rear rail are cut from the solid. Vertically grained fillets of red cedar are applied to the rear rail to support the vertically grained quarter-round glue-blocks. Two-part vertically grained quarter-round blocks support the front legs. The knee-blocks are glued to the legs but not nailed. The shell of the front rail is applied and the rail is shaped to support it. The slip seats have white cedar rails mortise-and-tenoned together. The inside edges of the slip seat frame have been shaped into a cloverleaf cutout.

The shoe is separate and the splat is seated directly in it. Both splats have been repaired, having been damaged at their widest points. The back of the crest rail is rounded along the top and bottom edge and flat in the middle. The backs of the stiles are U-shaped, but flatten as they reach the crest rail.

Literature: Chairs from this set are illustrated in Montgomery and Kane 1976, 155; Comstock 1962, no. 263; Hipkiss 1941, no. 86

Exhibition: Richmond, Virginia Museum 1979–1980

8

Side Chair
(one of a pair)
1755–1780
Philadelphia
Mahogany
39½ x 23½ x 21⅜ in.
ACC. NO. 72.12 a, b

These chairs and the pair in cat. no. 7 afford a wonderful opportunity to compare two interpretations of a single design. Each element and the overall form are alike, while the result is entirely different. Both pairs show the hand of a well-trained carver and chairmaker, and while we may be tempted to see one as earlier or later, city or country, there is no evidence to support such conclusions.

The carving of cat. no. 7 is robust and deep, with a naturalistic flow that gives a sense of movement to the design. The shells are full and the acanthus leaves spill over the legs, crest, and splat while with this pair the carving is highly refined, more lapidarian than botanical. A series of shallow gouge cuts along the lower edge of the crest rail and upper edge of the splat indicate the line of a scroll, whereas full volutes turn the ears out on cat. no. 7. The design of the crest stresses the unity of an abstract design rather than the naturalistic effects usually stressed by rococo decoration. This design is created by using a series of scrolls over a diaper-work background within a stylized shell. The joining of the crest rail to the stiles and splat shows a much greater effort to integrate the elements than do those in cat. no. 7. Similar differences show up in the legs, with this pair using smaller knee-blocks and tightly formed leafage in contrast to the expansive carving of the other.

One of these chairs is marked VIII on the rear rail; the other is unmarked. A third chair from this set, in a private collection, is marked VII on the rear rail and VIII on the slip seat.

These chairs reflect more than different hands interpreting a common pattern; they reflect different aesthetic interpretations of the prevailing taste.

Provenance: Charles H. Gershenson Collection, Detroit; Israel Sack, Inc., New York

Construction and condition: The front and side rails are tenoned to the front legs and the joints secured by pins. The side rails are tenoned through the stiles but not pinned. The horizontal shaping of the rails is cut from the solid. A rabbet is cut in the front and side rails for the slip seat. The rear rail is thinner than the stiles. Two pins in each stile secure the rail. Returns are cut in the rear rail from the solid. The inside lower edge of all the rails is chamfered. The glue-blocks and slip seats are replacements. The knee-blocks are glued and nailed in place. The front-rail shell is applied, with the rail shaped in a conforming pattern to support it.

The shoe is separate and the splat is seated directly in it. The edges of the splat are square to the face and not chamfered. The crest rail is fully shaped in the rear.

9

Side Chair
(one of a pair)
1765–1785
Philadelphia
Mahogany; yellow pine, red cedar, poplar
38⅜ x 23¾ x 22 in.
ACC. NO. 74.13 a, b

English designers integrated Gothic motifs with the prevailing rococo style to produce a popular eighteenth-century hybrid —Gothic rococo. In the colonies this Gothic influence was most often seen in chair splats and a few fretwork patterns. The plainer the design the more the Gothic was emphasized; but as quatrefoils and Gothic arches became encrusted with C-scrolls and leafage the distinctive Gothic rococo emerged.

One of Philadelphia's most high-style interpretations of the Gothic rococo is seen here. The splat may be based upon plate XVI of the 1762 edition of Chippendale's *Director*. The Gothic elements of the interlaced splat are highlighted by delicately carved C-scrolls. The piercings of the splat extend into the crest rail, integrating the two and lightening the crest. This integration of crest and splat is further emphasized by the stiles, which are only molded. The teardrop-shaped piercings below the quatrefoil open the splat at its base as it joins the shoe. The carved leafage that encircles the ears of the splat are especially well done. The front rail is cut out and incised with the profile of the crest rail.

Four chairs from this set are in the Philadelphia Museum of Art and another is in a private collection. The backs of these chairs are identical with those of a set made for the Edwards family of Philadelphia (Downs 1952, no. 138). The Edwards family set has a carved front rail and differs in the layout of the knee carving.

Provenance: The Wharton family genealogy that came with these chairs lists a number of family members of sufficient wealth to have been the original owners. Also, throughout the late eighteenth and nineteenth centuries the Whartons intermarried with other families prominent in colonial Philadelphia, broadening considerably the list of possible original owners.

These, or chairs from this set, are pictured in Hornor 1935, pl. 362, with a Wharton family history and there is a late nineteenth-century photo of three of the chairs in the parlor of C.W. Wharton's house on Spruce Street, Philadelphia.

The chairs bear several inscriptions. On one chair is the following:

9/16/40 Date of purchase of these chairs by Rodman Wharton. They stood in the house of his grandfather, Charles Wharton— second above Spruce Street—being discarded by his daughters as too old fashioned. Rodman placed them in the parlor at 336 Spruce Street till the death of his mother in 1888, when they came to his own family in their houses—911 Pine Street and 910 Clinton Street. Two of these were given to their son William Rodman Wharton on the eve of his marriage June 22, 1894. [signed] Susan D. Wharton

On the other chair:

This chair, left me by cousin, Clara Wharton, is now in the property of Charles W. Wharton, Jr. as of date, December 25th, 1962. [signed] Charles W. Wharton

Inscribed on both chairs:

This Philadelphia Wharton ancestral chair belongs to Charles W. Wharton, Fairview, Jamestown, Rhode Island

Israel Sack, Inc., New York

Construction and condition: The front and side rails are tenoned to the legs. The side rails are tenoned through the stiles. Two pins at each stile secure these joints. The horizontal shaping of the rails is cut from the solid. A rabbet is cut in the front and side rails for the slip seat. The rear rail is a vertical lamination of mahogany and poplar as thick as the stiles. Two pins in each stile secure the rails. The bottom edge is straight across with no shaping. Vertically grained quarter-round red cedar glue-blocks support the joint of the rails and stiles. Two-part vertically grained quarter-round red cedar blocks support the front legs. The knee-blocks are glued in place. The slip seats have yellow pine, rails mortise-and-tenoned together.

The shoe is separate and the splat is seated directly in it. Quarter-round horizontally grained mahogany blocks are applied at the joint of the splat to the crest. The back of the crest rail is flat at the ears and in the center and rounded in between.

Literature: Hornor 1935, pl. 362; I. Sack n.d.–1979, 4:1086

10

Side Chair
(one of a pair)
1768–1770
Philadelphia
Mahogany; *white cedar glue-blocks
36⅞ x 24½ x 23¼ in.
ACC. NO. 74.16 a, b

These chairs are the highest achievement of Philadelphia rococo chairmaking. They give us a clear picture of the height of fashion in 1770. John Cadwalader (1742–1786), for whom they were made, was a man out to impress. He had married Elizabeth Lloyd of Wye Plantation in 1768. Her father was the wealthiest planter on Maryland's Eastern Shore. Cadwalader bought a house and proceeded to spend more on the architectural embellishments than he had for the house itself. He commissioned Charles Willson Peale to paint the family's portraits; the furnishings would be no less elaborate.

These chairs, numbered VIIII and X, are two of seven known from a set of at least twelve with a pair of card tables ensuite (PMA 1976, no. 91). Peale's portrait of John's brother, Lambert, shows a chair identical in form to these with a molded rather than carved stile. The entire set of furniture for the newly decorated house, all with hairy paw feet and highly carved, probably numbered thirty-two chairs, four card tables, and a number of sofas and fire screens (see cat. no. 32).

Unlike cat. no. 5, which represents a successful integration of rococo ornament into an earlier form, these chairs are undiluted rococo. The splat may be derived from two splats in Chippendale's *Director* (pls. XVI, 1754 ed., and XV, 1762 ed.) that show "Ribband back" chairs with splats joined to the stiles and the double figure eights. The carving is robust and full of movement. The leafage on the stiles twists and curls as it moves up to the crest. The splat branches out in C-scrolls and leafage to the stiles before it reaches the crest rail. The stiles flare outward just below the gently curved and simply carved crest rail; this creates a continuous flow for both the carving and the entire back. The finely cut and shaped skirt, with asymmetrical designs on the side rails and central cabochon, creates a sense of movement and lightness. The clarity of the carving almost frees the knee-blocks from the form of the chair. The overall scale and proportion of these chairs is often considered English. However the lower back, broader seat, and hairy paw foot relate more to their unique position in American furniture than to their "Englishness."

The chairs have long been attributed to Benjamin Randolph. One from this set, along with five other elaborate chairs, belonged to a descendant of Randolph's second wife and were dubbed the "sample" chairs, as they were thought to be too fancy for anything but display purposes. The appearance of five more in 1974, numbered VII, VIII, VIIII, X, and XI, dispatched the "sample" theory.

Commissions to furnish the newly redecorated Cadwalader house were parceled out among a number of shops. Bills show that John Cadwalader patronized Benjamin Randolph, Thomas Affleck, and William Savery, who in turn employed the carvers John Pollard, James Reynolds, Hercules Courtney, and the partnership of Bernard and Juigez; some of the carvers

Chippendale, *Director* 1754, pl. XVI

Frame, cat. no. 10

were employed directly by Cadwalader as well. With the cabinetmakers acting as general contractors to various carvers, these chairs and the entire suite are unique, both for design and for a collaborative effort by Philadelphia's finest carvers and cabinetmakers.

What we know of the owner and the probable craftsmen tells us that these chairs were absolutely the best that money could buy; rarely has the height of fashion been captured so perfectly.

Provenance: The chairs were made for General John Cadwalader of Philadelphia and remained in Philadelphia until at least the first decade of the twentieth century. This is confirmed by the inscription *Charles Hanlon* on the shoe. Hanlon was an upholsterer listed in the Philadelphia directories between 1901 and 1905. The chairs next attracted attention when five of the set were consigned to a sale at Sotheby's in London in January 1974 before they were withdrawn and sent to New York for sale. The consignor was a Major R.G. Fanshawe of Gloucestershire. The Major received the chairs from a friend who had acquired them at an estate auction in Ireland in the 1930s. The history of the chairs between the death of General John Cadwalader in 1786 and their reappearance at an estate sale in Ireland in the 1930s is a mystery. The first chair was found in Philadelphia early in this century, the seventh chair of the set in Italy in 1982, and a matching card table in Canada in 1968; none of these discoveries has simplified research efforts. SP-B, sale 3691, 16 November 1974, lots 1477–1479; Israel Sack, Inc., New York

Construction and condition: The construction of the chairs was one of the first clues to their Philadelphia origins when they were consigned to auction in London in 1974. The heavy mahogany rails with the carving cut from the solid, the side rails tenoned through the stiles, and the stump rear legs are features more common to Philadelphia cabinet shops than to London. The chairs are constructed entirely of mahogany with only the glue-blocks of white cedar to help localize their production. The blocks were identified by microanalysis, which strengthened the belief in their Philadelphia authorship.

The serpentine front rail is shaped on both sides. The top is dished to create a saddle seat. It is tenoned to the legs but not pinned. The side rails are tenoned to the legs and tenoned through the stiles. Two pins, at least one of which is modern, secure the rail to the stile, and one pin holds the rail to the leg. The top edge of the side rails are beveled toward the center for the saddle seat. The rear rail is thicker than the stiles. It is stepped, and the top and bottom edges are curved for the saddle seat. A pin through each stile secures the rail. Vertically grained fillets of white cedar are set between the rear and side rails to increase the surface area for the glue blocks. Vertically grained quarter-round white cedar blocks were set at the joint of the rail and stile. Most of these are missing. Two-part quarter-round white cedar glue-blocks support the legs. The knee-blocks are glued and nailed in place.

The splat is tenoned to the rear rail. Screws through the splat now secure the shoe. The splat is composed of three pieces. The first is the central vertical portion forming the lower two-thirds; this is tenoned to the horizontal section, which is thicker. At this joint blocks were added supporting the lower section and smoothing the transition. The thickness of the horizontal section gives support at the point of greatest stress and a cleaner line when it meets the stiles. The smaller top section is vertically grained and is set between the horizontal section and the crest. It is backed by blocks that make it as thick as the pieces it connects. The crest rail is bowed at the center, where it is thinnest and flat in back.

Literature: Chairs from this set are illustrated in Downs 1952, no. 138 and Hummel 1972, pl. 9; PMA 1976, no. 90; Kindig 1978, no. 61; SP-B, sale 4942, 23 October 1982, lot 71; Heckscher 1985, no. 59

The history of the chairs and their owners are discussed in the following: Wainwright 1964; Woodhouse 1975, 33–43; Loughlin 1978; Zimmerman 1979, 193–208

Shoe, showing inscription

11
Drop-leaf Dining Table
1730–1760
Philadelphia
Mahogany; oak, poplar
28¾ x 54⅛ x 56½ in.
ACC. NO. 81.1

Dining in the eighteenth century was not always confined to a specific room. The largest, the warmest, the fanciest, or whatever room was needed served the occasion. The drop-leaf dining table, which is portable and can be placed against a wall for easy storage, accommodated this practice.

This twelve-sided, drop-leaf table is one of the finest Philadelphia examples and one of only three known that are so fashioned (see Hornor 1935, pl. 64 and Fales 1976, fig. 250). The two other tables also have four legs but end in pad feet, and only one has shell carving on the knees. An eight-sided table with six legs is pictured in Elder 1968, no. 24.

The stylized stockings of the feet, the shell carving on the knees, the high arch in the skirt, and the raised molding of the leg where it meets the skirt—all indicate the table's Philadelphia origin. Faceting of the top was probably an expensive option given its rarity of occurrence and the quality of materials and craftsmanship used. The faceting simplified seating, as did the use of only four legs. Six or eight legs were common during the William and Mary period and continued to be so in New York throughout the rococo period.

Practicality was happily not the sole consideration for this table. The high arch, which opens up the deep skirt, forms a continuous curve that extends from the leg across the knee, up the skirt, and down to the opposite leg. The cabriole legs are well formed and the shells delicately carved.

Provenance: The table was originally owned by the Leedom family of Germantown, Pennsylvania. *Leedom* is inscribed three times on the underside of the top and the frame of the table. It descended to the Sharp and Williams family; Israel Sack, Inc., New York

Construction and condition: The table is built around its seven and a half inch deep frame. This consists of mahogany end rails tenoned and double pinned to the stationary legs. Poplar inner rails are dovetailed to the other side of the oak fly rails. These inner rails extend the length of the frame and are nailed to them. These are one and nine-sixteenths of an inch thick. They are tenoned and double pinned to the stationary legs and to the fly legs. The fly rails rotate on knuckle joints, and the fly legs overlap the end rails. The knee-blocks are a triple lamination of mahogany with two layers of poplar.

The top is secured by modern screws through the frame. The leaves originally rotated on rule joints. At some time the rule joint was planed flat and the hinges replaced. The top and leaves now simply butt. This has reduced the overall width of the top by approximately one and a half inches.

Literature: I. Sack n.d.–1979, 7:184

12
Tea Table

1755–1765
Newport
John Townsend 1732–1809, fl. 1765–1805
Mahogany, *poplar
27⅝ x 34 x 21⅛ in.
ACC. NO. 84.4

This table is one of the finest examples of American baroque sculpture. The dense wood has allowed the cabinetmaker to carve extraordinarily crisp edges on the cabriole legs, especially through the ankles. The tension expressed in the grip of the talons gives the effect of squeezing the ball into its elongated shape, thus lightening the effect of the mass it supports. The intaglio carving of the knees is tight and crisp without interrupting the line of the leg. The ogival curves of the skirt spread out behind the leading edge of the knee, while the molded edge of the tray top serves to cap and enclose the design.

The table is attributed to John Townsend on the basis of both interior and exterior characteristics. The system of dovetailed skirt braces is found on documented Townsend tables from the Colonial through the Federal periods, including the Pembroke table, cat. no. 67. The knee carvings and the shaping of the ball-and-claw feet relate to the signed Townsend highboy (Moses fig. 3, 99) and a signed Townsend card table (Cooper 1980, 24).

Six tables with this form are known, but this is the only one attributed to John Townsend. Three examples (Downs 1952, nos. 372, 373 and Carpenter 1954, no. 77) have open talons but differ in having a continuous horizontal skirt that hides the plinth of the leg. Two others (Warren 1975, no. 106 and Cooper 1980, 215) have closed talons with the rails tenoned into the legs.

Provenance: According to the previous owners, the table was acquired from a New York decorator/dealer about twenty-five years ago. The dealer indicated that the table had been purchased by her brother at an auction in Seattle, Washington, a few years earlier; Israel Sack, Inc., New York

Construction and condition: The mahogany rails are shaped on one side only and tenoned to the legs. Vertically grained blocks, now replaced, were glued to the joints. Two poplar cross braces, one of which remains, were dovetailed across the top of the frame. A single medial brace, now missing, was dovetailed across the bottom of the frame. The knee-blocks are glued in place. Two of them are replacements. The tray top is molded from the solid. The beaded lower edge is applied. The top is currently attached to the frame by both blocks and screws.

Literature: Moses 1984, frontispiece; I. Sack 1984, 42–43

13
Folding Stand
1760–1780
Philadelphia
Mahogany
27¾ x 24 in.
ACC. NO. 73.5

This compact and well-proportioned piece is not a smaller, uncarved version of Philadelphia's grandest tea tables. A manuscript of the Philadelphia price list of 1772 (Weil 1979, 187) identifies it as a folding stand, though it is most often referred to today as a tip-table or candlestand. All the options seen here, save the scalloped top, are described and priced:

Folding Stands
Stand 22 inches [presumably the diameter of the top] with a box plain top & feet	1:15:0
Ditto plain top & claw foot	2: 2:6
Ditto with leaves on the knees	2:10:0
Ditto fixed [top does not turn] 18 inches	1: 4:0
Ad for fluting the piller 5 s[hillings] & to Jurneyman [0: 2:6]	

Folding stands were a common form made throughout the colonies. All the hallmarks of the Philadelphia style are seen in this stand: the flattened ball beneath a fluted column, the bird cage (called a box in the price list), and scalloped top. There are several illustrated similar examples, with varying degrees of decoration (Downs 1952, no. 283, Rodriguez-Roque 1984, nos. 172, 173, and Heckscher 1985, no. 120).

The ball-and-claw feet and the shell-and-leaf work on the knees are typical mid-eighteenth century Philadelphia motifs. The scalloped top is borrowed from silver salvers of the period. The handling of the column reflects an interest in classical architecture and proportion that flourished throughout the eighteenth century. This combination of elements shows a pursuit of elegance and refinement based on "modern" decorations along with classical inspiration.

Provenance: Israel Sack, Inc., New York; Mr. and Mrs. Edmund Zacker Collection, Hartford; Israel Sack, Inc., New York; Lansdell K. Christie Collection, Syosset, New York; P-B sale 3422, 21 October 1972, lot 59; Israel Sack, Inc., New York

Construction and condition: The legs are dovetailed to the column and a triangular iron brace attached over the joints. The bird cage is made by vasiform balusters doweled through mahogany blocks. The battens are slightly bowed in length and rounded on top. The end of each batten is finished with an unmolded cyma curve and held by a screw. A circular brass catch locks the top to the bird cage. The top is cut from a single piece of mahogany and the piecrust molding is carved from the solid.

Literature: A. Sack 1950, 259

14
Card Table
1760–1780
Philadelphia
Mahogany; yellow pine, white cedar, poplar, oak
29½ x 34½ x 17 in.
ACC. NO. 80.9

This table perfectly exemplifies the spirit of the early rococo in Philadelphia. Like cat. no. 5 the turret end table is an earlier form updated by the application of rococo decoration. The highly carved legs, with broad knees and deep turrets, are the focus of the table. The canted skirt, with its series of C-scrolls and foliage over a diaper-work background, unites the two legs. Canting the skirt adds depth to the frame in a different plane from that created by the turrets and flanking ogee blocks. The acanthus leaves of the legs are outlined by a series of interlaced scrolls that terminate in a pendant bellflower. Naturalistic carving flows over each of the elements—turrets, legs, and skirt—uniting them in a richly sculptured example of Philadelphia rococo.

The mate to this table is in the collection of Colonial Williamsburg (Cooper 1980, fig. 213). Both have an engraved

plate stating they were bought by Joseph Parker Norris at the sale in 1788 of Solitude, John Penn's estate. Hornor attributed this pair to Thomas Affleck because he believed Affleck made all of Penn's furniture, though no documentary evidence supports the theory. A number of other highly carved Philadelphia turret-end card tables are known (Hummel 1976, fig. 103 [a pair], Hornor 1935, pl. 234, Warren 1975, no. 110, and one in the collection of the PMA, acc. no. 67-69-1). All have the same deep frame, carved turret ends, and a single drawer. Warren 1975, no. 110 varies the most in having a gadrooned edge. The pattern of carved decoration is different on each table.

Provenance: A brass plate attached to the table states that it was purchased by Joseph Parker Norris in 1788 at the sale of the contents of John Penn's estate, Solitude. The style of engraving is such that it may be contemporary with the purchase by Norris. The table descended through the Norris family of Philadelphia to Dr. Norris W. Vaux; Joe Kindig, Jr. and Son Antiques, York, Pennsylvania

Construction and condition: The yellow pine rear rail is dovetailed to the mahogany side rails. Large vertically grained blocks, the depth of the frame, obscure the joint of the side rails to the front and the attachment of the front legs. An oak fly rail is nailed and screwed flush to the rear rail. The rear legs are mortised and double pinned to the fly rail. The fly leg rotates on a knuckle joint. It overlaps the frame with a thumbrail molding that extends to the knee, where a dado is cut to accept the carved skirt. This section is set at an angle to the frame and glued to its lower edge. A series of two-part glue-blocks reinforce the joint. One part is glued to the frame and the other is glued to the carved skirt and the other block. Horizontally grained blocks support the carved pieces of the skirt below the vertically grained ogee blocks which flank the turrets.

The drawer opening is cut from the solid. The drawer is supported by L-shaped pine runners fitted between the front and rear rails at each end of the opening. The drawer has a mahogany front with an inset beading. The back and sides are poplar. The bottom is white cedar with the grain set side to side. The top is currently attached by glue-blocks and screws through the frame. The inside of the top and leaf are covered in old, but probably not original, red baize. Pockets for counters and candle sticks are carved out at each corner.

Literature: Hornor 1935, pl. 235. The mate to this table is illustrated in Cooper 1980, no. 213

Exhibition: Williamsburg, Virginia, Colonial Williamsburg 1982

15

Pembroke Table

1760–1770
Eastern Virginia
Mahogany; poplar, cherry, white cedar
28½ x 42⅝ x 31¼ in.
ACC. NO. 82.1

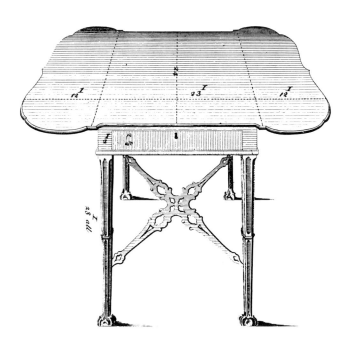

Chippendale, *Director* 1754, pls. 27, 53, 123, 133

Breakfast, or Pembroke, tables were a new form introduced around mid-century and pictured in the 1754 edition of Chippendale's *Director*, plate 53. Following English usage, "Pembroke" refers to the lady who first gave orders for such a table. The design of this one follows the basic form shown in the *Director*, in combination with Chinese, Gothic, and rococo motifs. The tassel-like feet may copy the guttae on classical cornices. In Chippendale, they are seen on the feet of chairs and cabinets in the Chinese taste (1754, pls. 27, 123, 133). The legs, which are chamfered on all four sides, and the pierced stretchers are in the Gothic manner. The stretchers are very similar to those used in a Philadelphia Pembroke table (Comstock 1962, no. 359). The serpentine top with porringer corners and cast brasses are typically rococo features.

The legs and feet are the table's most distinctly regional features. Several similar tables (see Comstock 1962, fig. 362) are thought to have been made in northeast North Carolina. A Williamsburg group has also been documented (Gusler 1979, fig. 94). The sophistication of design and quality of execution seen here suggest an urban center like Williamsburg or Norfolk rather than the Carolina group.

Provenance: Bernard and S. Dean Levy Inc., New York

Construction and condition: The sides of the frame are made of a thin poplar inner rail and a cherry fly rail. The inner rail is nailed to the fly rail. Together they are as thick as the legs. There is a single leaf support. It has an ogee profile with matching cutout and rotates on a knuckle joint. The far side of the frame is a plain piece of mahogany tenoned to the legs. The drawer side has two mahogany rails. The upper one is dovetailed to the legs and the lower one is tenoned. The drawer is supported by poplar strips glued and nailed to the inner rails.

The drawer has poplar sides and back with a white cedar bottom that is set front to back. The drawer front is mahogany veneered in mahogany with inset beading.

The stretchers are lapped where they cross and are tenoned to the legs. The guttae feet are applied. They were hollowed out at one time for castors. The top is highly figured and slightly thinner than usual. It is attached to the frame by white cedar glue blocks. Two hinges, each marked *SM-*, hold each leaf. The leaves rotate on a rule joint.

Exhibition: Williamsburg, Virginia, Colonial Williamsburg 1985–1986

16
Card Table

1760–1785
Philadelphia
Mahogany; poplar, oak, yellow pine, white cedar
29⅛ x 36⅛ x 17¾ in.
ACC. NO. 83.5

Straight legs and legs with Marlborough feet begin appearing next to the ubiquitous cabriole leg in the first edition (1754) of Chippendale's *Director*. While straight legs were used throughout the colonies, the Marlborough foot was used primarily in Philadelphia. Thomas Affleck (1740–1795), the Scots cabinetmaker who arrived in Philadelphia in 1763, is most often credited with popularizing the form. A manuscript of the Philadelphia price book of 1772 (Weil 1979) shows that by then most forms were offered with "crooked" (cabriole) or Marlborough legs. During and after the Revolution the chairs and desks made for the government offices in the State House all used Marlborough legs (Hornor 1935, pls. 97, 296–299).

The fullest development of Philadelphia's Marlborough school is shown in this card table. Each embellishment is described and priced in the 1772 price list, leaving little room for either improvement or imagination. The rope twist carving of the legs is a feature seen on only a few card and Pembroke tables (Heckscher 1985, nos. 106, 113, Hipkiss 1941, no. 62, and a card table at the Henry Ford Museum). The rope twist is also seen on chairs made by Thomas Affleck for the Supreme Court (Hornor 1935, pls. 298, 299). The fully serpentine top with conforming frame, the gadrooned edge, and carved legs share the robustness and vitality that infused all Philadelphia furniture during this period.

Provenance: G.K.S. Bush, Inc., Washington

Construction and condition: The rear rail is yellow pine and is dovetailed to the mahogany side rails. These are shaped on one side only. They are not perpendicular to the rear rail, but are set at an angle and tenoned to the front legs. The mahogany front rails are shaped on one side only. The upper rail is dovetailed to the legs and the lower rail is tenoned. The rear legs are mortised to an oak fly rail that is flush with the rear rail. The fly leg rotates on a knuckle joint and overlaps the frame, which has a corresponding rabbet. The gadrooning is shaped on one side only. It is glued and nailed to the lower edge of the frame. The brackets are replacements. The Marlborough feet are applied parallel grain to the legs. Some of the facings are replacements.

The drawer rides on pine supports glued and nailed to the sides. Pine guide strips are applied to the supports. The drawer has poplar back and sides. The bottom is white cedar with the grain set side to side. The drawer front is made of layers of mahogany horizontally laminated, shaped on both sides, and veneered in crotch mahogany. The beading on the top and bottom extends the full thickness of the drawers; on the sides it is inset. The brasses are replacements.

The top is held by a series of glue-blocks along the rails and screws through the front rail. There is one leaf-edge tenon.

17

High Chest
1700–1730
Boston
John Scottow, cabinetmaker, 1701–1790, fl. 1722–1770
Maple, white pine; white pine
64¼ x 40¾ x 22½ in.
ACC. NO. 75.5

Interest in oriental wares burgeoned in the English-speaking world during the reign of Charles II. This was naturally transferred to the colonies. By the early eighteenth century fashionable Bostonians had developed a taste for japanned pieces. Their sources were the same ones that would influence American taste throughout the century: design books, imported items, and immigrant craftsmen. The design book most often cited is *A Treatise of Japanning and Varnishing*, published by John Stalker and George Parker in 1688. Little is known of its use, if any, by Boston craftsmen. Yet advertisements and inventories record the presence of imported English examples, as do surviving pieces. At least one craftsman, William Price, advertised japanned pieces by one "late from London."

Part of the pleasure in viewing these highly derivative pieces is similar to that found in looking at the depiction of Westerners in Chinese export porcelain and trade paintings where the Westerners appear with oriental physiognomies. A world was created with western symbols in an oriental landscape. So it is with these pieces. Horses and hunters, fishermen and birds, wisemen and dragons as well as elephants inhabit a world more distant and unknown than the Orient that inspired it.

Other known William and Mary high chests with japanned decoration are illustrated in Fales 1972, fig. 79, Fales 1976, fig. 420, and Randall 1974, page 1128. Other examples are at Winterthur, SPNEA, and another in a private collection. The one at the Adams Historic Site (Randall 1974) is signed by its japanner, William Randle.

The size of the cornice and shape of the legs are the major variables of form within the group. The Kaufman example is distinguished by the faceted legs, each cut with six sides and so positioned that on the front four legs a facet faces forward. On the two rear legs the facets are set square with the sides. Each facet is decorated. Faceted legs are not known on other American pieces, but are seen on English examples (Kirk 1982, fig. 552).

Inscribed on the back of each of the drawers in chalk is the name *Scottow*. This represents the Boston cabinetmaker John Scottow. One of the japanned high chests (Randall 1974, 1128) is signed *Randle* in black paint. William Randle was a Boston cabinetmaker and japanner. A Queen Anne dressing table (Levy and Levy 1986, 15), now stripped of its japanning, is signed on the backboard *Scottow W. Randle* in black paint. This indication of a working relationship between the two suggests that Randle japanned this piece.

Provenance: The pieces were acquired from descendants of the Cogswell-Dixon family of Massachusetts. The japanned dressing table was acquired at the same time from the same family; Nathan Liverant and Son Antiques, Colchester, Connecticut; Israel Sack, Inc., New York

Construction and condition: The high chest is made in two sections. The upper case is made entirely of pine. The sides are dovetailed to the top and bottom boards. The back boards are two pieces of book-matched white pine. They are set in grooves in the sides and top and nailed to the bottom board. At the front there are three full-panel dust boards set in grooves in the sides. There is a rail set behind the cornice. The vertical partition which extends about six inches into the case, is set between the top dust board and the rail. A double-bead molding is applied to the edges of the sides, dust boards, and partition, outlining the drawer openings. The cornice is made in two pieces, vertically laminated. The upper case is raised on pine strips along the sides and front. The mid-molding is applied over these and the case. Short pine strips are glued along the front of the dust boards and bottom of the case to act as drawer stops.

The drawers have white pine sides, backs, and bottoms. The drawer fronts are maple. The bottoms are nailed to a rabbet in the front and along the bottom edge of the sides and back. Those of the upper case have strips added to the bottoms at the side, but those of the lower case do not. On the lower case drawers a small section of the bottom board extends beyond the back to act as a drawer stop.

The lower case has a pine backboard dovetailed through the pine sides. Vertically grained, square, pine blocks are glued at the bottom of these joints, allowing the legs to be doweled to the case. At the front vertically grained pine blocks are glued to the sides. A strip of veneer is glued over this joint to cover the end grain of the side and to make japanning easier. The front legs are doweled to this joint. The top rail is dovetailed to these blocks and the sides. The skirt is maple and is dovetailed through the sides. The center legs are doweled to vertically grained blocks applied to the skirt. White pine partitions are nailed to the skirt on each side of the center drawer. These taper in depth and extend to the back where they are set in grooves. Pine strips are set in the center of the drawer openings of the skirt and nailed to the back to support the drawers. Pine drawer guides are glued to the sides behind the leg blocks. A double-beaded molding is applied to the front to outline the drawer openings. These cover the partitions but not the top rail.

The top of the lower case is a U-shaped pine frame. Pine boards placed front to back are set in a groove on the inside of the frame and nailed to the top edge of the back board. The mid-molding is applied to the frame and encloses the upper case. The stretchers are lapped together. The convex parts of the front stretcher are applied. The side stretchers are cut from the solid. The legs are made in three pieces. The upper section extends from the case to the end of the faceted part. The middle extends from there to the stretcher. The last part is that below the stretcher.

The japanned surface and decorations are discussed in the *Construction and condition* notes of cat. no. 18.

Literature: Fairbanks and Bates 1981, 131–132

18

Dressing Table
1700–1730
Boston
Cherry, maple; white pine
30⅜ x 34⅛ x 21¼ in.
ACC. NO. 75.6

Japanned furniture was certainly the most delicate and perishable produced in the eighteenth century. It was more vulnerable than painted objects because of the raised decoration. There are fewer than forty pieces of Boston japanned furniture known and this is the only William and Mary japanned dressing table in the group.

The high chest (cat. no. 17) and this dressing table are not a matched pair, though they are thought to have been owned as a pair. The construction shows different hands at work and the japanning and decoration, while similar, also appear to be by different hands. The dressing table is thought to be later than the high chest because it is stylistically more refined. This is based on the ogival arches of the front skirt, shaped ogival stretchers, and the delicacy of the trumpet-shaped legs. Whether the two pieces were bought at the same time from different sources, or at later times as circumstances allowed, is likely to remain a mystery. The desire of the patron to acquire objects of the highest quality is present in each piece. The name *Milton* is inscribed in chalk on the back of the drawers. This is thought to refer to the cabinetmaker and not to the owner.

One of the most extraordinary features of the dressing table is the extent of the japanned decoration, which is applied over a black ground. (In the Queen Anne style black and red grounds imitating tortoise shell were more common.) Virtually every available surface is decorated. The sides have freehand flowers, the trumpets of the legs have leafage, and all the ball turnings, including those below the stretchers, have floral decoration. The tops of the stretchers are also decorated. The small size of the drawers and skirt limit the decorations to individual houses, birds, and people.

The glory of the japanning is in the top where a hunting scene is framed by diaper work and free-form floral decoration. Oriental in character, it is in no way foreign in story. Hunters on horseback and archers pursue a beast of obvious ferocity within a realistic landscape. The source for the scene is as yet unknown. The top presents the largest japanned picture of any piece known. Given the expanse, the painter took obvious pains to create a balanced and integrated design and not only a menagerie of motifs. The result is successful beyond any mere attempt to imitate oriental sources.

Provenance: This piece descended in the Cogswell-Dixon families of Massachusetts and was acquired along with the japanned high chest cat. no. 18; Nathan Liverant and Son Antiques, Colchester, Connecticut; Israel Sack, Inc., New York

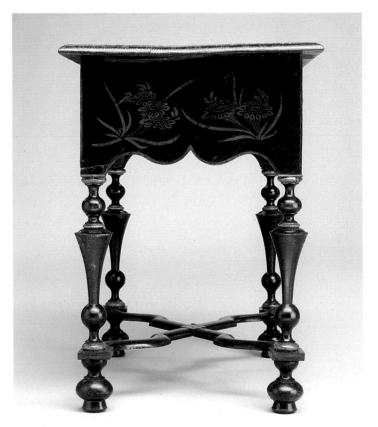

Construction and condition: The case has a white-pine back dovetailed to the cherry sides. These joints are reinforced by vertically grained pine blocks the height of the case, to which the rear legs are doweled. At the front vertically grained pine blocks are glued to the sides. Strips are glued over the end grain of the sides to make the japanning easier. The front legs are doweled to this block. The shaped skirt is cherry and it is tenoned to these blocks. White pine partitions are nailed to the skirt on each side of the center drawer. They extend to the back where the top inch is tenoned through. The drawer openings are outlined in applied beads which cover the pine partitions. Vertically grained pine blocks are applied behind the skirt as if to support turned pendants, but the beaded plinths are solid. The center drawer is supported by pine strips nailed to the sides of the partitions. The side drawers are supported by strips nailed to the bottom edges of the partitions. There are no drawer supports at the sides.

The top is made of two pieces with the underside painted white. Pins through the top secure it to the case. Strips of pine are glued to the inside upper edge of the case between the leg blocks. These once helped to hold the top, but have now shrunk away from it. The stretchers are cherry, lapped together in the center. Below the stretcher the leg is a plain dowel fitted with a hollow turning which acts as a collar.

The drawers have white pine sides, backs, and bottom boards. The drawer fronts are soft maple. The bottoms are nailed to a rabbet in the front and along the bottom edge of the sides and backs. Pine strips are glued to the bottoms at the sides.

Both the high chest and dressing table underwent conservation in 1976. The original paint had been applied directly to the wood, which resulted in few losses over time. The majority of these losses occurred in the raised gesso and gilt decorations of the top. The entire surface was cleaned of wax and grime, but the paint layer was left untouched. The surface was then saturated with an acryloid resin, the minor losses were in painted, regessoed and gilded, then recoated with an acryloid resin.

Literature: Fairbanks and Bates 1981, 131–132; Cooper 1980, pl. 22

Exhibition: Washington, NGA 1980 (In Praise of America)

19
High Chest
1725–1750
Boston
*Maple, *cherry, walnut; white pine
66⅛ x 38¾ x 21¾ in.
ACC. NO. 83.1

The earliest version of the New England Queen Anne high chest differed from its William and Mary predecessors primarily in the number and shape of the legs. The change from turned legs to cabriole legs also involved a change in construction from legs doweled to dovetailed cases, to panels tenoned and pinned to legs.

Transitional furniture is usually thought to mix the most fully developed elements of one style with the tentatively introduced elements of the next. In this high chest the cabriole legs are beautifully executed, showing all the delicacy the Queen Anne style achieved in Massachusetts. The shaping of the skirt shows a subtle refinement from the William and Mary period: the central arch is made of two arcs that intersect to form a pointed drop beneath the line of the escutcheons and drawer brass. In the William and Mary period this area was usually filled by a single plain arch. (For similar examples see I. Sack n.d.–1979, 7:201, A. Sack 1950, 177.

The facade is made of book-matched panels of walnut veneer, edged by a herringbone pattern of walnut veneer and walnut moldings. The sides and legs are maple and cherry. The present finish blends these, by staining, into a unified, if somewhat monochromatic, whole. The original finish may have employed graining or a painted finish on the sides and legs to simulate the more expensive and colorful veneers of the facade. A dressing table and high chest illustrated in Jobe and Kaye 1984, 186–188, show examples of this. Japanned pieces of the period are comparable in that the sides and legs are decorated and not just painted black. Refinishing has destroyed any internal evidence of this technique, and the exact nature of its original finish remains only speculation.

Provenance: Mrs. George Maurice Morris Collection, The Lindens, Washington; Christie's, sale 5262, 22 January 1983, lot 345; Israel Sack, Inc., New York

Construction and condition: This high chest is made in two sections. The upper case has maple sides dovetailed to white pine top and bottom boards. The back boards are two pieces of book-matched white pine, nailed to rabbets in the sides. At the front there are three pine rails with molded walnut facings. These are dovetailed through the sides. Walnut strips along the front edge of the side cover these joints. Beading is set in the sides between the rails. A pine rail behind the cornice is notched to the sides. The vertical partition is set between this and the next rail. The drawers are supported by strips of pine nailed to the sides. The bottom drawer rides directly on the bottom of the case. The cornice molding is made of two walnut moldings, vertically laminated. It is applied to the sides of the case and over the rail and edge of the top board in front. The upper case rests on pine strips applied to the bottom. The mid-molding is walnut and is applied over these strips, the sides of the case, and the front edge of the bottom board.

The drawers are made entirely of white pine. The dovetails are thick and widely spaced. The bottom boards are set front to back. They are nailed to a rabbet in the front and along the bottom edge of the sides and back. Strips are added to the bottoms of the sides for the upper case drawers but not for those of the lower case. The brasses are antique, but not original to the piece.

The lower case has cherry sides and a white pine back, all tenoned and pegged to the maple legs. The shaped skirt is white pine and tenoned to the legs. Pine partitions are nailed to the skirt on each side of the center drawer. They taper in height as they extend to the back. The top inch of the partition is tenoned through the back. Pine drawer guides are applied to the sides between the legs. The drawers are supported by pine strips set in the skirt in the center of the drawer openings and nailed to the back. A nailed walnut bead outlines the lower edge of the skirt. The pendants, which are new, are doweled to vertically grained pine blocks glued to the skirt. The top of the lower case is a U-shaped frame pegged to the legs. Two pieces of book-matched pine are set in grooves on the inside edge of the frame and nailed to the top edge of the backboard. Walnut moldings are glued and mitered to the frame enclosing the upper case.

Literature: Iliff 1979, 754

20
High Chest

1730–1760
Boston
Walnut; white pine
88¼ x 43 x 22½ in.
ACC. NO. 81.2

The Massachusetts high chest, or highboy as it is often called, reached its zenith during the Queen Anne period. It retained the decorative embellishments of veneer, inlay, and japanning of the William and Mary period and it incorporated the bonnet top, cabriole legs, and carved shells new to the period. The most distinctive features of the best of these pieces are the recessed, carved, and gilded shell drawers. About a dozen high chests are known that have either elaborate veneer or japanning, and shell drawers. Four other veneered versions have been published (Heckscher 1985, no. 157; Randall 1965, no. 54; Biddle 1963, no. 55—also shown in Comstock 1962, no. 183—and one in the Flayderman sale, 1930, lot 437). Three dressing tables (Heckscher 1985, no. 158 and Fales 1976 nos. 427, 428), though not mates to any of these, show the same high level of design and decoration. One of the high chests (Randall 1965, no. 54) is signed and dated 1739 by Ebenezer Hartshorne of Charlestown. Even without this example, however, the group could be closely dated. Account books of the 1730s record charges made for each of the decorations seen here. This documents both the style and a sophisticated trade in component parts and specialized labor.

As a group these veneered high chests have the same form and decorations seen in cat. no. 20. The sides of both the upper and lower case are crossbanded, outlined in stringing, and inset with compass stars. The stringing on the sides of the upper case forms an arch above the stars. This level of decoration is comparable to that of the japanned pieces, which are also decorated on their sides. The high chests show their greatest variety in the amount and handling of the decorative elements such as the shell carving, number of compass stars, arrangement of brasses, and types of finials. The Kaufman high chest has only one feature not seen on any of the others; the cornice above the pilasters starts to rise immediately rather than turning at right angles to the pilaster.

Provenance: The high chest was purchased from the family of an early Rhode Island collector who is thought to have acquired it early in this century; Nathan Liverant and Son Antiques, Colchester, Connecticut; Israel Sack, Inc., New York

Construction and condition: The lower case has pine sides and back, all tenoned to the walnut legs. The sides are veneered in vertically grained walnut and the legs are crossbanded in walnut veneer. The sides are outlined in string inlay and have a compass star inlaid in the center. In front the rails and partitions are pine faced with molded walnut. The top of the lower case is a U-shaped pine frame with pine boards set front to back in a groove along the inside edge of the frame. Walnut moldings are affixed to the edge of the frame enclosing the upper case. The pendants are replacements.

The drawers ride on pine strips notched into the rails in the center of each drawer opening and tenoned through the backboard. Drawer guides of pine are set between the legs on each side. The drawers are white pine throughout. The top edges of the drawer sides are beaded. The drawer bottoms are set front to back and nailed in place.

The upper case has two-board walnut sides dovetailed to the bottom board. The crossbanding of the lower case is continued on the upper case, as is the stringing and inlaid compass stars. The top is a closed cornice. The tympanum is pine, front and back. Pine boards conforming to the curve of the cornice are nailed in place. The section behind the central finial is U-shaped, with pine set over and in line with the sides of the shell drawer. The back has horizontally grained pine boards nailed to a rabbet. At the front, walnut strips are glued to the edge of the sides; along the outside they are crossbanded and inlaid with stringing. Walnut pilasters are set in the center of the strips. The rails are pine, faced with molded walnut. There are full pine dust boards, thinner than the rails, set in dadoes in the sides. Pine drawer guides are set behind the pilasters at each side.

The drawers of the upper case are constructed like those of the lower, except that pine strips are glued to the bottom of each side. All the locks of the upper case are new. The brasses are old, but not original to the piece. The original set of brasses had matching escutcheons, the shadows of which can still be seen. The shells are cut from the pine drawer fronts and have been regilded. The plinths and side finials are later additions.

Literature: Moses 1984, fig. 1.10; Jobe and Kaye 1984, fig. 1-23

21

Dressing Table

1735–1760

Massachusetts

Walnut; white pine *

30¼ x 34¼ x 21⅞ in.

ACC. NO. 77.4

The combination of blockfront form and veneer decoration seen here is unique among dressing tables and is one of only two such pieces known. Among blockfront dressing tables there are two easily distinguished groups. One group is associated with the cabinetmaker Joseph Davis who trained in Boston but worked in Portsmouth, New Hampshire. These have three raised panels rather than the raised and recessed blocking of cat. no. 21 (Jobe and Kaye 1984, I-34 and Copper 1980, fig. 244). The other group is characterized by raised and recessed panels, two tiers of three drawers each, and an extra row of brasses on the frame below the lower row of drawers (Downs 1952, no. 325, Montgomery and Kane 1976, no. 98, and Lovell 1974, fig. 65). There are also a number of highly veneered and inlaid dressing tables. These range from ones with high arches in the skirt, similar to cat. no. 19, to ones with carved shells or painted recesses similar to cat. no. 20. This dressing table is not closely related to either the blockfront or veneered groups.

The highly distinctive shaping of the legs and feet, however, does relate to a number of other pieces. The pad feet have a distinct offset as the ankle enters the foot, which, in turn, rests on a thin wafer. This feature is seen on a number of case pieces attributed to the Salem-Ipswich area (Fairbanks and Bates 1981, 117 and I. Sack n.d.–1979, 6:1644). The only other veneered blockfront piece, a slant front desk, has this type of foot as well. This feature is in no way conclusive of Salem authorship, but does indicate that it may have been made outside Boston.

Provenance: By tradition this table descended in the Munro family of Cambridge, Massachusetts, whose ancestors owned the Munro Tavern. The table is supposed to have been rescued in the 1880s by Alice B. Munro from the back shed of the tavern where it was being used as an ironing table; Israel Sack, Inc., New York

Construction and condition: The sides and back are roughly finished white pine panels tenoned and pinned to the walnut legs. The front has three pine rails. The top rail is shaped on one side and dovetailed to the legs. The middle rail is shaped on one side and tenoned to the legs. The lower rail is made from a single piece of pine shaped on both sides. The vertical partitions are pine. The sides and front are veneered, and the plinths of the legs are crossbanded, as is the bottom edge of the sides. The veneer behind each of the brasses and shell is crotch walnut.

The drawers are constructed entirely of white pine. The drawer bottoms are set front to back and nailed to a rabbet in the front and to the bottom edge of the backboard. There are strips glued to the bottoms at each side on which the drawers ride. The top-drawer front and two side-drawer fronts are shaped on both sides, but the center drawer is shaped on one side only. The drawer beads are walnut and applied. The carved and inlaid shell is also applied.

Pine drawer guides for both upper and lower drawers are set against each side between the legs. Strips are set behind the vertical partitions and attached to the back to support the drawers. Strips are also set at each side for the upper and lower drawers.

The top is pine, framed by molded walnut strips. These strips butt each other. The central section is made of four book-matched panels of mahogany edged by walnut crossbanding. Checkerboard inlay separates the two.

Literature: I. Sack n.d.–1979, 6:1462–1463; Cooper 1980, no. 232; A. Sack 1985, 189

Exhibition: Washington, NGA 1980 (In Praise of America)

22
Clothes Press
1760–1780
Boston
Mahogany; white pine
86½ x 41½ x 21¾ in.
ACC. NO. 81.3

Clothes presses and chest-on-chests superseded the high chest in English fashions by the mid-eighteenth century. The wealthy Boston merchant Charles Apthorp imported a bombé clothes press with mirrored doors before 1757 (Fairbanks et al. 1975, fig. 44). Despite this indication of interest in keeping up with the latest in English fashions, the clothes press was not widely produced in New England. The high chest and chest-on-chest remained the most popular tall case pieces of the period.

The clothes press is of the same overall form and design as a group of Massachusetts blockfront chest-on-chests. These include signed and strongly attributed examples out of shops from Boston to Salem (see Randall 1965, no. 40, Whitehill 1974, fig. 1, Lovell 1974, figs. 74, 76, and Nutting 1928–1933, 1: 315). This example has been attributed to Benjamin Frothingham of Charlestown. The presence of a large body of labeled examples by this maker has not yielded a set of criteria applicable to this piece. Among the other blockfront clothes presses known are two early ones (Lovell 1974, fig. 72 and Vincent 1974, 96). These are distinguished by their closed curved baroque pediments. An example closer in form to this one, but having arched panel doors under a broken-scroll pediment, was in the Christie collection (SP-B, sale 3422, 21 October 1972, lot 57).

Excepting the carved rosettes of the pediment, this piece presents a more restrained appearance than comparable chest-on-chests. This comparison can be easily made by simply opening the doors. The interior is composed of four drawers, graduated in height, topped by a fifth that has the same profile as the doors. The brasses, though they do not match those of the base, are of similar quality and there is a line of matching escutcheon plates. The layout of the interior suggests that the doors were primarily for aesthetic effect and that the maker chose the subtle modulations of raised panel doors rather than brasses or fan carvings. The doors offer a vertical emphasis, where graduated drawers stress balance. A progression from the three-bay facade of the base to the two doors leading to the central finial is created. The linen tray indicates that either craftsman or customer still had an eye on practical matters.

Provenance: Descended in the Robbins Family of Brush Hill, Milton, Massachusetts; Israel Sack, Inc., New York

Construction and condition: This clothes press is built in two sections. The lower case has two-board mahogany sides dovetailed to white pine top and bottom boards, faced with mahogany at the front. The back boards are white pine, set side to side, nailed to rabbets in the sides. At the front are three molded rails, dovetailed through the sides. The top rail is all mahogany and the lower two are mahogany facings on pine. All are shaped on one side only. On top a mahogany molding encloses the upper case. Pine strips have been added to the bottom of the case to support the base molding which is applied to the sides of the case. At the front an additional piece of mahogany is inset to accommodate the concave blocking. The front feet are mahogany, supported by a vertical block of white pine with two flanking horizontal blocks. The rear feet are mahogany with a white pine bracket at the rear and are supported like the front feet.

The drawers of the upper and lower case are constructed in the same fashion. They have white pine sides, backs, and bottoms. The sides have a double-beaded top edge. The bottom boards are set front to back. They are nailed to a rabbet in the front and to the bottom edge of the backboard and sides. Pine strips are glued to the bottom at the sides. The drawer fronts are mahogany and are shaped on both sides. The convex blocking of the top drawer is hollowed out. There are five drawers in the upper case. The top drawer has the same profile as the doors. It is partitioned into three sections by two boards set front to back. The other four drawers are graduated in height. The drawers have straight fronts and are solid mahogany. They have rococo plates with Queen Anne bails. Each drawer has a matching escutcheon though there are no locks.

The upper case has two-board mahogany sides dovetailed to a white pine bottom board. At the top, the sides are connected by the mahogany pediment and in the rear by a pine board of similar profile. This piece is arched at the sides and has a U-shaped central section. The front and back are connected by pine boards nailed between them. There are five rails at the front. The top four have molded mahogany facings on pine. The bottom rail is mahogany, with a full-panel pine dust board. The drawers ride on pine strips nailed to the sides. Beads are applied to the sides between the rails. Narrow pine strips are set against the sides behind the beads to act as drawer guides. The bottom drawer rides on strips on top of the dust board which is thinner than the rail. The linen tray is made entirely of mahogany, with mahogany stiles and rail with a flush panel. The doors are framed and paneled with solid panels raised on the face side only. The finials are made in two parts: urn and flame.

Literature: I. Sack n.d.–1979, 7:1872–1873

23

Desk and Bookcase
1760–1790
Salem
Abraham Watson 1712–1790
Mahogany; white pine
97⅜ x 45¾ x 26¼ in.
ACC. NO. KAF 79.3

Oxbow-front (also called reverse or double serpentine) case pieces became popular in New England late in the rococo period and continued to be produced until the turn of the century. Chests and desks with oxbow facades often used brasses with large plates and matching escutcheons.

Salem makers relied heavily upon the modulation of form to elaborate their designs. Ball-and-claw feet, simplified fans or pinwheels, and a small amount of highly stylized leafwork were their only concessions to the rococo preference for naturalistic details. Salem makers favored arched panel doors—a Queen Anne feature—throughout the rococo period. The pinwheel rosette in the tympanum is a feature used by other North Shore makers (Heckscher 1985, no. 180 and Jobe and Kaye 1982, 1-32). Salem artisans used it in combination with tiny pinwheels to finish the circular openings beneath a scrolled pediment rather than rosettes on the scroll itself. The interior of this desk is of the type found throughout eastern Massachusetts. The oxbow drawers, ball-and-claw feet, and pendant are typical of Salem in both the smooth line of the drawers and tightly controlled shaping of the feet. Similar examples are shown in I. Sack n.d.–1979, 3:753, and A. Sack 1950, 99.

This desk and bookcase matches one in Fales 1965, no. 44, except for two details: the piece in Fales has a tombstone-shaped mirror on its prospect door, and a slightly different pattern of drawer brasses. It retains the gilding of the pinwheel rosette in the tympanum and has its original urn-and-ball finial. It is thought to have been made by Abraham Watson of Salem. The desk and bookcase, a chest-on-chest (Lovell 1974, fig. 76), and a desk lost in a 1914 fire were made by him for his own use, possibly for the house he built in 1770. The pieces are still owned by his descendants. Watson must have been a man of some means to have kept furnishings of such quality. On the top of the desk section of cat. no. 23 the names *John Hurd* and *George Hurd* are inscribed by the same hand. Their identity is not yet known.

Provenance: This desk was presented to the Women's City Club of Boston in memory of Grace Sinclair Whittemore by her husband, Parker W. Whittemore. This was recorded on a brass plaque in the writing section; Women's City Club of Boston; Christie's, sale "Phyfe," 21 October 1978, lot 274; Israel Sack, Inc., New York

Construction and condition: The desk and bookcase is made in two sections. The desk section has mahogany sides dovetailed to pine top and bottom boards. A mahogany strip runs along the front edge of the pine top board. The back boards are pine set horizontally and nailed to rabbets in the sides. At the front are four rails and a writing board dovetailed to the sides.

The rails have a molded mahogany facing and are shaped on one side only. Beading is set between the rails. Pine drawer supports are nailed to the sides. The writing board has a mahogany front section and is pine underneath the pigeon holes. The front part is dovetailed to the sides, while the rest is dadoed. The desk section has two layers of moldings at the base. The cove and bead part is applied to the sides and over the front edge of the bottom board and rail. These rest on a plain mahogany molding backed by pine and applied to the bottom of the case. The feet and knee-blocks are mahogany. The knee-blocks are backed by horizontally grained shaped pine blocks. The carved pendant is mahogany and is backed by a shaped pine block.

The drawers have white pine sides, backs, and bottoms. The upper edges of the sides are shaped with two raised beads. The bottom boards are set front to back. The fronts of the three lower drawers are mahogany, shaped on both sides. The top drawer front is mahogany; the convex ends are hollowed out and the concave center is straight across. The top two drawers have two mahogany partitions each. They are set in grooves in the front and nailed to the backboard. The lid supports are pine, tongue and grooved to vertically grained pieces of mahogany. The lid is mahogany, tongue and grooved to mahogany battens with thumbnail molded and lipped edges on the top and sides.

The desk interior is made in two tiers. These are separated by a pine rail with a molded mahogany facing. The lower tier has three drawers separated by vertical partitions of pine with molded mahogany facings. The drawers are supported in front by a mahogany strip that raises them above the writing surface. Pine strips are set behind the mahogany at each side and under the vertical partitions.

All the interior drawers have white pine sides, backs, and bottoms with mahogany fronts. The bottom boards are set front to back.

The upper tier is set back from the lower. It is divided into five sections separated by four vertical partitions of pine with molded mahogany facings. The fan carved pigeonhole valances are drawers. The prospect door and flanking pilasters are the facade of a removable box, held in place by a spring lock released through a finger hole in the top. The box is mahogany dovetailed together. The prospect door is mahogany, with a gilded frame and mirror applied. There are two drawers behind the door, and the upper one has a carved fan. There are document drawers behind the pilasters, but they open at the rear of the box and not the front.

The upper case is not attached to the lower. Mahogany moldings nailed to the top of the lower case enclose the upper case.

The upper case has mahogany sides. The bottom board is tenoned to the sides just above the candle slides. It is pine with a mahogany facing. Mahogany strips are set below the joints at each side. A mahogany strip is applied at the front, and the candle slides are set in it. Just below the pediment a white pine board, with a shaped and molded mahogany facing, is dovetailed to the sides from the front. The tympanum is mahogany. Arches are cut in the tympanum just above the board, and a pair of concave carved fans are set in them. The pediment is connected to a similarly shaped pine backboard by pine boards set front to back and nailed in place to conform to the curve of the pediment. A U-shaped well made of white pine boards set front to back is set behind the finial.

The backboards are white pine set side to side and nailed to rabbets in the sides. The frames and panels of the doors are mahogany as are the applied pilasters. The arched panels are raised on the face side only.

The interior of the upper case is a series of pigeonholes, shelves, and drawers. All the partitions are white pine with mahogany facings. The top row of pigeonholes conforms to the curve of concave fans. All the valances are mahogany. There are three adjustable pine shelves with mahogany facings. Three drawers, set along the bottom, have white pine sides, backs, and bottoms, with mahogany fronts. The drawer bottoms are set side to side.

Literature: I. Sack n.d.–1979, 6:22, 1941

Exhibitions: New York, MMA 1980–1986; Norfolk, Virginia, Chrysler Museum 1979–1980

24
Chest of Drawers
1765–1785
Newport
Goddard-Townsend families
Mahogany; white pine, chestnut, yellow pine
31⅝ x 37⅛ x 21½ in.
ACC. NO. KAF 80.10

Newport block and shell chests of drawers apparently came in two models: three-drawer or four-drawer. A number of the four-drawer variety are either signed or are strongly attributed to John Townsend (see Heckscher 1985, no. 139). Three-drawer chests show a greater variety in their execution. One (Downs 1952, no. 219) has a desk section behind the shell drawer. Two chests (GSE 1929, no. 602 and Rodriguez-Roque 1984, no. 4) have drawers with lipped edges. The most common drawer treatment in Newport is a plain drawer fitted in an opening outlined by beading. Other chests (Hipkiss 1941, no. 37 and Ott 1965, no. 51) are distinguished by the handling of the shells or the shaping of the feet. Examples similar to this one are illustrated in Moses 1984, figs. 7.24, 8.8, and 8.9.

This chest of drawers has the distinction of being signed by one man, inscribed with the name of another, and authenticated to a third. Inside the case, written in ink on the bottom board, is the name *James Goddard, Jr.* within a scribed circle interlaced with inscribed arcs. *John* is written in chalk on the back of a drawer. *John* is also written on the bottom boards inside the case. Indecipherable script is found on the bottom of the case and the letter *T* on another drawer back. Michael Moses authenticates the piece to Edmund Townsend (Moses 1984, 16–17). He believes that Goddard, who was apprenticed to Townsend, signed it during that time. The signature is, he thinks, a doodle rather than a sign of authorship. This much information makes a generic Goddard-Townsend school attribution a safe one.

This three-drawer chest is decidedly less square in proportion than its New York counterpart, cat. no. 28. The slightly greater width of the case in relation to the height gives a smooth flow to the outline of the shells and prevents them and the blocking from appearing to protude too much. The use of only three drawers presents a more unified facade that balances the boldness of the blocking with the horizontal drawers. The base and feet are subtly brought together by the addition of the molding, which connects the raised blocking of the feet. Their termination in a carved scroll is the type of finishing detail that highlights the best work of the Goddard-Townsend school.

Provenance: Joe Kindig, Jr., Antiques, York, Pennsylvania; Mr. and Mrs. Walter B. Robb Collection, Buffalo; SP-B, sale 4478Y, 22 November 1980, lot 1290; Israel Sack, Inc., New York

Construction and condition: The case has mahogany sides dovetailed to the pine top and bottom boards. The mahogany top is attached to the pine top but the method is hidden. The fillet, cove, and bead molding are applied to the sides and over the straight top rail and front edge of the pine top. Three shaped and molded rails are dovetailed to the sides. These are chestnut with mahogany facings. The upper two drawers are supported by yellow pine strips nailed to the sides and white pine rails dovetailed to the back of the case. White pine strips are nailed to the sides above the top drawer, to prevent it from tipping when opened. Thick pine strips are set on the bottom, at the sides, to support the bottom drawer. Beading is set in the sides between the rails. The back boards are chestnut. Two of them are tongue and grooved together. They are nailed to rabbets in the sides and in the pine top. They are also nailed to the pine rear rails and the bottom board.

The drawers have pine sides and backs. The drawer bottoms are chestnut set front to back. They are set in grooves in the front and nailed to the bottom edge of the back. Strips are glued to the bottoms at the sides. The drawer fronts are mahogany. The lower two are shaped on both sides from the solid. The top one is shaped on one side and has applied convex shells. The brasses are replacements.

The base molding is in two parts. The upper section of the ogee and plain vertical strip are one piece and applied to the case. The rounded section between the feet is nailed to the bottom of the case. It is shaped on one side only. The front feet are backed by a vertically grained, shaped pine block flanked by two horizontally grained, shaped pine blocks. A chestnut bracket is slotted to each rear foot. The rear feet are supported in the same way as the front feet, and the rounded molding set between the front feet is also between the front and back feet.

Literature: A. Sack 1950, 103; Gaines 1968, 484; Moses 1984, pl. 19

Exhibition: New York, MMA 1982–1986

25
Bureau Table
1760–1790
Newport
Goddard-Townsend families
Mahogany; white pine, poplar, chestnut
33 x 37½ x 21 in.
ACC. NO. 75.4

Newport blockfront, shell-decorated bureau tables, which to-day are often called kneehole desks, have become the icon of American pre-Revolutionary artistic achievement. Their independence of European fashions has come to be regarded as the artistic statement of the political struggles of the period. The work of the Goddard and Townsend families is distinctly American in a way that other Americans of the time would have thought provincial. Newport's cabinet trade never seems to have attracted significant numbers of foreign-trained craftsmen. Cities like Philadelphia and Charleston prided themselves on their acquaintance with current London fashions; new craftsmen in town sought clients with advertisements such as "late of London," or "London trained." Members of the Goddard-Townsend clan appear to have trained with each other and not with craftsmen influenced by London fashions. Such clannishness easily accounts for the localized construction details peculiar to Newport. The great mystery lies with the patrons and their interaction with the craftsmen. Newport was based on maritime wealth acquired through privateering and the triangular trade. Its merchants had access to all the colonial, Caribbean, and British ports; had these men and their families sought the latest in London fashions they could have easily acquired them. Newport's aesthetic preferences have been attributed to its Quaker community, but the argument collapses when one turns to the products of Quaker Philadelphia. Why the mercantile elite of a city, whose wealth was based on international trade, should invest that wealth in the products of a highly competent, but provincial, group of cabinetmakers is as mysterious as the results are beautiful.

This bureau table is first and foremost a piece of functional sculpture. Its practical uses are dwarfed by its artistic intentions. The storage capacity of a bureau table is considerably less than a chest of the same size. Where the central recess of kneehole offers some leg room, a dressing table or lowboy offers more. Blocking demanded more materials and workmanship, but did not increase available space. The shells have absolutely no functional value. The craftsmanship and expenditure of materials is just as extravagant and representative a display of wealth as any carved Philadelphia dressing table or Boston bombé chest.

All this effort, of course, achieves a vastly different effect than it would in Philadelphia or even Boston. The craftsman of the bureau table has shown a concern for the overall manipulation of form and a subtle handling of details. This orchestration of elements can be seen in the blocked drawers made of a highly figured light mahogany that contrasts with the darker, more tightly grained wood of the shell drawer and door. The back edges of the rear feet have an ogee profile, and while the piece is intended to stand against a wall, these give it a more freestanding appearance when viewed from the side. The inner curve of the blocked feet comes to a point to mark the transition from the horizontal to the vertical plane. The molded top is supported by a fillet, cove, and bead molding that allows the vertical line started so smoothly in the feet to move into the top and across the case. This fluidity of line is expressed in the shells, which are a kind of leitmotif of Newport craftsmanship. The balance of lobe and fillet, convex and concave shell, is a perfect expression of the form in the decoration.

This bureau table is a masterpiece, not because it is uniquely American or because of any technical virtuosity; it is a masterpiece because it could not be formed in any other way and express what it does; each line and curve is a part of the whole and unable to admit alteration or addition.

Provenance: Purchased in 1948 by Israel Sack from the Belknap family of Flushing, Long Island. Mrs. Belknap inherited it from her grandfather, Captain Morin, who married Miss Thorndike of Boston; Mr. and Mrs. Walter B. Robb Collection, Buffalo; Israel Sack, Inc., New York

Construction and condition: This bureau table is constructed as a chest of drawers with a recess and not as separate pedestal units. The mahogany sides are dovetailed to white pine top and bottom boards. The mahogany top is fitted to sliding dovetails from the sides; nails through the pine top secure it. A cove-and-bead molding is applied to the case on the sides, and over the top rail and the front edge of the pine top. Chamfered poplar blocks are glued between the top rail and pine top.

The facade of the case is built around the rail supporting the shell drawer and the partitions that form the sides of the recess. The rail is a half-panel pine dust board dadoed to the sides, with a molded and shaped mahogany facing dovetailed

to them. The dado extends only as far as the dust board. In the rear there is a pine rail dovetailed to the sides. The bottom board of the case is cut out for the recess. The mahogany partitions are dovetailed to it and nailed to the shell drawer rail. Vertically grained pine partitions extend from the mahogany partitions to the back of the case. These form the sides of the cabinet behind the door. A board is set between the shell rail and rear rail to form the top of the cabinet. There are two mahogany shelves in the cabinet. Mahogany strips are mitered and nailed in the recess to form a frame for the door. These strips have beading cut from the solid. The bottom rail of the frame is shaped on one side. A poplar board is set behind it to form the bottom of the cabinet. The door is made without framing or battens. The recess and shell is cut from the solid, with no shaping in the back.

The drawers have poplar sides and backs with white pine drawer bottoms. The bottom boards are set side to side. They fit in grooves in the front and sides and are nailed to the bottom edge of the back. Strips are applied to the bottoms as they join the sides. The drawer fronts are mahogany, and shaped on both sides. The shell drawer front is shaped on one side only, with applied shells. The bottom boards of the shell drawer are set front to back. The brasses are replacements.

Six pine rails, with molded and shaped mahogany facings, support the blocked drawers. They are dovetailed to the sides and to the mahogany partitions. The drawers are supported by pine strips nailed to the sides and to the mahogany and pine partitions. The base molding is applied to the sides of the case. At the front it is applied to the mahogany partitions and to the lower edge of the door frame and of the bottom board.

The front feet are carved from the solid. They are supported by vertically grained and shaped pine blocks flanked by horizontal chestnut blocks. The back edge of the rear feet is shaped to match the profile of the feet. The rear feet have pine brackets supported by the same blocking as that used for the front feet. The left rear foot has a replaced bracket and blocking. The rounded molding set between the front feet and below the recess is also set between the front and rear feet. It is nailed to the bottom of the case.

Literature: I. Sack n.d.–1979, 5:1206; Moses 1984, fig. 1.16

cat. no. 24, detail

26
Chest-on-Chest
1765–1790
Rhode Island
Mahogany; white pine, chestnut
86¾ x 41½ x 21¾ in.
ACC. NO. 85.1

This piece forms a group with two other blockfront, shell-decorated case pieces that are distinguished by their stepped pediments. The other pieces are the nine-shell chest-on-chest (Downs 1952, no. 183) and the nine-shell desk and bookcase (Ott 1965, no. 67). Some of their other common characteristics are lipped drawers, the pattern of the feet, and style of shell. The shells are carved from the solid, and the convex ones are outlined and undercut. All the pediments are constructed in the same way, using the same moldings, plinths, and finials.

In neither construction nor execution of the embellishments do these pieces appear to be part of the Goddard-Townsend school. They have continually been attributed to them on the basis of family associations and the belief that all Rhode Island block and shell pieces were either Goddard or Townsend. The theory has been raised that these pieces represent a Providence school and possibly the work of the Carlyle family (see Moses 1984, 303). They are also said to be early examples of the style.

There is reason to agree with the idea of a Providence group, but conclusive evidence or the ability to make an attribution to an individual shop is not yet possible. The only other Rhode Island pieces that have stepped pediments are a group of tall case clocks. These clocks show great variation in their execution and do not appear to be from a single shop. Beyond their stepped pediments, the only other common characteristics are a raised panel with a convex shell on the door and chamfered corners on the base.

At least twelve of these stepped pediment tall clocks are known. Seven have painted dials, a feature that was first introduced in the 1770s but did not become widely available until after the Revolution. Published examples include *Antiques*, July 1933, 4 and September 1982, 437; E. Miller 1937, No. 1809; GSE 1929, No. 633; and I. Sack, n.d. 1979, 4:852. Three have works signed by Caleb Wheaton (1757-1827) of Providence who started working on his own no earlier than 1778 (*Antiques*, July 1933, 4; Ott 1965, no. 67; and I. Sack, n.d. 1979, 7:2017). One is signed by Edward Spaulding (1732–1785) of Providence. While Spaulding's earliest works date from the 1750s, this case has a band of blind fretwork set below the hood, a feature that did not become popular until late in the Colonial period. One is thought to have been made for Jabez Bowen of Providence by John Goddard in the 1760s

(*Antiques*, May 1984, 989). This clock has English works. One of the Wheaton clocks (*Antiques*, 1933, 4) has been associated with John Goddard or his son Townsend Goddard by a 1786 bill of sale.

All the clocks in this group are either associated with a Providence clockmaker, Providence patron, or have the later painted dials that as previously mentioned became popular after the Revolution when Providence had overtaken Newport as the economic center of Rhode Island. The evidence from these clocks indicates the possibility of a Providence school of block and shell designs possibly inspired by Newport makers that pre-dated the Revolution and evolved into the stepped pediment case pieces that include catalogue no. 26.

The argument that these stepped pediment pieces are an early version of the form is based on an incorrect comparison with Newport examples. The evolution of Newport shell designs, from the solid to applied, in no way proves that another shop had to follow that progression. Further, the design of these shells could not have been executed separately from the drawers. The outlining and undercutting is done in the drawer face to give greater depth to the shells. Nothing in their construction indicates a production as early as the 1750s, which has been suggested.

Even within the context of Rhode Island chest-on-chests this piece is still in a small group. Only five other chest-on-chests with block and shell bases are known (Downs 155, no. 183, Comstock 1962, no. 305, Rodriguez-Roque 1984, no. 13, SP-B, sale 3467, 24–27 January 1973, lot 947, and one in the Cleveland Museum of Art).

Provenance: By tradition this piece was originally owned by John Brown, the great merchant of Providence. It is first pictured in Luke Vincent Lockwood, *Colonial Furniture in America,* as the property of Nathaniel Herreshoff of Bristol, Rhode Island. Captain Herreshoff was the great grandson of John Brown through his grandmother, Sarah Brown Herreshoff, John's daughter. In the 1950s John Nicholas Brown purchased the piece from his cousin many times removed, Westcott Herreshoff Chesborough, a relative of Nathaniel Herreshoff; The Nicholas Brown Foundation

Construction and condition: This piece is constructed in two sections. The upper case has mahogany sides dovetailed to a white pine bottom board. The sides include the boxed ends. The cornice molding is applied to the sides and is held by screws from the inside. The sides are connected at the top by the front and back boards of the cornice. The front piece is mahogany. It starts above the capitals of the quarter columns and is rabbeted to the sides. It includes the boxed ends, and the moldings of the pediment are applied to it. The backboard is white pine. It begins at the line of the top rail and is nailed to vertically grained blocks glued to the sides. The back piece is flat at the ends, with quadrants behind the scrolled pediment and a U-shaped central section. The front and back boards are connected by chestnut boards over the boxed ends and the shell drawer. The quadrants and vertical panels of the U section are white pine. The central plinth is backed by a strip extending down behind the tympanum and screwed to it. Two chestnut back boards are set side to side and nailed to rabbets in the sides.

At the front the columned corners are made in three parts. The quarter columns are glued to the edges of the sides and are flanked by mahogany strips. These are backed by vertically grained white pine blocks. The rails are white pine with mahogany facings. They are set in the pine blocks of the sides. The top rail is a full-panel pine dust board. The vertical partitions are mahogany, nailed to the tympanum and set of grooves in the top rail. Drawer guides are attached to the sides behind the quarter columns. Strips nailed to these support the drawers. For the bottom drawer, these guides and strips are applied to the bottom board at the joint with the sides. Pine blocks are glued behind the bottom rail and to the bottom board to stiffen the rail and support the drawer. Strips are set between the front and back boards of the tympanum above the top row of drawers to prevent them from tipping when withdrawn. The mid-molding is applied to the side of the case and over the bottom rail and front edge of the bottom board.

The drawers have white pine sides, backs, and bottoms. The drawer fronts are mahogany. The bottom boards are set front to back. They are nailed to a rabbet in the front and to the bottom edge of the back. They are set in rabbets in the sides, and pine strips are applied along the bottom at the joint. The drawers have three lipped edges which overlap the rails and sides. The fronts of the lower case drawers differ. The lower two have mahogany fronts shaped on both sides, with an additional piece of mahogany glued behind the recessed section. The shell drawer is cut from the solid. The convex shells are hollowed out in the back and the concave shell is raised.

The lower case has mahogany sides dovetailed to white pine top and bottom boards. The back boards are chestnut set side to side and nailed to rabbets in the sides. At the front there are four rails. The middle two are pine with shaped mahogany facings. These are dovetailed to the sides. The top rail is mahogany, notched to the sides. The bottom rail is mahogany, shaped on one side only and notched to the sides. Pine blocks are set under this rail on the bottom board as supports. Pine strips nailed to the sides support the upper two drawers. Strips set on the bottom board support the bottom drawer. Pine strips nailed to the sides behind the top rail prevent the top drawer from tipping when opened. The waist molding is nailed to the sides and to the front rail and edge of the top. It encloses the upper case. The base molding is applied to the sides and over the bottom rail and edge of the bottom boards.

The front feet are backed by vertically grained pine blocks and flanked by horizontal ones. The rear feet have pine brackets and the same blocking.

Literature: Lockwood 1926, 121; Nutting 1928–1933, 1:no. 321; E. Miller 1937, 1:no. 881; Ott 1965, no. 56; Moses 1984, pl. 4, fig. 8.23 a, b, c

Exhibition: Providence, John Brown House Loan Exhibition of Rhode Island Furniture, 1965

27

High Chest
1765–1795
Newport
Mahogany; poplar, maple, chestnut, yellow pine
82¾ x 39¾ x 22¾ in.
ACC. NO. 86.1

American craftsmen and patrons continued to be interested in the high chest as a form long after the English ceased to produce them. In Newport, craftsmen and patrons continued to favor baroque designs well into the rococo period. The combination of these factors produced another example of the distinctive style of Newport furniture. While adopting the bonnet top, Newport craftsmen were unwilling to change their basic approach to the form. They incorporated their versions of rococo decorations, shells, and intaglio carving into the design without altering the line. Thus the sharp line of the knee is undisturbed by the carving, and the talons of the ball and claw feet flow perfectly into the four corners of the legs (see cat. no. 12). Both the upper and lower outlines of the concave shell smoothly carry the line of the arched skirt. Though the shell is carved from the solid, the shaping of the lower edge gives it an almost floating appearance. Newport craftsmen were unwilling to abandon the earlier pad feet. The combination of ball and claw feet in the front and pad feet in the back is seen on high chests, dressing tables, and card tables. The Newport craftsman's interest in the baroque approach to design is seen in the handling of the scroll pediment. The tympanum is filled by raised panels with the lipped edges matching those of the drawers and conforming to the curve of the scrolls. This approach successfully carries the line of the drawers smoothly through the pediment to the central finial. The continuation of the line of the scroll pediment is achieved by moldings applied on the outside edge of the circular openings beneath the scrolls. Another example of the craftsman's control of the form can be seen at the mid-molding. A progression is created from the knee of the cabriole leg to the lower case and from it through the mid-molding to the upper case. In other regions, mid-moldings are applied to both the upper and lower case making them wider than both and creating a horizontal emphasis. These features show the Newport craftsman's refusal to let decoration dominate the form.

This high chest follows the documented work of John Townsend very closely. It varies from his standard pattern in having a thirteen-lobed shell instead of a fourteen, the pattern of the knee carving, and the shaping of the sides of the lower case. In matters of construction and style of decoration, this piece follows Townsend completely. A closely related example (Ott 1965, no. 60) follows Townsend's documented work more closely and has his distinctive handwriting as well. Catalogue No. 27 may be John Townsend's handiwork, but it also may represent a related member of the Goddard-Townsend family who trained with him and successfully replicated his style.

Provenance: Pierce Annesley Chamberlain, Jr., New Jersey; SP-B, sale 4180, 16–18 November 1978, lot 1073; Bernard and S. Dean Levy, Inc., New York

Construction and condition: The high chest is made in two sections. The lower case has a maple backboard dovetailed to mahogany sides. At the front there are two rails and a shaped skirt. The rails are maple with mahogany facings. The upper rail is dovetailed to the top of the sides. The other rail is dovetailed to the front edge of the sides. The shaped skirt is mahogany, with the shell carved from the solid. It is dovetailed to the sides. The pilasters above the front legs are mahogany veneer. Chestnut strips are set between the shaped skirt and the top rail and notched into the middle rail, all of which is covered by the mahogany veneer of the pilasters. The vertical partitions between the lower row of drawers are maple with mahogany facings. They are rabbetted to the shaped skirt and extend the depth of it. They are secured by nails through the middle rail, nails through the partitions into the skirt, and have a large rosehead nail at each end. The legs are mahogany. They extend up behind the corners of the case and are supported by glue blocks on each side. They were once removable but have been glued in place. The left rear leg is a replacement. The legs have lost about three-eighths of an inch in height. The knee-blocks are applied.

The upper drawer is supported by maple strips set behind the rail at each side and in the middle. The lower row of drawers are supported by poplar strips dovetailed to the shaped skirt in the center of each opening and nailed to the backboard with supporting glue blocks. Yellow pine drawer guides are glued to each side and set behind the vertical partitions.

The drawers have poplar sides and backboards with mahogany fronts. These have thumbnail molded edges lipped on three sides. The top row of drawers of the upper case have poplar bottoms set front to back with the remnants of spring locks nailed to the bottoms. The bottoms of the rest of the upper case drawers and top drawer of the lower case are set side to side in grooves cut in the sides and front and nailed to the backboard. The row of drawers in the lower case has bottoms set front to back and nailed in place. The brasses of the two end drawers of the lower row are replacements.

The upper case has single board mahogany sides dovetailed to maple top and bottom boards. The backboards are poplar set side to side and nailed in rabbets cut in the sides. The mid-molding is applied to the sides and front edge of the upper case. Guide strips are glued and nailed to the bottom of the upper case to align it when it is seated on the lower case.

The scrolled pediment has a mahogany tympanum and a poplar backboard. The pediment is dovetailed to the sides with book-matched panels of mahogany glued to its face. The closed area behind the central finial is made of a piece of pine cut to shape and glued to the pediment. A mahogany backboard is glued to this. The inside edge of these circular openings have mahogany crossbanding. A stretcher is set between the scroll and backboard on each side. Poplar boards set front to back and nailed in place enclose the top of the pediment. The caps of the plinths and the finials are replacements. The cornice and pediment moldings are glued and screwed in place.

At the front of the case, vertically grained mahogany strips are glued and nailed to the sides. The quarter columns are set in the rabbets created at the joint of the strips and sides. The rails are maple with mahogany facings. They are dovetailed to the side strips. The bottom rail is mahogany. Glue blocks are set behind it as it joins the bottom board. Guide strips are glued to the sides behind the rails. The drawer supports are nailed to these. The bottom drawer is supported by strips set on the bottom board. The top row of drawers are separated by a vertical partition of maple with a mahogany facing. These drawers are supported in the center by a strip set between the front rail and rear rail, which is set between the drawer guides.

Literature: Moses 1984, fig. 1.19, 1.19a

28
Chest of Drawers
1760–1780
New York
Mahogany; poplar, pine, maple
35⅝ x 35½ x 21¾ in.
ACC. NO. 77.2

Prior to the Revolution New York craftsmen and patrons adhered to English forms and proportions more closely than did Boston or Philadelphia. One indication of this is the scarcity of high chests and dressing tables and the preference for chest-on-chests and clothes presses. Another indication is the generally squarer, less vertical orientation of New York designs. In decorations, however, they showed a more local preference. All the embellishments of this chest of drawers are executed in typically New York fashion. The ball-and-claw feet are squarish, full, and tightly molded. There are no volutes or returns on the knee brackets. The gadrooning is smooth, with no contrasting fillets. The fluted chamfers with carved lamb's tongues are found in the most sophisticated New York rococo pieces, though they would be considered "early," or less expensive, if found in Philadelphia. They are also seen on Charleston pieces, another city with a preference for English forms. Blind fretwork, popular throughout the colonies, in New York pieces is typically found in the upper case of high chests, chest-on-chests, and desks and bookcases. In chests of drawers only an unrelated example by William King of Salem, at the Henry Ford Museum, has it set horizontally in a frieze below the top. The fretwork on cat. no. 28 uses intersecting arcs exclusively to form a pattern of diamonds and pointed ovals. The more common pattern combines straight lines and arcs (Randall 1965, no. 39).

Another New York chest of similar form but different proportions is illustrated in Downs 1952, no. 147. The facade of cat. no. 28 is within an eighth of an inch of square. The fretwork frieze, chamfered sides, and deep molding of the skirt give it a compact, almost compressed appearance. The use of only three drawers, each with three brasses, adds to this compact squareness. The cabinetmaker, it seems, tried to make up for some of the lost storage space by a visual trick. The rail beneath the bottom drawer is actually part of the drawer and the drawer rests on the molding. The visual balance is preserved, and more storage is added.

Provenance: This piece was acquired from descendants of the Townsend family of Long Island; Bernard and S. Dean Levy, Inc., New York

Construction and condition: The case has mahogany sides dovetailed to poplar top and bottom boards. The back is made of two poplar boards set horizontally, tongue and grooved together, and nailed to rabbets on the side. The visible top is a separate piece of mahogany held by screws through the poplar top.

The moldings at the base are attached to the sides and front of the case. The feet and gadrooning are attached directly to the bottom of the molding. The fretwork and adjacent moldings are glued and nailed to the case.

The chamfered corners are made in four sections: the chamfered and fluted piece is glued to the edge of the side; another piece of mahogany is glued to the front side of the chamfered one; these two pieces are supported from behind by a vertically grained strip of pine; behind these strips are vertically grained triangular pine blocks.

The rails are mahogany and tenoned to the chamfered corners. The drawer supports are replaced. Drawer guides above the top drawer prevents it from tipping down when open. The bottom rail is actually part of the drawer front. The drawer, including its false rail, rests on a maple rail backing the moldings.

The drawers have poplar sides, bottoms, and backs. The grains of the bottom are set side to side. The drawer fronts are mahogany.

29

High Chest
1750–1770
Philadelphia
Mahogany; poplar, yellow pine, white cedar
94⅜ x 43¾ x 24⅛ in.
ACC. NO. KAF 80.7

High chests and dressing tables, or highboys and lowboys as they are often called today, were often made to match. This high chest and cat. no. 30 have been reunited after a long separation. As the term dressing table implies, these pieces were not meant to be used in the parlor. The sliding tray in the base of the high chest confirms its use for clothing and linen storage.

There is greater emphasis on a tight verticality here than in the typical Philadelphia high chest. It is achieved through the design of three areas: the skirt rises into the case instead of descending below it, the arrangement and smaller size of the drawers lightens the base, and the chamfered and fluted corners extend uninterrupted from the knees to the cornice. On other pieces these are most often drawn to a point, or lambstongue carving, at the waist and cornice that interrupts continuity and emphasizes the horizontal elements (I. Sack n.d.–1979, 7:1792). The key element in the design of the pediment is the shell drawer. The size of it controls the pitch of the pediment. Shell drawers in this location are usually as large as the drawer below them, if not larger. Often the central drawer in the top row is larger than its neighbors in response to the shell drawer. A larger drawer accommodates a larger carving plan and the scrolled pediment must accordingly rise more steeply or scroll down more quickly to accommodate it. Here in cat. no. 29 the shell drawer is smaller than usual and the scrolled pediment well proportioned around it.

Cat. nos. 29 and 30 fit the aesthetic criteria devised to distinguish between Maryland and Philadelphia rococo styles (Downs 1952, Nos. 192, 199). These criteria follow the logic outlined in cat. no. 6. They are insufficient to justify a Maryland attribution without a family history or other documentation given the existence of similar pieces with Philadelphia histories (I. Sack n.d.–1979, 7:1792).

Provenance: Louis G. Meyers Collection, New York; Colonial Williamsburg, Inc., Williamsburg; Joe Kindig, Jr. and Son Antiques, York, Pennsylvania

Construction and condition: The high chest is built in two sections. The lower case has two-board mahogany sides and a yellow pine backboard, all tenoned and pinned to the legs. At the front are three rails and a shaped skirt, all of mahogany tenoned to the legs (the top rail alone is pinned). There are three mahogany vertical partitions, each tenoned to the rails. Behind the partitions are yellow pine boards nailed in place. These are tenoned through the back. Pine strips nailed to the sides of the lower partitions support the center drawer. Strips nailed to the bottom of the lower partitions support the end drawers. At each side L-shaped pine strips are nailed to the legs to support the drawers and linen tray. The top of the base is two poplar boards, their grain set side to side. These are enclosed by the waist molding which is lapped over them. The waist molding is in turn supported by another molding attached to the sides and front rail. All the carving of the skirt is applied. The knee-blocks are glued and nailed in place.

All the drawers in the piece are constructed in the same fashion. They have poplar sides and backs, with white cedar drawer bottoms. These are set front to back. The bottoms are set in grooves in the sides with strips set on the bottom and chamfered at the rear. The drawer fronts are mahogany veneered in mahogany. The brasses have been replaced. In the upper case the shell is carved from the solid and the leaf work applied. The linen tray of the lower case is a mahogany frame.

The upper case has two-board mahogany sides dovetailed to a yellow pine bottom board. At the top a yellow pine board is dovetailed to each side. They are secured to yellow pine boards set between the front and back boards of the tympanum on either side of the shell drawer. The rear board of the tympanum follows the line of the front but stops below the return of the scroll where it angles down toward the shell drawer and is flat in back of the cartouche. The pediment is closed by poplar boards nailed between this and the front. The back boards are poplar set horizontally and nailed to rabbets in the sides.

The chamfered and fluted corners are supported by yellow pine strips. The rails are mahogany and are fitted to these strips. There are full-panel poplar dust boards, which are thinner than the rails. These are dadoed to the sides and fit in grooves in the back of the rails. Drawer guides of pine are set at the joint of the dust boards and the sides. The vertical partition between the upper pair of drawers is mahogany tenoned to the rails. The partitions for the row of three drawers are mahogany tenoned to the rail below and notched to the tympanum. Behind each partition is a yellow pine board which extends to the back. The opening for the shell drawer is cut directly in the tympanum. The carving flanking the shell drawer and the cartouche are replacements. The molding is cut from a single piece of mahogany and not built up.

Literature: GSE 1929, no. 622; Winchester 1959, 78

Exhibitions: New York, GSE 1929; Williamsburg, Virginia, Colonial Williamsburg 1930–1976; Norfolk, Virginia, Chrysler Museum 1982–1986

30
Dressing Table
1750–1765
Philadelphia
Mahogany; poplar, yellow pine, white cedar
29¾ x 34¾ x 20¾ in.
ACC. NO. KAF 80.8

The arched skirt and arrangement of the drawers are features usually associated with the Philadelphia Queen Anne style for high chests and dressing tables. If this piece had trifid feet and a plain skirt it would be unquestionably Queen Anne. A number of Philadelphia Queen Anne chairs have ball-and-claw feet and pierced splats, typical rococo features, but are without a doubt Queen Anne chairs. The distinction among dressing tables and high chests is not so clear.

The earliest dated Philadelphia rococo high chest that is known is signed by Henry Cliffton and Thomas Carterer, 14 November 1753 (Colonial Williamsburg acc. no. 1975.154). It has a pendant skirt, ball-and-claw feet with acanthus-leaf knees, chamfered and fluted corners that go straight through and do not end in points or carved lamb's tongues, and a shell drawer in the tympanum beneath the scrolled pediment. The chamfered and fluted corners and shell drawer in the tympanum can be identified as features of the early rococo style. The arched skirt of these matched pieces (cat. no. 29) is seen on only a few other high chests (Nutting 1928–1933, 1:no. 372 and I. Sack n.d.–1979, 7:1792). These also have chamfered and fluted corners and shell drawers in the tympanum. This type of applied convex shell is also considered an early feature, often seen on chairs with strapwork splats (see cat. no. 6).

All these features argue strongly that this piece and its matching high chest are among the earliest surviving examples of the rococo style in Philadelphia.

Provenance: Mrs. Henry W. Breyer, Jr., Collection, Haverford, Pennsylvania; Joe Kindig, Jr. and Son Antiques, York, Pennsylvania

Construction and condition: The dressing table has mahogany sides and a yellow pine backboard, all tenoned and pinned to the legs. There are two rails and a shaped skirt in the front. These are mahogany and are tenoned but not pinned to the legs. The vertical partitions are tenoned to the rails. Yellow pine boards are nailed in place behind the partitions. These are tenoned through the backboard. A yellow pine strip nailed to the bottom of the upper partition supports the drawers. Pine strips nailed to the sides of the lower partitions support the central drawer. Strips nailed to the bottom support the side

drawers. All the carving is applied and the knee-blocks are glued and nailed in place.

The drawers are constructed in typical Philadelphia fashion. They have poplar sides and backs. The bottoms are white cedar, with the grain set front to back. Strips are glued at the joint of the bottom and sides to support the joint and are chamfered at the rear. The drawer fronts are mahogany with mahogany veneer. The brasses are replacements.

The top is attached by glue-blocks and supported by the applied molding beneath it. It is also secured by pins through the top into the legs.

Exhibition: Norfolk, Virginia, Chrysler Museum 1982–1986

Chippendale, *Director* 1754, pl. 78

31

Desk and Bookcase
1755–1765
Philadelphia
Mahogany; yellow pine, white cedar, poplar, white oak
114¼ x 53¾ x 26⅞ in.
ACC. NO. 75.1

One of the luckiest accidents an author can have is to describe and discuss a group of, say, seven objects and be rewarded by the discovery of the eighth. Such was the case for Robert C. Smith who wrote "Finial Busts on Eighteenth-Century Philadelphia Furniture" in the December 1971 issue of *Antiques*. Soon after its publication, a letter arrived informing him of this extraordinary and previously unknown example.

Thomas Chippendale's name became synonymous with the decorative arts of the rococo period by the publication in 1754 of *The Gentleman and Cabinet-Maker's Director*. His designs were rarely copied directly in the colonies. This desk and bookcase is the most elaborate and ambitious piece of American furniture derived from the *Director*. The design of the desk section is copied from plate 78 of the 1754 edition. Chippendale offered alternative patterns of decoration for his designs. These were shown on opposite sides of symmetrical objects. The Philadelphia craftsman and patron chose the more elaborate details and went a step further by using carved moldings where Chippendale showed them unadorned. The blind fretwork of the pilasters flanking the prospect door is copied from plate 151.

The interior of the desk follows a pattern seen in other Philadelphia desks in the Queen Anne and early rococo style. The pattern has four carved drawers over eight pigeon holes over four drawers. The plain prospect door and fretwork pilasters, however, are atypical. Other desks and bookcases with this style interior are shown in Dorman 1980, plate 34, *Antiques*, November 1979, 977, and *Antiques*, March 1979, 537. Among later Philadelphia Chippendale desks the interior of cat. no. 31 is less common. The interiors shown in the *Director* are very plain and more like those seen in Philadelphia desks of the 1770s. The maker of this piece departed from Chippendale and followed local preference.

Smith (1971) described the bookcase as "at once the enigma and chief glory of the desk and bookcase." He felt its architectural quality reflected the designs of William Kent, Abraham Swan, and Batty Langley rather than Chippendale. He cites the cabinet made for Governor Penn's air pump in 1739 (Fales 1976, 125) as an example of this style. While its fluted pilasters and deeply carved, pitched pediment exemplify the style, it is not closely related to this piece. Chippendale's third edition of

the *Director* (1762) has elements indicating that Chippendale himself had not totally abandoned this style at a time when designs in the classical revival manner were first being produced. His plate 107 shows a desk and bookcase with pitched pediment and urn-decorated plinth similar to the air-pump cabinet. Plate 104 shows a chamber organ that has pilasters with ionic capitals, a pitched pediment with a bust in the center, and a carved swag similar to the one used here on the plinth.

The bookcase, especially by reason of its deep, elaborately carved frieze and cornice moldings, reflects an architectural preoccupation that was superseded in the later rococo. Smith postulated that the piece could have been made in the late 1750s or early 1760s, but dismissed the idea on stylistic grounds. For him the "enigmatic" bookcase places the piece around 1770 or later. His 1770s theory is based heavily on a presumption of Benjamin Randolph's authorship, which was highly speculative then and remains so now. The use of the early interior arrangement renews the possibility of an earlier date. The pediment is closed and integral to the bookcase, features that had changed by the 1770s.

Provenance: The history of this desk, from its manufacture in the mid-eighteenth century until the late nineteenth century, is unknown. It was thought to be owned by the Reverend Edward Craig Mitchell (1836–1911), A Swedenborgian minister who lived in Philadelphia and moved to St. Paul, Minnesota in the 1870s, where he died. The desk and bookcase was owned by Robert Dunn, whose mother had acquired it from the Reverend Mitchell. The piece was brought to the attention of Robert C. Smith by the Dunns after the publication of his article in *Antiques* (Smith 1971); Bernard and S. Dean Levy, Inc., New York

Construction and condition: The desk and bookcase are made in two sections. The bookcase has mahogany sides connected by four horizontal and two vertical boards and the back boards. The bottom board is yellow pine. It is set in the sides with sliding dovetails at a line just below the bottom edge of the doors. Behind the doors are three shelves, two of which are fixed. They are pine with beaded mahogany facings. The middle shelf is adjustable in grooves in the sides. There was a row of drawers along the bottom that has been removed. The pine top board is dovetailed to the sides behind the upper line of the cornice moldings. The cornice is mahogany and is attached to the front edges of the sides. All the moldings and carvings are

mahogany and are applied to the cornice and the sides. The pediment is fixed to the bookcase and is not removable. It is entirely closed and appears to be attached internally. The bust is fixed to a turned base and doweled to the plinth. A rail is attached to the front edges of the sides just below the doors. The base moldings are applied over this and the sides. The back boards are white cedar set side to side. They are nailed to rabbets in the sides. Two L-shaped pine blocks, set front to back, are attached to the bottom board at each side. These are designed as a locking mechanism with similarly shaped pieces on the desk. Those were missing when the desk was found.

The desk section has mahogany sides dovetailed to yellow pine top and bottom boards. The top board has a mahogany front edge. The interior writing board is mahogany, with yellow pine underneath the pigeonholes; both are dadoed to the sides. The lower case of the desk is built around the partitions flanking the graduated drawers. These are mahogany, set vertically, extending the full depth of the case. They are attached to the bottom and writing board and reinforced by chamfered pine blocks at the top. The partitions are notched to accommodate the carved ogee waist piece which rests on a mahogany rail fixed to the partitions. This rail is covered by the carved molding. Three mahogany rails are dadoed to the partitions below that. The upper two have full-panel white cedar dust

boards the thickness of the rails dadoed to the partitions. The bottom rail has no dust boards. Pine strips are set along the bottom at the partitions to support the drawer. Cross-grain strips are set in grooves behind the uppermost rail to prevent the drawer below from tipping when opened. The lid-support drawers rest on a mahogany rail and full-panel white cedar dust board set between the sides and partitions. Behind each door is a single mahogany partition that extends the depth of the case. It is set in the rail and dust board above and in the bottom board. A false bottom is set at the level of the doors' lower edges. The doors are mahogany and the carving is applied. The locks are set in the center of the doors and held by catches in the partitions.

The base molding is applied to the sides and over the front edge of the bottom board and rail. The feet are mahogany, backed by a vertically grained triangular pine block that is topped by a horizontally set pine square. Horizontal blocks flank these. At the rear a horizontally set pine bracket is fixed to the foot with the same blocking that is used for the front feet.

The drawers are constructed in typical Philadelphia fashion, with yellow pine sides and backs. The bottom boards are white cedar set front to back. Strips are glued to the bottom, at the sides, and mitered at the back. The drawer fronts are mahogany with inset beading. The brasses and escutcheons are replacements. The pigeonhole drawers have white oak sides and backs. The drawer bottoms are white cedar and are set front to back. The bottoms are set in rabbets in the sides, backs, and fronts. The drawer fronts are mahogany, shaped on one side only. The far left drawer of the bottom row is a nineteenth-century replacement. The drawers behind the prospect door are constructed in the same way. The far left drawer of the bottom row is a replacement.

The prospect door and flanking fretwork pilasters are part of a removable box that enclosed the drawers behind the prospect door. This box is dovetailed together and is made of mahogany. When the box is removed it reveals two white cedar document drawers behind the pilasters. Two shelves in the center may have contained drawers. The partitions separating the document drawers from the central cavity are poplar.

Within the desk section the angled mahogany sides are rabbeted for the lid. A mahogany strip is nailed to the front edge of the top for additional support. The lid is mahogany with mitered battens. The bottom inch of the lid along the hinges has been rebuilt, and the area around the escutcheon has also been repaired. The lid is outlined with an applied bead.

Literature: Smith 1973, 129–135; Snyder 1975, cover and 128–134; Fairbanks and Bates 1981, 185; Cooper 1980, no. 149 (finial bust only)

32
Fire Screen
1765–1775
Philadelphia
Mahogany
63⅜ x 18⅞ x 16¾ in.
ACC. NO. KAF 80.9

In the eighteenth century the fire screen had the very practical purpose of protecting one from the heat and glare of a fireplace. The form was rendered obsolete by the introduction of central heating. Aesthetically it was the perfect way for a lady to display her needlework and a craftsman his turnings and carving.

Furniture with hairy paw feet is rare in Philadelphia, and most of it has been associated with John Cadwalader's house (see cat. no. 10). The same virtuosity and rococo exuberance seen in those side chairs are found in this fire screen. The carver has ornamented every available surface. The leafage on the knees spills over the sides and extends down the ankles to the hairy paws. The shaft alternates bands of highly carved convex surfaces with clear concave ones that are topped by a fluted, slightly tapered column. The screen molding is totally carved, as well. Thomas Affleck, in a 1771 bill to John Cadwalader that included two commode card tables (PMA 1976, no. 91), also listed four mahogany fire screens. At the end of the bill he listed a separate charge for the same items from carvers James Reynolds, and the partnership of Bernard and Jugiez. The 1904 sale of Cadwalader possessions included "2 fine antique mahogany fire screens"; at least two other screens have Cadwalader family histories not connected with this sale (see Heckscher 1985, no. 13). Just as there are more surviving chairs and tables with hairy paw feet than there are surviving bills of sale, so it is with the fire screens. Three others are in public collections (Downs 1952, 236, PMA 1976, no. 80, Heckscher 1985, no. 133) and a few in private collections (Hornor 1935, pl. 105). A closely related screen, with the same carved shaft but ball-and-claw feet with light scoring on the claws, is shown in Downs 1952, no. 238.

Provenance: Joe Kindig, Jr. and Son Antiques, York, Pennsylvania

Construction and condition: The legs are dovetailed to the column and an iron plate is attached to support the joints. One of the paw feet has been replaced. The pole, which is doweled into the column, is of a different wood from the rest of the piece and may be a replacement. The finial is a replacement. The screen consists of a frame made of three stiles and two rails. The central stile has two brass fittings to adjust the height of the screen. Eighteenth-century fabric covers the screen. The carved molding is grooved to fit over the fabric-covered frame and nailed in place.

Literature: Beckerdite 1985, 504

Exhibition: Norfolk, Virginia, Chrysler Museum 1981–1982

33
Fire Screen
1760–1775
Newport
Mahogany
55 x 19½ x 16¾ in.
ACC. NO. 73.4

This fire screen is from a group of Newport pieces in which legs ending in small cat's-paw feet support a platform that in turn supports a pedestal or column; alternatively, the legs attach directly to the column. The Newport group, which encompasses the work of both Goddards and Townsends, includes tilt-top tea tables (Hipkiss 1941, no. 59), kettle stands (Downs 1952, no. 288), basin stands (Downs 1952, no. 278), and fire screens. Five of the known fire screens are this highly developed. Three of them (Heckscher 1985, no. 123, Moses 1984, 72, and one in a private collection descended from John Brown) have a plain turning between the reeded caps and the twist-reeded lower ball, and one has a fluted column (Rodriguez-Roque 1984, no. 290).

By tradition cat. no. 33 was owned by Joseph Wanton, the last colonial governor of Rhode Island. He fled to New York with his son where both died before the conclusion of the Revolution. A number of Wanton's possessions were sold, or given in payment for past debts. John Townsend appeared before a notary in 1782 to collect $6.13 owed him by Wanton for a plain fire screen and a mahogany card table and lining made in 1774 (Carpenter 1954, 18). Unfortunately no further documentation exists.

This fire screen and cat. no. 32, the Philadelphia example, offer an interesting comparison of the tastes of two cities in the decade prior to the Revolution. The Philadelphia craftsmen, possibly Affleck and Bernard and Jugiez judging by the carved decoration, created a new shape out of an unadorned form. In Newport the craftsman, possibly John Townsend, chose to emphasize clean lines and the interplay of different masses: shallow carving, scratch beads, reeding and fluting enhance and delineate the underlying form. Both fire screens are beautifully proportioned and executed, and each has achieved a full development of the same form in a different style.

Provenance: By tradition this piece was owned by Governor Joseph Wanton of Rhode Island. It was purchased at a small estate auction of a member of the Hathaway family of New Bedford, Massachusetts, around 1960; Harry Arons Antiques, Ansonia, Connecticut; Israel Sack, Inc., New York; Lansdell K. Christie Collection, Syosset, New York; P-B, sale 3422, 21 October 1972, lot 48; Israel Sack, Inc., New York

Construction and condition: The legs are dovetailed to the triangular platform. A modern, three-pronged iron brace replacing an earlier one is attached to the underside. The column has a threaded shaft screwed to the platform. The pole, which is doweled to the column, is a replacement. The needlework and brass fittings are antique but the frame is not.

Literature: Ott 1965, pl. 93; Moses 1984, 240, fig. 5.27

Exhibition: Providence, John Brown House Loan Exhibition of Rhode Island Furniture, 1965

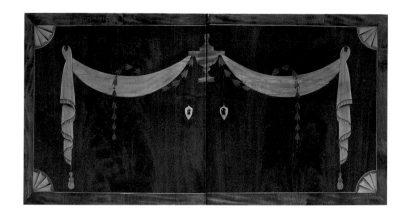

The Neoclassical Style in New England and New York, 1785–1840

Wendy A. Cooper

For centuries, throughout the world, changes in fashion and style have been cyclical, whether the focus is on clothing, literature, architecture, or furniture. Furniture styles in America seemed to change every twenty-five to thirty years, following shifts of fashion in England and on the Continent. By the 1760s a dramatic change was gaining momentum in England, manifesting a preference for lighter, more linear shapes very different from the three-dimensional qualities of the boldly sculptural rococo style.

The impetus for this change in furniture (as well as other media) was occasioned by a renewed awareness of early Roman society and culture brought to light by excavations at Herculaneum and Pompeii. Roman forms and decorative motifs were quickly adopted by architects, designers, and craftsmen to meet the desires of avant-garde patrons. Even well-to-do colonials were aware of this trend to the antique as numerous sons of the American elite journeyed to Europe and participated in "the Grand Tour" experience. However, the outbreak of the Revolution seems to have been a major deterrent in the trans-Atlantic transmission of this new style. First of all, trade with England was abruptly curtailed; and secondly, many a colonial craftsman exchanged his tradesman's tools for wartime pursuits and active military service.

American regionalism continued to prevail both during and following the Revolution. Probably the new style took hold in some regions long before it became widely recognized in others. This time factor in the transmission of styles was due to numerous variables, including the importation of objects in the new style, travel abroad, the migration of English and European craftsmen, and imported design books and other printed sources. Evidence exists that this new neoclassical style had taken hold in regions south of New York by the out-break of the Revolution. Soon after the fighting ceased, however, northern merchants like John Brown of Providence were ordering "plated tea urns" from France, and craftsmen like Paul Revere were fashioning teapots in this new and different style.

By the mid-1780s the importation of neoclassical objects into New England was more frequent, and English-trained craftsmen like John Seymour and his son Thomas were finding new homes and clients on this side of the Atlantic. While no dated examples of New England furniture from the 1780s in this new style are known, a letter written in January 1787 is suggestive. In anticipation of his impending marriage and setting up a household, David Spear of Boston wrote to his fiancée, Marcy Higgins, in Barnstable, to assure her that "Mr. Bright, who is an old Friend and Acquaintance of my Father's is to make all the mahogany Furniture . . . and I doubt not but that we shall have very good furniture from him—the chairs are different from any you ever saw, but they are pretty, of the newest Taste (Fairbanks et. al. 1975, 159-161)."

Exactly how was this neoclassical style (or Federal as it is also called in America) "of the newest Taste" "different from any you ever saw?" While the style change from baroque or Queen Anne to the rococo or Chippendale was seemingly a natural progression, the shift from rococo to early neoclassical styles was a dramatic about-face. Curvaceous sculptural forms with prominent surface carving were exchanged for very linear and geometric forms of tremendous lightness and delicacy. Where ornament was formerly part of a three-dimensional whole, it was now applied to a two-dimensional surface as a thin veneer and in delicate inlaid patterns. The legs of chairs and tables seemed almost fragile in comparison to earlier styles. Square and tapering, or turned with a taper and perhaps reeded ornament, these vertical members suggested a lightness or verticality unlike any elements of previous styles. The shape of chair backs and table tops was thinner, lighter, and more geometric, with the ornament receding into the surface rather than protruding outward in the former robust, sculptural manner.

Even as each region expressed individual preferences in forms as well as ornament, there was a dependence on and derivation from, English designs of George Hepplewhite, Thomas Sheraton, and later George Smith and Thomas Hope throughout the emerging American republic. Since individual interpretation was significant in each geographic region, the strongest contribution of these English sources may have been in the introduction and adoption of new forms. Just as new forms gained popularity with the adoption of "antique" styles, similarly by the end of the eighteenth century there were new forms to accommodate the demands created by more leisure time, increased wealth, and greater social activity and entertainments. The proliferation of card table forms, the introduction of the sideboard (replacing the simpler slab-top serving table), work tables for ladies' sewing and writing activities, commode dressing tables, cylinder-front desks, library tables, tambour desks, basin stands and "wash-hand" tables, cellarettes, and pier tables added new elegance and variety to this changing American aesthetic.

By the early nineteenth century the new style began to exhibit a change similar to that which had occurred in the shift from the Queen Anne or baroque, to the Chippendale or rococo style. Extremely linear forms and the use of highly figured veneered surfaces gave way to stronger, more demonstrative forms, bolder shapes with sweeping curves, and the use of more turning and robust carved ornament. The sources of both forms and ornament were derived more directly from archaeological examples than had been the case earlier. The vocabulary of design motifs employed a greater use of animal images—eagle and lion masks, paw feet, anthemion leaves, carved drapery, vigorous bowknots binding bunches of wheat and revived forms such as Grecian couches, Greek klismos chairs, and the curule X-form. While this later neoclassical style (often called the Empire style) might seem dramatically different from the earlier Federal style, clearly it represented a natural outgrowth or progression.

The early neoclassical furniture produced in Boston and Salem expresses the epitome of elegance, lightness, and grace signaled by the advent of this new and different style. David Spear's new chairs in 1787 might have resembled in overall form a shield-back example like cat. no. 34. The distinctive use of highly patterned, superior veneers and inlay is notable in two card tables (cat. nos. 70, 71). Both exhibit the almost unstable lightness of numerous card tables of this period, while

showing contrasting manners in the handling of the shaped top, the patterned skirt, and the tapered legs. These tables are two of the finest examples from many variations on this popular New England form.

Among the varied and innovative furniture forms produced in New England is the tambour writing desk. Two extraordinary examples of this form, cat. nos. 83, 84, both incorporate finely figured veneers and regionally distinctive inlay. Presumably this form emerged in the latter years of the 1790s and was almost singularly favored by New England patrons and craftsmen. An interesting comment by young Susannah Clarke, attending school in Salem in 1797, suggests the fascination the new form must have held for many young and style-conscious Americans: "Dr. Prince has a new kind of desk and I wish Papa would permit me to have one like it—the lower desk that is a parcel of drawers hid with doors made in reeds to slip back and in the middle a plain door, 'tis the handsomest thing in the kind I ever saw and most beautifully varnished" (Ott 1973, 131). The use of tambour doors is also seen on sideboards and pot cupboards, and not surprisingly found its inspiration in English designs popular in the 1790s.

One might be tempted to presume that New England ladies spent all their time either sewing or writing, given the popularity of ladies' work tables in that region. Another new form introduced with the Federal style, cat. no. 80, demonstrates how New England cabinetmakers could make a boxlike form, of little overall interest, virtually shimmer through the use of patterned veneers and string inlay. A handsome shirred or pleated silk bag suspended beneath the drawers would have further enhanced this seemingly simple yet utilitarian furniture form. While virtually unique in American furniture, the Boston gaming table (cat. no. 79) is closely related in overall form and ornament to the work table, and distinctly a New England product.

Directly derived from high-style, sophisticated English precedents a brief vogue for delicately painted furniture flourished in the Boston area in the 1790s and early 1800s. Quite different in style and execution from the later interest in painted furniture in Baltimore, this preference is illustrated in the curly maple nest of tables with painted tops and the two side chairs with oval, painted backs (cat. nos. 36, 37).

The later neoclassical style in the Boston area continued to embody a delicacy of form and ornament, while manifesting a greater sculptural quality through the use of more turning, reeding, and carving. Turned and reeded legs swelled a bit more generously, and carved swags, leafage, and animal masks represented more commanding mass and weight (cat. no. 72). The later and more purely classical manifestation of the Empire style in Boston furniture has only recently been recognized and appreciated. A pair of side chairs (cat. no. 51) ex-

cat. no. 83

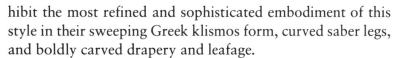

cat. no. 84

hibit the most refined and sophisticated embodiment of this style in their sweeping Greek klismos form, curved saber legs, and boldly carved drapery and leafage.

Boston area craftsmen in the Federal era were noted for their brilliantly innovative efforts in the fabrication of timepieces. No other American geographic region exhibited the adventuresome talent that was principally led by the Willard family of clockmakers, located in the Roxbury area adjoining Boston. Among Simon Willard's masterful achievements, cat. no. 100 has a case which presents the most superior Boston/Roxbury cabinetwork and ornamentation. The Willards and the apprentices they trained were known for their creativity in developing a variety of smaller wall-mounted clocks as well as the magnificent table model, the lighthouse clock. The girandole clock (cat. no. 101) by Lemuel Curtis, represents not only an original American form, but also the fine talents so prevalent among Boston's early nineteenth-century carvers, gilders, and ornamental painters.

The aesthetic talent and skill in Newport cabinetmakers following the Revolution did not diminish. However, the economic climate and thus local patronage was not nearly as

strong and favorable during the Federal period. As in earlier decades of the eighteenth century, there continued to be specific parallels in the regional preferences of Rhode Island and New York patrons and craftsmen. For example, Newport and New York craftsmen occasionally chose to use six legs on their half-round or demilune card tables (cat. nos. 64, 68). While the inlay used in Rhode Island remained regionally distinctive, there were similarities with New York inlays in motifs such as tassels and delicately formed bowknots. Newport craftsmen such as John Townsend and Holmes Weaver worked in this new style (cat. nos. 67, 69), but their pieces were less innovative than they had been. A set of four side chairs labeled by John Townsend could be taken for New York ones, were it not for the label.

While Newport makers exhibited a keen sense of aesthetics and design, the work of Providence craftsmen was different from their Newport or New York counterparts in this early neoclassical style. The extraordinary sideboard (cat. no. 85), made for Oliver Wolcott of Connecticut, and the Providence sideboard (cat. no. 86), are of similar shape and form and both are elaborately inlaid using several common motifs. While both designs show regional and probably client preference, the craftsman's skill and the availability of superior materials was also an obvious factor.

New York craftsmen and patrons embraced the late neo-classical style, or Empire period, with great enthusiasm and a special aesthetic virtuosity that firmly established its popularity. A distinct preference for ancient forms—the klismos (cat. no. 49), curule (cat. no. 57), and Grecian couch (cat. no. 58)—manifests itself in the production of purely classic forms overlaid with a regional style of carved motifs. The scroll-back side chairs of klismos form, with boldly carved eagle backs (cat. no. 49), are representative of this New York interpretation. They also exhibit the finely tapered reeding and acanthus-leaf carving characteristic of New York craftsmanship. While the klismos form was universally used in the new republic, the New York interpretation is quite different from that of Boston (cat. no. 51) and Philadelphia (cat. no. 50) craftsmen.

Elegant sweeping lines marked many New York forms in this style, with the characteristic tapered reeding lightening the broad curves of curule settees (cat. no. 57) and graceful Grecian couches (cat. no. 58). Though somewhat restrained in overall presentation, crest rails and seat rails were often ornamented with motifs typical of New York, with bunches of wheat, or thunderbolts tied with delicate bowknots. Motifs of carved festoons and bowknots continued in fashion, and appear on seating furniture (cat. no. 57) as well as card tables (cat. no. 74) and other forms. Card tables with elliptical tops were especially favored, with double or triple ellipses available at additional cost.

New York furniture in its latest expression of the Empire style became extremely vigorous and heavily embellished with fantastic animals. Dolphins, griffins, winged eagles—even swans and sea horses (cat. no. 97)—can be found on a variety of forms in different interpretations. The profusely carved and gilt convex mirror (cat. no. 97) epitomizes this late neoclassical extravagance. Ironically, this final Empire exuberance seems to hark back to the florid sculptural qualities of the rococo style, while embracing the exotic animalistic motifs of the Greco-Roman revival.

cat. no. 86, detail

The Neoclassical Style in Philadelphia and the South, 1785–1840

Gregory R. Weidman

There were dramatic changes in the design of American furniture following the Revolution, as the neoclassical styles first attained popularity. Nowhere are these differences more apparent than in Philadelphia, where the sculptural, three-dimensional, highly carved rococo forms of the Chippendale style were superseded by the flat linear, veneered, and geometric forms of the early Federal style. Philadelphia furniture of the 1790s is in general more conservative than its pre-Revolution cabinetwork and the contemporary productions of the newer style centers of the Federal era.

The reasons for the change in the character of Philadelphia furniture after the Revolution were both economic and cultural. The city had suffered from occupation and economic stagnation during the war. Yellow fever epidemics in the 1790s ravaged the population, disrupting commerce and trade. Another significant factor causing Philadelphia's economic power to decline was competition in its markets by the younger and more rapidly growing city of Baltimore. Several local cultural factors also led to the conservatism of Philadelphia Federal cabinet wares. Philadelphians, by the Federal era, were an established society with fewer recently made fortunes. Such stable groups tend to prefer less flamboyant, more conservative goods. Philadelphians' preference for the Chippendale style led to its persistence after the arrival of the Federal style. In the early 1790s Thomas Affleck's commissions for the city's government buildings in the Marlborough style document Chippendale furniture being made in the Federal era. Other conservative forms persisted in popularity, notably ladder-back chairs and transitional versions of Marlborough-leg tables. With less demand for the newer and more stylish forms, Philadelphia craftsmen produced fewer avant-garde pieces.

Still, the records show that stylish Federal furniture was being made in Philadelphia at an early date. Indeed, the first introduction to the city of the English neoclassical styles predates the Revolution. (The famous Richard Humphries neoclassical silver tea urn made in 1774 is the most notable example.) As early as January of 1785 Samuel Claphamson, "late from London," was advertising new Adamesque forms such as commode sideboards, oval and circular card tables, and oval breakfast tables. Surviving furniture made for the Penn estate, Solitude, in 1788 is thoroughly neoclassical in style. By 1795 standard Federal forms such as the heart-back chair are recorded in the Philadelphia book of prices. Catalogue nos. 63, 87, and 88 demonstrate the interest of some Philadelphians in sophisticated early Federal forms.

Identifiable characteristics of Philadelphia's early Federal cabinetwork include the use of broad plains of veneers, sometimes of highly contrasting color, framed by inlays. These large fields give more emphasis to the broader geometric form of a piece than do the smaller units of contrasting veneers seen on New England furniture. This subtle manipulation of form and emphasis on shapes distinguishes stylish Philadelphia Federal furniture. The pieces often show refined geometric interplays in veneering, banding, and stringing, particularly in the form of interlaced ovals, rectangles with concave corners, and elongated arched panels. The general lack of elaborate pictorial inlay is also notable and very different from the comparable work of Baltimore cabinetmakers.

Philadelphia's stylish early Federal furniture is often closely derived from English design books. Some examples are based on more than one printed source, such as the combination of Thomas Shearer and Thomas Sheraton seen in the tambour writing table (cat. no. 87). Philadelphia's Federal cabinetmakers used a variety of exotic fancy woods in addition to richly figured mahogany. West Indian satinwood, ebony from Madagascar, and even a species of Casuarina from Australia are seen. In addition to this richness of surface, the overall form of some early Federal cabinetwork is quite innovative and unusual. Besides the new but comparatively common tambour closing for desks and writing tables, one finds rarer forms such as cabinet desks and secretaries, some of highly unusual design. In these characteristics of sources, woods, and innovative forms the work of Philadelphia early Federal cabinetmakers is related to the contemporary work of Baltimore craftsmen.

The Philadelphia cabinetmaker's early use of the designs of Thomas Sheraton has been noted above. The reliance on this source becomes even more pronounced after 1800, coinciding with an upswing in the city's fortunes. The Sheraton-derived works by Philadelphia masters such as Ephraim Haines, Henry Connally, Joseph Barry, and their contemporaries have survived in greater quantity and are better known today than their early Federal counterparts. The later works in Federal style also tend to be fairly restrained, relying on neat reeding and flat, fluid carving for most decorative effects. The popularity of this Sheraton school, most generally seen in square-back chairs with turned stiles and legs (cat. no. 45) and kidney-shaped card tables with turned legs, continued through the end of the first decade of the century.

Related to this late Federal Philadelphia style, but more sophisticated and refined, is the group of furniture influenced by French designs filtered through English sources (cat. no. 46). The importation of French furniture to Philadelphia (such as the noted set of furniture from Versailles acquired by Gouvenor Morris) and the importance of French culture in the city during the Federal period has long been noted. Indeed, only in Philadelphia was the Louis XVI style taken up in a serious way. This preference may have begun quite early. In 1787 both Samuel Clapham and William Long advertised that they made and sold "French chairs."

The advent of the Empire style in the second decade of the nineteenth century saw the popularity of furniture that continued the neoclassical tradition, but in a much more archaeological and romantic manner. Many forms were actually referred to during the period as "Grecian," although they were often combinations of Roman and Egyptian motifs as well. The later work of Sheraton plus newer designs of Thomas Hope, George Smith, Rudolph Ackerman, and James Barron brought the English Regency style to Philadelphia. French designs also continued to find a receptive audience in the city, in contrast to Baltimore where there was very little direct influence by French Empire works.

Although Philadelphia Federal furniture was somewhat conservative in general, the city's cabinetmaking industry ex-

perienced a great revival when the Empire style was in vogue. A large and rich body of work survives, again showing a stylishness and exuberance such as there was in the colonial era. One large group of pieces, typified by those of French émigré Anthony G. Quervelle and his school, features florid, fully carved objects in the "antique" style. Pieces in this Philadelphia group are often very robust and three-dimensional, carved with bold dolphins, lion's paws, cornucopias, eagles, and heavy acanthus leaves. These Philadelphia Empire works are often quite closely related to contemporary examples of the other principal cabinetmaking centers of New York and Boston. Philadelphia pieces showing the classical lyre motif (cat. no. 73) are in this mainstream of the American Empire style. The Philadelphia examples can be distinguished by highly figured veneers, crisp lines, and the broad character of the carving.

In contrast to this first and dominant group of Philadelphia Empire furniture is a second specialized group whose highly distinctive pieces are notable for their classical severity, often being both architectonic and archaeological in feeling. Their more restrained classicism contrasts with the first group by emphasizing form and proportion rather than three-dimensional decoration. Within this second group are several important subgroups. One is the rare group of pieces embellished with brass inlaid in contrasting woods called "boulle" work (cat. no. 90). These extraordinary pieces, which are among the finest works of Empire furniture produced in this country, demonstrate a strong kinship to contemporary English Regency cabinetwork where such metal inlays are frequently seen. Another significant Philadelphia subgroup are the architectural *secretaires à abattant* (cat. no. 91). Here, too, one discerns a European (as opposed to American) aesthetic. The cabinet tops and broad proportions distinguish the Philadelphia examples from comparable Boston secretaries.

Turning now to the neoclassical furniture made in post-Revolutionary Maryland, one finds pieces long renowned for their sophistication and quality. The large body of identifiable work from Federal Maryland contrasts greatly with the region's production in the colonial era. Baltimore, in particular, remained a small city prior to the Revolution, one whose two principal cabinetmakers, Gerrard Hopkins and Robert Moore, both trained in Philadelphia. This dominating influence changed dramatically after the Revolution when Baltimore became the fastest growing city in the country, going from a population of three thousand in 1770 to twenty-five thousand in 1800. The great increase in trade and commerce occasioned by complex geographic, social, and economic factors drew new residents to Baltimore, creating a large market for fashionable furniture. Craftsmen from Europe and America were attracted to the thriving city, and dozens of new cabinetmaking firms were founded by the turn of the century.

Based on a sizable group of extant examples, the distinctive characteristics of Baltimore early Federal furniture can be discerned. The large number of immigrants, both craftsmen and patrons, may in part account for the close design relationship between Baltimore and English neoclassical furniture. The "Englishness" of Baltimore Federal cabinetwork has often been noted, not only in the literal adaptation of the designs of Hepplewhite, Sheraton, and Shearer, but also in the adoption of such thoroughly English forms as the oval-back chair. The most popular of the wide variety of forms available in Federal Baltimore was the card table, the half-round shape being the favored one. After card tables, among the most frequently surviving forms are dining furniture—sideboards, sideboard tables (cat. no. 76), and Pembroke tables (cat. no. 60) in particular—and desks or secretaries with bookcases.

Perhaps the most noteworthy group of Baltimore early Federal furniture (and also the most English in design) are the famous group of ladies' cabinet desks. Generally based on Sheraton's designs, most of these pieces feature the use of *verre églomisé,* reverse painting on glass panels. This highly unusual type of decoration, though not exclusive to Baltimore furniture, was used there in the manner of shaped panels set into furniture, similar to pictorial inlay and painted decoration (cat. no. 77).

The predominant decorative embellishments of Baltimore early Federal furniture were veneers and inlays. In general the pieces are distinguished by a rich and subtle use of mahogany veneers. Frequently, round, oval or rectangular panels are edged with satinwood crossbanding or patterned inlay and set into mitered frames. Satinwood crossbanding also outlines the tops and aprons of tables and is used to form half-panels or "carrot"-shaped panels on tapered legs. The Baltimore bell-flower is the most famous of the inlay patterns, but one also sees a rich variety that includes conch shells, ruffled paterae, eagles, lilies-of-the-valley, thistles, tassels, and grapevines. Many, though not all of these inlays, were produced in Baltimore by one of the city's three known inlay-makers or ebonists (Thomas Barrett, William Patterson, and Francis Garrish). Since most of the leading cabinetmakers patronized these craftsmen, the attribution of a piece of furniture based on inlays alone is very difficult. In contrast, however, are a group of pieces associated with Levin S. Tarr (fl. 1799–1815) which are consistent not only in the types of inlay but also in other very distinctive features of decoration and construction (cat. nos. 54, 60, 61, 76). They are highly significant in being part of the largest group of Baltimore Federal furniture that can be firmly attributed to a shop.

While the name of Levin S. Tarr has been unknown until recently, the name of Annapolis cabinetmaker John Shaw (fl. c.

cat. no. 87

1767–1816) has long been renowned. The Scots émigré began his six-decade-long career in Annapolis when the town was the economic and cultural center of the colony. At that time the flourishing community supported a group of cabinetmakers, several trained in England, who produced fairly sophisticated wares closely related to English prototypes. Almost all of Shaw's plentiful documented work, however, dates from the 1790s, when Annapolis' power and prestige were in decline. At a time when the most sophisticated Federal pieces were being manufactured only thirty-five miles to the north in Baltimore, Shaw made conservative, "transitional" furniture for his clients. Cat. no. 62 is a particularly fine example of his work, one that is more up to date and refined than many.

The boom in Baltimore continued through the first decade of the nineteenth century. At the time when Sheraton-inspired late Federal mahogany furniture was dominant in Philadelphia, Baltimorians were enthralled by painted or "fancy" furniture. Perhaps the leading craftsmen in the country for this type of ware, Baltimore's painted furniture manufacturers produced a large and splendid body of work notable for its sophisticated designs. The furniture was made in a wide variety of forms and colors and was decorated with both real and imaginary landscape scenes, musical and weapons trophies, bows and quivers of arrows, grapevines, and swags.

The work of Baltimore's cabinetmakers in the late Federal and early Empire styles is in general more conservative than in

the earlier period, reflecting the slowed growth, economic problems, and established population following the War of 1812. The furniture is closely related to English Regency prototypes, with little or no direct French influence discernible (such as one sees in New York and Philadelphia). The dominant decorative element of Baltimore late Federal and Empire furniture is a heavy, sometimes pointed reeding. Many pieces gain their aesthetic impact through the high contrast of dark mahogany with bird's-eye maple. Rather than elaborate carving, another large group (principally desks, sideboards, sideboard tables, and serving cabinets) features Gothic-arched, veneered panels, some examples having "mummy-headed terms" (often called caryatids).

Baltimore continued to produce fine pieces of painted furniture in the Empire style. These later works are as stylish and refined as the Federal examples, though quite different in form and decoration. The most typical decorations are stylized motifs (such as spearlike anthemions, swirled rosettes, scrolled vines, winged thunderbolts) gilded on vivid rosewood graining (cat. no. 59). A large group of tables are known with this type of embellishment, many having barrel-turned shafts and X-frame bases. An immense number of side chairs were produced that featured clusters of ring turnings on the stiles and legs; other painted seating furniture, such as sofas, Grecian couches, window seats, and ottomans were also popular.

Charleston, South Carolina, was a very wealthy and sophisticated city in the colonial era and continued to prosper through the end of the eighteenth century. The city's craftsmen produced what was probably the most thoroughly English of all furniture made in America before the Revolution, reflecting extraordinarily strong social, economic, and cultural ties to the mother country. Similarly, much of the Federal furniture made in Charleston was also strongly influenced by imported wares, but of domestic origin. Newspaper advertisements and customs records show extensive importation of cabinetwork from both New York and Philadelphia. A few craftsmen from the northern cities even opened "branch offices" in the south. Some Charleston furniture, for example shield-back side chairs, are nearly indistinguishable from their New York counterparts; history and secondary woods are the determining factors. Other characteristics of New York furniture found in Charleston pieces are inlaid quarter-fans set in the corners of doors and panels, book inlays over legs and on cornices, and engraved husk inlays.

Charleston Federal furniture was by no means entirely imitative, however, and a number of distinguishing local characteristics can be identified. These include canted corners on case pieces and straight bracket feet with inlay. Other notable inlays are the unusual blossomlike motifs found in the corners of doors, and floral sprigs in small oval panels. Some distinctive forms of furniture evolved in Charleston also, including a particularly fine group of case pieces such as the Holmes family library bookcase and cat. no. 89. These show that although perhaps less survives than in other regions, and still less is currently recognized, the neoclassical furniture of Charleston is of a quality comparable to that of the newer and better-known northern cities

These varied manifestations of the neoclassical impulse in American furniture persisted until about 1840. By that time many new factors were affecting the cabinetmaking business and, in turn, furniture design. The late Empire or "Pillar and Scroll" style that became dominant in this country in the 1830s was derived from the French *restauration* style of the previous decade. Significantly, the predominant elements of this last of the classical styles (smooth curved surfaces, broad planes of veneer, and plain columnar forms) were well suited to benefit from steam-powered advances in manufacturing techniques. Quantities of furniture in its mass-produced version thus became readily available to the burgeoning American middle class. As this trend developed, the regional differences so apparent in the previous decades became less and less distinctive. John Hall's *The Cabinet Maker's Assistant*, published in Baltimore in 1840, was the first book of furniture designs published in this country and led further to the nationalization of furniture design. Other factors in this process were increased export trade by the principal manufacturing cities, improved transportation, machine-produced standardization of products, and the growth of large midwestern centers. By the advent of the romantic revival styles of the mid-1840s, the American furniture industry was entering the modern era, leaving behind the world where the small shop and hand craftsmanship were dominant.

34
Side Chair
1790–1800
Massachusetts
Mahogany; *ash and *birch rails
38 x 21½ x 20¾ in.
ACC. NO. 76.3

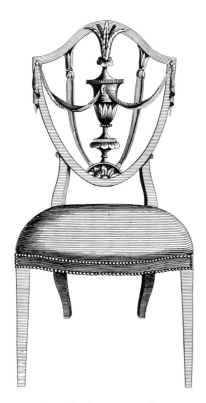

Hepplewhite 1794, pl. 2

Plate two in the 1794 edition of Hepplewhite supplied the inspiration for this chair, while the decoration came from the cabinetmaker and carver. Hepplewhite's design indicates a carved splat with plain shield and legs. The cabinetmaker-carver has enriched that design. He has balanced the shield by narrowing its crest and pointing the tip. The face of the shield now has beaded edges and a hollowed center supported by molded stiles. Carving has been added to the splat and also to the legs in the form of bunches of carved grapes. The legs have pendants of leaves and grapes suspended from delicate bows, and the spade feet are made of ebony appliqués. The result is one of the finest chairs of the Federal period.

Other chairs from this set include Randall 1965, no. 165 (a pair), Hipkiss 1941, no. 91, Warren 1975, no. 139 (a pair), Montgomery 1966, no. 14, Davidson and Stillinger 1985, fig. 208, and one is in the Cleveland Museum. The carved leaf and grape motif of the legs is seen on a number of pieces owned by the great Salem merchant Elias Hasket Derby and include a sofa, card table, urn stand, and side chairs (Hipkiss 1941, nos. 75, 92, 120). The pair of chairs illustrated in Randall 1965, no. 165 have a Derby family history. The Derby family patronized the designer/carver Samuel McIntyre, and this group has long been attributed to him.

Provenance: C.K. Davis Collection, Fairfield, Connecticut; John Walton, Inc., Griswold, Connecticut

Construction and condition: The side rails are ash and the front rail is birch. They are shaped on both sides. The rear rail is birch, veneered in mahogany. The upholstery is nailed to a rabbet at its upper edge. The front legs have been rebuilt at the joints. The spade feet are appliqués of ebony. None of the original glue-blocks remain. The brass nail pattern is not based on original evidence; it may have originally been a single row of nails along the bottom edge. The splat is made of five pieces. The three vertical banisters are tenoned to the crest and stay rails. The drapery work is made of two pieces, notched to the stiles and the urn and lapped over the two flanking banisters. All the carving is cut from the solid.

Literature: Chairs from this set are discussed in Hipkiss 1941, no. 91; Randall 1965, no. 165; Montgomery 1966, no. 14; Warren 1975, no. 134; Davidson and Stillinger 1985, fig. 208

35
Side Chair
(one of three with one armchair)
1795–1805
Boston
Maple; birch rails
Side chair: 35 x 22¼ x 23⅛ in.
Armchair: 35 x 20¼ x 21⅛ in.
ACC. NOS. KAF 79.9 a–c and 78.12

In Federal Boston, curly maple found great use contrasted with mahogany, such as the tambours of cat. nos. 83 and 84 and the inlaid panels of the labeled Seymour card table, cat. no. 70. Curly maple is used in contrast with painted decoration in cat. no. 78. Nonetheless these chairs, originally part of a set of at least fourteen (four others are illustrated in Randall 1965 no. 173), are the only high style, all-maple Boston Federal chairs known. A variety of cuts of maple are found here, with bird's-eye maple panels inlaid in the legs, stiles, and crest rail, while a dark curly maple is used as a cuff and a border on the rails. The desirability of the cut of the wood is seen in the use of curly-maple veneer on the birch rails when the difference in price between maple and birch was minimal.

The back seems to be derived from plate 13 of the 1794 edition of Hepplewhite. The Boston cabinetmaker has chosen to emphasize the interplay of geometric forms by eliminating a tablet seen in the plate. The carved floral squares frame and enclose the back, adding depth to it.

The interlaced ovals within a square, double-tapered legs, maple inlay, and the use of a light-colored primary wood all combine in a simple and elegant statement of the Boston Federal style.

Provenance: Tradition and a brass plaque on the rear rail of the armchair have made these chairs the possession of John Hancock; however they do not appear in the inventory taken after his death in 1793 and are more likely the property of his widow, Dorothy Quincy Hancock Scott, who remarried. After her death in 1830, they appear in the probate records as a set of fourteen bird's-eye maple chairs with damask seats. They were purchased at the family auction by the Bullards, relatives of Dorothy Quincy Hancock Scott. The four chairs, illustrated in Randall 1965, no. 173, were owned by Bullard descendants. These chairs were consigned to Sotheby Parke-Bernet by Brewster D. Doggett; two of the chairs bear a paper label with the inscription *Mrs. Grace M.D. Doggett*; SP-B, sale 4180, November 1978, lot 980; Israel Sack, Inc., New York

Construction and condition: The rails are birch, veneered half over with curly maple. The front and side rails are shaped on both sides. A few of the rails are made of two pieces, horizontally laminated. The side and front rails are shaped on both sides. Modern horizontally grained triangular pine blocks support the leg joints. The splat is made of two pieces joined at the top and bottom of the central oval. The carved floral squares of the back are applied.

Literature: Chairs from this set are illustrated in Swan 1937, 119–121; Randall 1965, no. 173; Stoneman 1965, no. 210; Bishop no. 374; Michael 1986, 72, 77. The chairs of cat. no. 35 are illustrated in Tracy 1980, 363, fig. 2; Davidson and Stillinger, figs. 77, 78

Exhibitions: New York, MMA 1979–1986 (a pair); New Haven, Connecticut, Yale University Art Gallery 1980; Norfolk, Virginia, Chrysler Museum 1980–1986; Houston, Texas, Houston Museum of Fine Arts 1979–1985 (armchair)

Hepplewhite 1794, pl. 13

36
Side Chair
1795–1800
Salem
Maple; oak, cherry rails
38⅝ x 21⅝ x 22⅞ in.
ACC. NO. 84.1

Delicacy in form and decoration characterize this painted Federal side chair. The oval back supported by gently curved stiles, the curved side rails, bowed center rail, and sharply tapered legs ending in spade feet make this one of the simplest and most direct of Federal forms. Embellishments that would have been lost in mahogany or walnut are the painted feathers gathered by a blue bow, the strings of leaves and flowers across the crest and central plume, and those hanging from another pair of blue bows on the legs. These naturalistic elements are framed within the geometric form of the chair.

The chair descended in the family of Elias Hasket Derby, the great Salem merchant. Two versions of this chair exist—this one with five plumes in white, and another with seven plumes in black (cat. no. 37). Within the white set there are two different decorative schemes (Montgomery 1966, no. 7, Hipkiss 1941, no. 105). Only the white set has a firm line of descent from Elias Hasket Derby. The larger set, of which cat. no. 36 is a part, has long been associated with a bill of 1796 to Derby from Joseph Anthony and Co. of Philadelphia for "24 oval back chairs, stuffed seats covered with haircloth, 2 rows brass nails" (Swan 1931, 280–282). In Philadelphia at that time "oval back" was a term used to describe bow back Windsor chairs. An examination of this chair unupholstered shows no evidence of brass nails. No Philadelphia versions or prototypes have been found, while a number of related Salem examples in mahogany exist (Montgomery 1966, no. 16). The incurvate legs and narrow rails are features found in a variety of Salem chairs, but not Philadelphia ones. The chairs without the bill would not be attributed to Philadelphia, and the evidence does not confirm that the bill describes this chair.

Provenance: This chair, along with KAF 79.7 (not in this exhibition), and a third chair which appeared at SP-B, sale 5208, 30 June 1984, lot 699, share the same line of descent: Elias Hasket Derby (1739–1799); John Derby, his son; Mary Jane Derby (1807–1892), his daughter, married Ephraim Peabody (1807–1856); Anna Huidekoper Peabody (c. 1840–1920), their daughter, married Henry Whitney Bellows (1814–1882); Ellen Derby Bellows (c. 1880–1972), their daughter, married Samuel Robinson; Katherine Lambard Robinson, their daughter; Christie's, sale 5484, 21 January 1984, lot 321; Israel Sack, Inc., New York

Construction and condition: The front rail is cherry and the side rails are oak. They are shaped on both sides. The tenons into both front legs have been rebuilt. The rear rail is cherry and the upholstery is nailed to a rabbet in its upper edge. Vertically grained quarter-round pine blocks support the rear legs and modern, horizontally grained triangular pine blocks support the front legs. The spade feet are applied.

The splat is made in three pieces. The largest section includes the central plume and upper two feathers and bow. Each of the lower two feathers is notched to the central section and tenoned to the stiles. The crest rail joins the stiles at a line just below the upper pair of feathers.

The painted surface was cleaned of two layers of white overpaint and the original paint layer was consolidated and coated with an acryloid resin. Lost floral decoration on the crest rail was repainted, and minor losses on the stiles and splat were inpainted.

Literature: Chairs from this set are illustrated in Hipkiss 1941, no. 104; Fales 1972, 92; *Antiques,* October 1983, inside cover

unupholstered frame shown on p. 255

37
Side Chair
1790–1800
Salem
*Soft maple
38½ x 21½ x 22 in.
ACC. NO. 74.6

For chairs, a new and very elegant fashion has arisen within these few years, of finishing them with painted or japanned work, which gives a rich and splendid appearance to the more minute parts of the ornaments, which are generally thrown in by the painter. Several of these designs are particularly adapted to this style which allows a frame work less massy than is requisite for mahogany; and by assorting the prevailing colour to the furniture and light of the room affords opportunity, by the variety of grounds which may be introduced, to make the whole accord in harmony, with a pleasing and striking effect to the eye.

So said George Hepplewhite in his comments on chairs in *The Cabinet-Maker and Upholsterers' Guide* (1794 edition). No more apt description of this chair, its purpose, and execution could be made. This chair, like cat. no. 36, uses the same simple form but with more decoration. Oval-back chairs were popular in England but were favored in only Baltimore and Salem. Baltimore's oval backs are all executed in mahogany.

Though this chair and others from this set (Tracy 1970, no. 7, Randall 1965, no. 160, and Montgomery 1966, no. 18) have no history of ownership in the Derby family, they have been associated with a bill, dated 1801, to John Derby, Elias Hasket Derby's brother, from John Stillé, Jr. and Co. of Philadelphia for "6 gold and green chairs and 6 gold and black do [ditto]" (Montgomery 1966, 18). No mention of shape is made. The association is based on the assumptions (not proven) concerning the Elias Hasket Derby white oval-back set (see cat. no. 36). There is no reason to expect a sequence of production between the two sets—either could have been made first.

Regardless of when, where, or for whom, the chair is a successful interpretation of the new fashion so accurately described in Hepplewhite's guide.

Provenance: Mr. and Mrs. Mitchell Taradash Collection, Ardsley on Hudson, New York; Israel Sack, Inc., New York

Construction and condition: The rails are maple. The side and front rails are shaped on both sides. The upholstery is nailed to a rabbet along the upper edge of the rear rail. Vertically grained quarter-round pine blocks support all the leg joints. The spade feet are applied.

The splat is made in five pieces. The largest one includes the central section, the uppermost pair of feathers and the bow. Each of the lower four feathers is notched to the central section and tenoned to the stiles. The crest rail joins the stiles at a line just below the uppermost pair of feathers. Losses in the background color along the edges of the stiles have been inpainted.

Literature: Chairs from this set are illustrated in Montgomery 1966, no. 18; Randall 1965, no. 160; Tracy 1970, no. 7. This chair is illustrated in I. Sack n.d.–1979, 5:1389 (rev. ed.)

38

Armchair

(from a set of six including two armchairs and four side chairs)
1785–1800
New York
Mahogany; ash rails
40⅝ x 23½ x 21 in.
ACC. NO. 73.20 a-f

This chair, like cat. no. 39, shows the classic New York shield-back form with a narrow shield, high arch to the crest, and sharp point at the base. The sharply tapered leg with a wide spade foot is another New York feature. New Yorkers seemed to prefer their chairs without stretchers, though this is not a singularly New York characteristic. There is no known published design source for this type of splat, but English examples do exist. It is seen on other New York shield backs including Montgomery 1966, no. 56 and a closely related set in Levy and Levy 1984, 29. This splat works best with heart-back chairs (Fales 1976, no. 145 and I. Miller 1956, no. 79), where the spreading fan flows into the flanking arches of the crest and the flanking banister flows into the central arch, giving the back an interlaced effect. Here the banister flows into the central arch alone, emphasizing the splat and the narrowness of the shield. The carved bellflowers, or husks as they were called, are done in a slightly overlapping fashion similar to stylized New York husks in inlay (see cat. no. 39).

Provenance: Ginsburg and Levy, Inc., New York

Construction and condition: The front and side rails are ash, shaped on both sides. The rear rail is ash, veneered in mahogany. The upholstery is nailed to a rabbet along its upper edge. Hardwood open braces are set in the rails at each leg. Modern, horizontally grained triangular blocks are glued and screwed to the rails below the open braces.

The carved bellflowers are cut from the solid and are on the front and sides of the legs. The spade feet are applied. The legs of the armchairs are rebuilt below the spade feet. The stay rail includes the point of the shield and the fan, though the carved section is applied. The splat is made of three separate pieces, each tenoned to the crest and stay rail. The crest rails have been rebuilt where the center and side banisters of the splat meet. The arm supports are held by screws to the rails and tenoned to the arms which are held by screws to the stiles.

39

Side Chair
1785–1800
New York
Mahogany; *birch and *ash rails
38⅝ x 21 x 21⅛ in.
ACC. NO. 74.11

This chair has all the most distinctive elements of the New York shield-back chair. Every aspect of its design and execution also show it to be among New York's finest. The shield's molded face, sharp point, and high arch are classic New York style. The tightly handled drapery and central plume are again typical of New York. Both the shield and the splat emphasize the vertical, and the tapered, outflaring legs add a touch of delicacy to the form. The overlapping husks inlaid in the legs are a New York characteristic (see Montgomery 1966, no. 447) typically found on tables and case pieces and rarely on seating furniture.

Outflaring legs are seen in combination with shield backs in a number of Hepplewhite's plates. A curious note is that these designs often include incurvate rear legs. The outflaring legs became fashionable in New York, while the incurvate legs became fashionable in Salem (see cat. nos. 34, 36), but neither area favored the other or both features. Though the shield-back chair with outflaring legs found the greatest favor in New York, Newport examples in the New York manner, including four chairs labeled by John Townsend (Warren 1975, no. 141), are known.

Provenance: John S. Walton, Inc., New York

Construction and condition: The side and front rails are birch, shaped on both sides. The rear rail is ash. The upholstery is pulled over all four rails. None of the original blocking remains. The brass rail pattern is not based on original evidence. The splat includes the carved fan and is cut from a single piece of mahogany. The curve of the legs is cut from the solid.

40
Armchair
1785–1800
American
Mahogany; oak rails
37⅞ x 23¼ x 20½ in.
ACC. NO. 73.10

Various individual features common to a number of different style centers are found in this chair, making a regional attribution difficult. The splat is found on chairs from New York (Montgomery 1966, no. 53), Newport (Warren 1975, no. 141), and Salem (Bishop 1972, no. 387) and on English examples as well. The shape of the shield, with a molded face, though not quintessentially New York, is seen there and in Rhode Island as well. Neither the carving, the inlay, nor the arms are particular to any region. The incurvate rear legs are most often seen in Salem, though Salem seems to have preferred a hollowed rather than a molded face for its shield backs. Internal evidence offers little guidance. There are no open or medial braces that would favor the New York or even Newport school. One might be tempted to split the differences between New York and Salem and settle on Rhode Island, for by the Federal era Connecticut is no longer the warehouse of the unclassifiable. Instead, one may accept the chair as simply American and judge it on its merits. It is a prototypical Federal shield-back armchair and contains all the necessary elements, successfully combined, to make a pleasing whole.

Provenance: Israel Sack, Inc., New York

Construction and condition: The rails are oak. The side rails are curved and the front rail is serpentine. They are shaped on both sides. The rear rail is veneered with mahogany and the upholstery is nailed to a rabbet along its upper edge. None of the original blocks remain. Glue marks indicate that small, vertically grained blocks were used. The brass nail pattern is not based on original evidence. The inlaid cuffs are replacements. The splat is cut from a single board and tenoned to the crest and stay rail. The arm supports are held by screws to the rails and are tenoned to the arms which are held by screws to the stiles.

41

Side Chair
1790–1805
New York
Mahogany, ash rails
36⅛ x 21⅜ x 20¾ in.
ACC. NO. 73.9

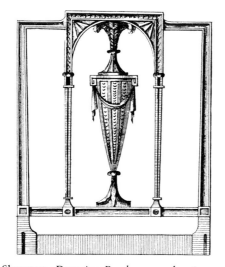

Sheraton, *Drawing Book* 1793, pl. 36, no. 1

Large numbers of chairs in this pattern survive, indicating their original popularity. This chair is based on plate 36, no. 1, of the 1793 edition of Sheraton's *Drawing Book*. The drawing indicates a carved back, though inlaid (cat. no. 42) and painted versions exist as well (Montgomery 1966, no. 36, Fales 1976, fig. 183). The carved version is both the most common and successful of the three interpretations.

The New York interpretation is slightly more abstract than the original. Here, as in most New York versions, the urn splat is indicated by three bars rather than a solid carved urn. This opens the back up and de-emphasizes the urn. The raised beads of the stiles and crest, along with the finely handled drapery, fans, and plume, add depth to the flat plane of the back. The relationship of the urn to the arch and the arch to the back give a proportional order to the back, while the pattern created by the columns, urn, and stiles molds the space into a complete unit. The reeded legs and spade feet are added refinements.

Provenance: Israel Sack, Inc., New York

Construction and condition: The front and side rails are ash, shaped on both sides. The rear rail is ash, veneered with mahogany. The upholstery is nailed to a rabbet along its upper edge. Open braces are dovetailed across the top of the rails at the front legs and across the bottom of the rails at the back legs. (The technique is illustrated in Levy and Levy 1984, 34.) Vertically grained quarter-round pine blocks support the front legs.

The front legs are reeded on two sides, and the spade feet are cut from the solid. The most common form of rear leg is carved. Here the stiles continue perpendicular to the rails for two inches below them and are then set at an angle rather than curved.

42
Side Chair
1790–1805
New York
Mahogany; *ash rails
36¼ x 21 x 20⅝ in.
ACC. NO. 72.2

Like cat. no. 41, this chair is based on plate 36, no. 1, of Shera-ton's *Drawing Book*, 1794 edition. "Square-back chairs" of this design are described in New York price books of both 1796 and 1802 (Montgomery 1966, 103). The pattern exists in varying levels of quality, indicating that it was produced by a number of shops (Levy and Levy 1984, 34, Hipkiss 1941, no. 108). The inlaid and carved versions were probably produced contemporaneously by shops with access to different special-ists. Differences in interior details show that this chair and cat. no. 41 are the work of different hands.

The use of inlay adds contrast to the back and is also more abstract than the carved version. The inlay here has only slight indications of shading and relies more on engraved details, as in the plume, for effect. This technique is seen on other New York pieces in the collection, such as cat. nos. 64, 73, and 85. This choice of inlay no doubt allowed for the use of tables and case pieces in a unified decorative scheme.

Provenance: Ginsburg and Levy, Inc., New York; P-B, sale 3371, 19–20 May 1972, lot 105

Construction and condition: The front and side rails are ash, shaped on both sides. The rear rail is ash, veneered with ma-hogany. The upholstery is nailed to a rabbet along its upper edge. The chair originally had open braces dovetailed across the tops of the rails at the legs. Now vertically grained quarter-round pine blocks are set at the leg joints. A cherry medial brace is dovetailed to the rails. It is dished on top and straight across the bottom.

The spade feet are cut from the solid. The most common form of rear leg is curved. Here the stiles continue perpendicu-lar to the rails for two inches below them and then are set at an angle rather than curved.

43

Armchair
1795–1810
New York
Mahogany; *ash, cherry
37½ x 21⅜ x 22⅝ in.
ACC. NO. 80.3

This armchair matches a set of six chairs (two armchairs and four side chairs; see Bishop 1972, nos. 295, 298). American Sheraton style open armchairs are few and the majority seem to have been made in Philadelphia (see cat. no. 46). Several clues indicate, however, that this chair was made in New York: the use of a shaped medial brace was favored in New York but not in Philadelphia; the drapery carving of the tablet, and floral squares of the legs, arms, and crest are typically New York features; lastly, the shaping of the arm, arm support, and leg is very close to a number of New York, but not Philadelphia, sofas (see Bishop 1972, no. 332, Comstock 1962, no. 530, and Montgomery 1966, no. 275).

Plate 61 of Sheraton's *Drawing Book* (1802), plate 32 of the Appendix and plate 8, no. 2 of the 1803 *Cabinet Dictionary* show chairs very similar to this one. The temptation to see them as the basis for this chair must be tempered by an interesting inquiry in *Antiques* concerning a chair identical in form, but made in satinwood with inlay rather than mahogany with carving (*Antiques* 1926, 28–29). The owner stated that the chair was brought over from England and descended through her family. While this may have been the true prototype for cat. no. 43, such evidence cannot be accepted without examination, but neither can it be ignored.

Provenance: Thomas Schwenke Antiques of New York purchased this chair at the estate auction of Esther Thurber Broughton of New York City; Israel Sack, Inc., New York

Construction and condition: The rails are ash, with molded mahogany facings applied over the lower third of the rails. The side and front rails are shaped on both sides. Vertically grained quarter-round glue blocks support the rear legs but only glue marks remain at the front. A cherry medial brace is half dovetailed to the rails. It is dished on top and straight across the bottom. Modern horizontally grained quarter-round blocks are set on top of the rails and notched to fit around the legs. These are usually applied to support a spring seat. The arm supports are integral to the legs and are tenoned to the arms which are tenoned to the stiles. The carving on the crest rail is cut from the solid.

Literature: I. Sack n.d.–1979, 7:1744, 1805

unupholstered frame shown on p. 254

44
Armchair
1795–1810
Mid-Atlantic
*Walnut and *ash
36⅜ x 22¾ x 23¾ in.
ACC. NO. 76.2

This chair presents a mystery. The woods are American and other examples may still exist, but little else is known. American furniture in the Louis XVI style is very rare. The best-known set was made for Edward Shippen Burd of Philadelphia and includes a sofa and twelve armchairs (PMA 1976, no. 170). This set also is painted and gilded. From the late 1780s until the 1830s there are contemporary references to Louis XVI style furniture being both produced and imported, but little of it can be documented today.

Photographs document the existence of other chairs and a sofa in this pattern. Unfortunately the present whereabouts of these objects is unknown. A photograph taken in 1945 of the upper parlor of a Baltimore townhouse shows a similar small sofa and three armchairs covered in a damask and painted white. Family tradition held that the set and other New York neoclassical furniture, also seen in the photo, had been acquired by Robert Smith, a prominent Baltimore merchant and government official in the early nineteenth century. The house in which this picture was taken was built by his son. The photograph was taken prior to the dispersal of the objects by auction in the spring of 1945.

Two armchairs are pictured in an article by Marie Kimball (*Antiques* 1929, 33–36) on the original furnishings of the White House. The chairs were owned by the Kimballs and are pictured in a room at Lemon Hill in Philadelphia in an arrangement that suggests their use at the White House. The caption for one of the armchairs says it was originally painted and gilded, and attributes it to Philadelphia.

This chair does not exhibit strong regional aesthetic characteristics, though the leaf carving of the arms is similar to numerous New York examples (cat. nos. 49 and 74). It may, then, represent a New York interpretation of the Louis XVI style, though other areas cannot be ruled out. Research by photographs alone is a risky endeavor and any conclusions about this chair must await further research.

Provenance: This chair descended in the Button family of New York and Connecticut; Israel Sack, Inc., New York

Construction and condition: The rails are walnut. The lower half of the rails is molded, and the upper half is rabbetted to accept the upholstery. The front rail is shaped on both sides. The legs and stiles are ash. There are no glue-blocks or braces. The gilding obscures the joints and types of wood used in the crest and stay rails, banisters, and arms. The gilded decoration is a replacement; originally the piece was probably painted white with gilt highlights.

45
Side Chair
(one of four)
1800–1810
Philadelphia
Mahogany; *ash rails
36 x 18¼ x 17 in.
ACC. NO. 72.11 a–d

These are as fine a set of chairs as Federal Philadelphia produced. They are part of a larger set that includes armchairs and a four chair-back settee now in the collection of the White House. The skilled hands of a turner, carver, inlay-maker, upholsterer, and chairmaker are revealed in every detail. Elements of their design are found in plate 6 of the Appendix of Sheraton's 1802 *Cabinet-Maker and Upholsterer's Drawing-Book*. Two related examples are known: one that differs only in having the oval of the back upholstered (Montgomery 1966, no. 93); the other (Halloway 1937, pl. 55) has a carved rather than inlaid center. Ephraim Haines produced a similar set of chairs, armchairs, settee, and a table in ebony for the merchant Stephen Girard in 1807. Girard supplied the lumber, and Haines acted as general contractor with the specialist craftsmen. This set has not been attributed to Haines, though it may have been produced in the same fashion.

Cat. no. 45 offers a wonderful interplay of elements. The leaf carving has a smoothed, almost rubbed quality, which complements the gentle swell of the turnings. The floral squares and leafage on the crest add a naturalistic touch that softens the lines of the back, while the inlaid vase and flower form a counterpoint to both carvings and turnings. The design of the back reflects the interest of the era in geometric forms, with the inlaid oval within the larger oval within the rectangle of the splat within the square of the back. This interplay is enhanced by the repetition of the stiles in the turnings of the splat.

Provenance: By tradition these chairs were a wedding gift from James and Elizabeth Sloan to their daughter Mary Sloan (1796–1866) who married William Frick (1790–1855) of Germantown, Pennsylvania. The couple soon moved to Baltimore where Frick pursued a career in the law; Mary Carol Frick Montgomery (great-granddaughter); Israel Sack, Inc., New York

Construction and condition: The front and side rails are ash, shaped on both sides. The rear rail is ash, veneered in mahogany. The upholstery is nailed to a rabbet along its upper edge. Modern horizontally grained triangular glue-blocks support the leg joints. The splat is made in three pieces: the two turned and carved columns, and the carved and inlaid central section. All three pieces are tenoned to the crest and stay rail.

Literature: I. Sack n.d.–1979, 2:533; PMA 1976, no. 174. Armchairs and a settee from this set are now in the collection of the White House, and are discussed in White House 1962, pl. 5; Fitzgerald 1982, figs. 5–26; Fairbanks and Bates 1981, 241; A. Sack 1985, 186–187

Exhibition: Philadelphia, PMA 1976 (Three Centuries of American Art)

46
Armchair
1795–1810
Philadelphia
Ash
36½ x 20½ x 21⅞ in.
ACC. NO. KAF 81.1

Gilded American furniture is rare and is usually considered French in style. However this Philadelphia example has more in common with English and other Philadelphia chairs than with any known French ones. The stepped arms are found on the armchairs and settee ensuite with cat. no. 45 which in turn is based on plate 16 in the Appendix of Sheraton's 1802 *Drawing Book*. The handling of the turnings is also seen on other Philadelphia chairs. The composition ornament is derived from English architectural books of the late eighteenth century. They may have been manufactured by Robert Welford's American Manufactory of Composition Ornament in Philadelphia.

This chair is a part of a set of which seven are known (Montgomery 1966, no. 92, and five in private collections). Family tradition concerning four of the chairs held that six were purchased at auction in the early nineteenth century in Philadelphia, at which time they were said to have been owned, along with a matching sofa, by Robert Morris, who had been an envoy to France. He was thought to have received them from the king of France. While numerous American officials are known to have brought furniture from France, including examples from the royal court, this is certainly not one of them. The other six chairs have a combination of white paint with gilt decoration unlike the chair seen here, which is covered entirely by a later oil gilding.

Provenance: The chair was found at auction in eastern Massachusetts; SP-B, sale 4529Y, 31 January 1981, lot 1514; Israel Sack, Inc., New York

Construction and condition: The chair is constructed entirely of ash. All the carved ornaments are applied composition. All four rails are curved and shaped on both sides. The molded strips flanking the ornaments on the rails are applied. There are no blocks or braces. The arm supports are integral to the legs and are tenoned to the arms which are tenoned to the stiles. The banisters, crest, and stay rails are rounded on the back.

The fabric is a replacement, but the upholstery substructure is original. At the time of its purchase a modern layer of filling obscured the sharper lines of the original triple-stitched French edge. Both the back and arm pads retain their original stuffing. The seat is built up from six strips of herringbone-pattern linen webbing. This is covered by a linen or canvas platform filled with horsehair, which is covered with yet another piece of canvas/linen, which is nailed to the rails and triple stitched to form a hard, sharp edge. The modern printed label of *Wilfert Brothers/Interior Decorators/and/ Painters/Furniture Antique and Modern/Repaired and Refinished/Upholstery*, with the oval stamp of *Wilfert Brothers, Boston, 27 Cambria Street*, is glued to the bottom of the seat.

The chair was originally painted white, with gilt decoration on the composition ornaments, and highlighting of other elements. It has subsequently been gilded all over at least once and probably twice. When purchased there was flaking down to the wood on all the reeded surfaces. There was also water damage to the front feet and lower rear legs, and losses on the rear of the crest rail and along the edges of the arms. The only major composition loss was the lower half of the right front leg panel. All these losses have been infilled and patinated to conform to the existing tone of the chair.

Literature: Another chair from this set is illustrated in Montgomery 1966, no. 92

47
Side Chair
1800–1815
Boston
Mahogany; *birch rails
35⅞ x 20⅛ x 21⅜ in.
ACC. NO. 83.6

The scroll-back chair was the first step in seating furniture away from the Adamesque-inspired designs of the early classical revival and toward the more archaeologically correct designs of the Regency and Empire periods. New York examples quickly abandoned the use of inlays and contrasting veneers in favor of carved motifs. This chair and the side chairs in cat. no. 48 show that Boston cabinetmakers were quick to adopt the new form but in combination with the dominant decorative schemes of the region. The result is one of the most finely crafted and sophisticated chairs of the early nineteenth century.

Scroll-back chairs appear in the 1802 London price book and most of the embellishments pictured here are listed there. The legs are flawlessly turned and reeded; this does not imply an earlier date of manufacture than the saber-leg chair would have (cat. no. 48). Turned legs were a stylistic option throughout the period and were used in klismos chairs where they reflected a Roman rather than Greek inspiration. This chair is more generous in its use of wood and sophisticated in its joinery than are those in cat. no. 48.

The handling of the back is masterful. The stay rails and stiles, with inlaid panels of crotch satinwood and carved floral squares, frame the splat and create an interplay of elements with the curves of the diamond, a treatment similar to that used in cat. no. 35. A carved and reeded plume motif ties the splat to the crest. All the embellishments of the chair are united in the reeded and inlaid crest rail. A progression from the large rectangle around the splat to the small one around the plume emphasizes movement up the stiles to the scroll and crest rail.

Provenance: Israel Sack, Inc., New York

Construction and condition: The front and side rails are birch, with molded mahogany facings applied to the lower half. The rails are shaped on both sides. The rear rail is birch veneered in mahogany. The upholstery is nailed to a rabbet along its upper edge. Modern blocks support the legs. The turned "bulls eyes" on the legs at the rails are applied.

The diamond-shaped splat is made in four pieces, one for each section of curve. The pieces are joined at the points, and these joints are covered by an appliqué of carved leafwork and a bead. The V-shaped piece below the crest is made of two pieces but the carved floral squares in the stiles are cut from the solid.

The crest rail is curved towards the rear rather than straight across. The central tablet is fully rounded in back, and the turnings are complete though they are reeded only three-quarters of the way round. The turned buttons on the stiles at the crest are applied.

Literature: Another chair from this set is illustrated in Tracy 1970, no. 14; Stoneman 1965 no. 211; Bishop 1972, no. 376

48

Side Chair
(one of a pair)
1800–1815
Boston
Mahogany; *birch rails
34¾ x 18⅞ x 20⅜ in.
ACC. NO. 83.11 a, b

Saber-leg chairs in this pattern normally have the front legs canted at the corners rather than facing ahead as they do here. The other saber-leg seating pieces fall into two groups. The first includes a five chair-back settee, a pair of chairs, a double chair-back settee (Montgomery 1966, nos. 37, 38, 39) and a pair of chairs (Hipkiss 1941, no. 116). The second group includes a pair of chairs (Warren 1975, no. 142), a single chair (Kane 1976, no. 154) and a second pair of chairs (Stoneman 1965, no. 57). These groups differ primarily in that the former have more inlaid flame birch panels than do the latter. The two groups show the same hand in the shaping of the legs, splat, and crest rail, which is different from the handling of cat. no. 47 (see *Construction and condition* for cat. no. 47).

No evidence indicates that these forward-facing saber-leg chairs are more closely linked to the later klismos style chairs than are the canted-leg versions. They are more probably the result of consumer choice than a stylistic progression. Hipkiss, in the caption to his no. 16 (1941), attributed these chairs to the Seymours "based on details of carving, inlays and their applications," but confirmation of this attribution has yet to be found.

Provenance: Phillips Gallery, sale 510, 20 October 1983, lot 714; Israel Sack, Inc., New York

Construction and condition: The rails are birch, veneered in mahogany. The upholstery is nailed to rabbets along the upper edges of the rails. The side and front rails are shaped on one side only and their upper edges have been rebuilt with poplar. Modern glue-blocks support the legs which are rounded in back.

The diamond-shaped splat is made in four pieces, one for each section of curve. The pieces are joined at the points. Unlike cat. no. 47 the leafwork at the points is cut from the solid. Modern, shaped mahogany blocks are glued behind the points to reinforce them. The V-shaped piece below the crest is cut from a single piece of wood. The carved floral squares of the stiles are carved from the solid.

The crest rail is curved toward the rear rather than straight across. The central tablet is slightly rounded in the rear, and none of the turnings are complete except the rings next to the stiles. The buttons on the stiles at the crest rail are applied.

49
Side Chairs
(two of four)
1805–1820
New York
Mahogany; *oak, *maple
32½ x 18½ x 21¾ in.
ACC. NO. 78.10 a, b and KAF 79.8 a, b

The klismos chair was a new form in the Graeco-Roman style introduced to America in the first decade of the nineteenth century. One innovation was the use of figural elements such as dolphins, caryatids, animal feet, and lyres. In these eagle-back chairs the newly imported style received a distinctly American interpretation.

The eagle, while not an inspiration to European designers, as evidenced by its meager showing in design books and total absence in price books, was the symbol of the new republic. Standing in full glory with wings spread one eagle faces right, the other left, so that when paired they face each other. Seen from the front, the stance of the chair legs reinforces the standing eagles; the simple klismos form is united with the naturalistic and robust American symbols.

A matching set of eight chairs (Tracy 1970, no. 25) descended from the family of George Clinton, brother of DeWitt Clinton. The Clinton brothers married the Franklin sisters, Maria and Hannah, who were half-sisters to Susan Kittredge Field from whom these four chairs descended. The other eight chairs are identical in every detail but have been reduced by three-quarters of an inch in height. These four and the eight are numbered consecutively I–XII and originally were a set.

Provenance: By tradition these chairs were made for Governor DeWitt Clinton of New York. The line of descent from DeWitt Clinton is as follows: Mrs. DeWitt Clinton (Maria Franklin Clinton) to her half-sister, Susan Kittredge Field; Moses Augustus Field (son of Susan Kittredge Field); Mrs. Henry Wilmerding Payne (née Mary Field, daughter of Moses Augustus Field); Augustus Field (brother of Mary Field Payne, by inheritance from his sister); Malcolm Graham Field (son of Augustus Field); Mrs. Malcolm Graham Field of Sloatsburg, New York; Christies, sale "Phyfe," 21 October 1978, lot 266; Israel Sack, Inc., New York

Construction and condition: The chairs employ the standard joinery of the day for klismos style chairs. The mahogany side rails are tenoned to the stiles and legs. The front and rear seat rails are oak and maple, faced with mahogany and double tenoned to the legs and stiles. The stay rail and crest rail are also tenoned. The eagles are carved on the face side only and held in place by mahogany pins rather than tenons. Two pins go through the stay rail and three hold the eagle to the crest rail. The turned buttons on the legs and stiles are applied. Panels of crotch-grain mahogany veneer are set in the crest rails. The maple slip seats are held by screws through the seat rails.

Literature: These chairs are illustrated in Nutting 1928–1933, 2:no. 2401–2402; McClelland 1939, pl. 254; I. Sack n.d.–1979, 6: 1642–1643; Cooper 1980, fig. 295; Carson 1979, 73, fig. 5. Chairs from this set are illustrated in Tracy 1970, no. 25, and Bishop 1972, no. 455

Exhibitions: New York, Museum of the City of New York 1943; New York, MMA 1939, 1979–1986 (KAF 79.8 a, b)

50
Pair of Side Chairs
1815–1825
Philadelphia
Mahogany; *ash rails and *white pine slip seat
33¼ x 19 x 23⅛ in.
ACC. NO. 74.7 a, b

The strict archaeological taste of the neoclassical period is reflected in these boulle-work chairs. Unlike most klismos-type chairs, which create the illusion of a continuous line from the top of the stiles to the bottom of the front legs, these chairs do the opposite. The crest rail rests in front of the stiles and is not enclosed by them. The stay rails are parallelograms that rise with the back and add to its sweep. The legs appear to be mortised into the seat frame which along with the free-standing slip seat give a platform effect to the seat. Designs for chairs of this form appear in Hope 1807, plate 25, and elements of the back and crest rail appear in a design executed by Benjamin Henry Latrobe for the White House in 1809 (Fales 1972, pl. 245). The simplicity of the form belies the quality of the decoration and execution. Brass inlay and boulle work (brass and ebony panels) was more than twice as expensive as wood according to the Philadelphia price book of 1828. It heightened the antique effect without disturbing the line.

The pattern of stars and anthemions in the crest rail relates to a side table in which they are inlaid in the frieze (Montgom-

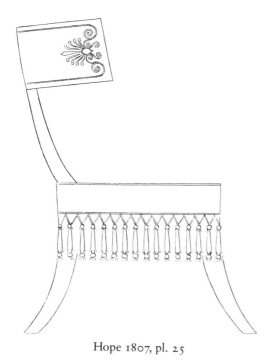

Hope 1807, pl. 25

ery 1966, no. 351). The panels of the skirt are similar to a group of Philadelphia boulle-work case pieces (see PMA 1976, no. 221 and cat. no. 90). There has always been some question as to whether the boulle work found on these chairs was of American manufacture or English, as was the case with many inlays during the Federal period. Examination of an English Regency sofa with four anthemions and two rosettes of identical size and design seems to indicate that at least this pattern was available as an import. Philadelphia boulle-work pieces have often been attributed to Joseph Barry (1757–1839) on the basis of an 1824 newspaper advertisement offering boulle-work pieces for sale (PMA 1976, 266), but no firmer connection has yet been established.

Twelve chairs of this set survive: the two Kaufman chairs, four in museums (Warren 1975, no. 177 and PMA 1976, no. 222a), and six in another private collection.

Provenance: Descended in the Hare family of Philadelphia; R.T. Trump and Co., Flourtown, Pennsylvania

Construction and condition: The rails are ash, tenoned to the legs and stiles. The rear rail is veneered in mahogany. Strips of mahogany are applied over the side and front rails, including the tops of the legs. Mahogany veneer is applied on top of the rails and over the legs as well. The slip seats are pine. They are notched at the rear corners to fit between the stiles and are secured in front by a steel pin set in the top of the rail that fits in a corresponding hole in the seat. The stay rails are tenoned to the stiles and are parallelograms in cross section. The stiles are notched and set in the crest rails.

The boulle work in the front rail is worked with rosewood. The rosettes in the stiles are brass and ebony. In the crest rail, brass stringing outlines a rosewood panel inset with more stringing, stars, and an anthemion. The stars and anthemion are brass and ebony.

Literature: Chairs from this set are illustrated in Warren 1975, no. 177; PMA 1976, no. 222a; Fitzgerald 1982, figs. 6, 7

51

Pair of Side Chairs
1810–1825
Boston
Mahogany; birch
32¼ x 18⅞ x 22¼ in.
ACC. NO. 85.3 a, b

Hope 1807, pl. 24

This interpretation of the Greek klismos chair, with its carved swag and scrolled splat was confined to Boston. The design may be based on the early nineteenth-century designs of Sheraton, which show sofas and chairs with swags of fabric draped across their backs (*Encyclopedia* [1804–1806] pls. 8, 12 and *Household Furniture* [1812] pl. 59). The crest rail is closely modeled on plates 4 and 24 of Hope (1807) though he calls for the design to be executed in boulle work (advice followed more closely in Philadelphia—see cat. no. 50). The common denominator of this Boston style—the crest and splat—are seen in chairs in the collections of SPNEA (acc. no. 1963.342B), at Gore Place in Waltham, Massachusetts, and at Dartmouth College. A window seat with these elements is shown in Israel Sack, n.d.–1979, 4:891.

The Kaufman chairs have the additional features of twist-reeded and carved front rails. The handling of the stiles, however, is their most distinctive feature. Set on the platform of the seat, they continue to the front where they terminate in carved volutes. The area below the stile at the rear of the seat is filled with a series of carved darts that emphasize the sweep and rise of the back and show the careful attention to detail that marks these chairs as among the finest examples of the form.

Provenance: Christie's, sale 5484, 21 January 1984, lot 176; Stuart P. Feld Collection, New York

Construction and condition: The front and rear rails are birch with mahogany facings. They are double tenoned to the legs. The side rails are mahogany and are single tenoned to the legs. The stiles start at the seat rails. They are tenoned to the rails and to the tops of the rear legs. The line of the stiles is continued in a separate horizontally grained piece glued to the top of the rails and front leg. It is molded with the stile and terminates in a carved volute. The splat is carved from a single board and tenoned to the stiles. The stiles are notched and fitted to the crest rail which is carved from the solid with an applied panel of crotch-grain mahogany veneer. The slip seat is birch and is held by screws through the rails.

52
Lolling Chair
1795–1810
North Shore of Massachusetts
Mahogany; birch
47⅜ x 25¼ x 20½ in.
ACC. NO. 80.4

The lolling, or "Martha Washington" chair as it is called to-day, is a distinctly American innovation of the Federal period. Chairs with upholstered backs and open arms were favored in England and the Continent through the third quarter of the eighteenth century. European designers did not update the form to fit in with the new classical ideals, and it died out. Upholstered-back, open-arm chairs were used throughout the colonies as well. After the Revolution only the craftsmen of Massachusetts and coastal New Hampshire updated and adapted the form to the new Federal aesthetic. The pre-Revolution New England version had a high back, often with a serpentine crest, ball-and-claw or pad feet, and scrolled arms with swept back supports (Downs 1952, no. 21). The next phase saw the introduction of tapered legs and a continuous line to the arm and its supports. The form reached its apogee in the evolution to turned leg and arm supports. The finest of these chairs have high narrow backs with serpentine crests. The turned legs have fine reeding. Continuous with the legs are the turned arm supports that join the curved and shaped arms. The delicate transitions between post and arm, from the round to the rectangular, is a highlight of the form. The best examples were produced in the coastal towns of Salem, Newburyport, and Portsmouth. Two very similar examples are illustrated which have slightly less elaboration (Montgomery and Kane 1976, 178 and Jones 1977, 980).

C-scrolls and stop-fluting are embellishments usually found on pieces from the rococo period. The stop-fluted, bulbous arm supports are a perfect counterpoint to the reeded legs, and the C-scrolls support and accentuate the transition from post to arm. This combination of elements is as distinctive as the chair itself and attests to the vitality of the form despite the influence of English design books on American furniture during the Federal era.

Provenance: H. W. Weeks, Framingham, Massachusetts; Harry Arons Antiques, Ansonia, Connecticut; Israel Sack, Inc., New York; Teina Baumstone Antiques, New York; Col. Edgar William and Mrs. Bernice Chrysler Garbisch Collection, Pokety Farm, Maryland; SP-B, sale H-2, 24 May 1980, lot 1114; Israel Sack, Inc., New York

Construction and condition: The description of the back of the chair is based on photographs taken when it was reupholstered. The rails are birch. The serpentine front rail is shaped on both sides. Modern blocks support the leg joints. The mahogany rear legs continue above the rails. The stiles are spliced and nailed to them. There is a stay rail tenoned to the stiles just above the splice. The serpentine crest rail is shaped on one side only and tenoned to the stiles.

The leg and arm support are one piece connected to the arm by a diagonally grained piece of mahogany carved into a C-scroll. The arm is tenoned through the stiles. Both the arms and arm support are tenoned to the C-scroll piece.

Literature: Nutting 1928–1933, 2:no. 2363

shown unupholstered on p. 254

53

Sling-Seat Armchair

1805–1825

Mid-Atlantic

Mahogany; poplar, pine

38½ x 24 x 33⅛ in.

ACC. NO. 74.5

Few pieces of antique furniture have design sources as ancient as this sling-seat armchair. Slung seats over X stretchers were used in ancient Egypt. The curule form with more curves and less X shape became a Roman magistrate's chair. Seventeenth-century Spain developed a version with turned stretchers, S-shaped arms, and a tooled leather seat. Thomas Jefferson enjoyed the Spanish variety—a campeachy chair—which he received from a friend in New Orleans. He had two of them at Monticello and commissioned a number in curly maple. In 1837 Joseph Bradley and Co. of New York was awarded a diploma for their "Spanish Chairs." The form continued to be popular throughout the century and on into this one with the contour chair.

The chair draws upon the neoclassical vocabulary with its curule shape, bold reeding, and volutes on the arms, crest, and seat rails. It is closely related to two others—one in Montgomery 1966, no. 120 (pictured unupholstered in Otto 1965, no. 37) and the other in Miller 1937, 1:no. 491. The three differ both in details and dimensions. The chair shown here has an overhanging crest and triple reeding that outline the frame. The crest rail of the other two is contained within the stiles, and a series of five reeds outline the frame. The one in Miller has a mahogany front rail and unupholstered arms, while the others are upholstered over the rail with padded arms. On the basis of the design and delicacy of the reeding Montgomery attributed the chair to New York, but the use of yellow pine and poplar is uncharacteristic of New York chairmaking. This chair also uses yellow pine and poplar and the overhanging crest rail and bolder reeding is more typical of Philadelphia. Given the scarcity of examples and provenances, the places of manufacture within the mid-Atlantic region are uncertain.

The appeal of the form, with its crosses and curves, elegance of line, and simple comfort is, one can say as a matter of fact, both timeless and universal.

Provenance: Mrs. Myrtle C. Shallow, Philadelphia, Pennsylvania; R.T. Trump and Co., Flourtown, Pennsylvania

Construction and condition: The construction of this chair is simplicity itself. The stiles and legs are combined into a roughly X-shaped unit made of two pieces secured by an angled lap joint at the cross. These units are joined by four stretchers: the crest rail, a bowed mahogany stretcher (shaped on both sides) just below the arms, a yellow pine stretcher at the cross, and a two-piece poplar front rail. The arm supports and arms are tenoned to these leg and stile units. The leather seat is nailed to rabbets along the reeded edges that have been repaired with mahogany in a number of places.

54
Sofa
1795–1805
Baltimore
Attr. Levin Tarr group
Mahogany; poplar, oak
36⅜ x 84 x 25 in.
ACC. NO. 71.8

The most sophisticated curvilinear design of the Federal era is the cabriole sofa. The inlaid legs, shaped arms, and molded crossbanding extending across the back to delineate the form create a unity of line and decoration. The serpentine front rail extends the curvilinear design to the seat. Only the Queen Anne chairs of Philadelphia show the same emphasis on continuity of line and curvilinear form.

Plate 24 in Hepplewhite (1794) shows a sofa of this form, but with no text commentary. Contemporary accounts and price books describe it as a cabriole sofa. Its greatest popularity was in New York and Baltimore. New York sofas use the same outflared arms seen on New York armchairs (see cat. no. 38). This breaks the continuity of line from back to arms, seen in this Baltimore piece.

Cabriole sofas are rare today and were probably so in the eighteenth century because of their high cost. Their popularity was brief, and some areas went from camelback sofas with classical decorations to Sheraton square sofas skipping the form entirely. Both structurally and aesthetically the cabriole sofa is a delicate form. The curve from the back to the arms, the key to its beauty, is also its weakest point. Like the oval-back chair, another delicate form popular in Baltimore, the appeal is purely aesthetic, not practical.

The inlaid husks and banded oval seen here are the same as those on the Levin Tarr group of tables (cat. nos. 60, 61, 76). Three other Baltimore cabriole sofas (Montgomery 1966, no. 266, Montgomery and Kane 1976, no. 130, and SP-B, sale 5208, 28 June 1984, lot 724) also have this distinctive pattern of inlay and the same construction techniques as this sofa. While no two of the four sofas are exactly alike, the consistency in form, decoration, and construction justifies their inclusion in the Levin Tarr group.

Provenance: Israel Sack, Inc., New York

Construction and condition: The description of the back and arms is based on photographs taken when the sofa was reupholstered. The serpentine front rail is made of three layers of horizontally laminated poplar. The rear seat rail is also poplar. The side rails are oak. All the rails are shaped on both sides and tenoned to the legs at each end. The two center rear legs are tenoned to the rail, while the two center front legs have an open-faced, dovetail-shaped tenon and a rectangular tenon set in the rail. Each of the end legs is reinforced by modern blocks. Oak open braces are set behind the front legs. Two large, poplar medial braces are dovetailed to the rails over the center legs. They are curved top and bottom.

The molded arm supports are part of the legs. The arm supports are tenoned to the mahogany arms. The transition between the arm and crest rail is made by a piece of poplar, shaped to the curve. The crest rail is a single piece of poplar, shaped on both sides. The stile of the rear corner legs is lapped and screwed to the shaped piece of poplar. The crest rail is supported by two bannisters. These are positioned just outside the center rear legs. They are tenoned to the rear and crest rails and a stay rail is tenoned between them. Stay rails following the curve of the seat rails are set between the arm supports, rear corner legs, and bannisters. A post is notched between the arm and side stay rail on each side.

The band across the crest rail to the arms is cross-grained, molded mahogany, glued to the edge of the frame. The molded face of the arm supports and arms is cut from the solid.

unupholstered frame shown on p. 252

55
Sofa
1790–1810
Boston
Mahogany; maple
35½ x 58 x 26 in.
ACC. NO. 73.12

This sofa appears to match a pair shown in Montgomery 1966, no. 273, both in decoration and construction. The pair are extensively discussed in Stoneman 1959, 20–23, 329. Montgomery and Stoneman attribute the pair to the Seymours on the basis of connections between them and the original owners of one of the sofas. The labeled Seymour satinwood tambour desk (Stoneman 1959, 48) descended through the same family. This sofa and one of the pair have no documented history. Montgomery mentions that the turnings are similar to pieces attributed to the Seymours. They are similar to cat. no. 79 as well, which has been attributed to the Seymours. Turnings, however, were available from specialized shops and seating furniture has not yet been documented to the Seymour shop. This type of turning may be over-attributed to the Seymours, but it is nonetheless typical of Boston.

Hepplewhite and Sheraton both show designs for "square" sofas. Sheraton shows a number of free-standing, turned arm supports such as are used here. This design proved to be the most popular in America. These pieces are smaller than most sofas, which generally are between six to six and a half feet long. They originally may have been used as window seats, or in niches flanking a fireplace or doorway.

Provenance: Israel Sack, Inc., New York

Construction and condition: The description of the back and arms is based on photographs taken when the piece was last upholstered. The back and arms retained an early, possibly original, upholstery substructure. This consisted of a single strip of herringbone-pattern webbing across the back, but none for the arms. There was a linen/canvas platform across the back and on each of the arms. These were filled with horsehair and covered with another sheet of linen/canvas. The frame has maple rails tenoned to the mahogany legs. These joints are supported by horizontally grained, triangular glueblocks. The front legs and arm supports are continuous, as are the rear legs and stiles. The center rear leg is tenoned to the rail, and a bridle joint holds the center front leg. The castors are replacements. Two birch medial braces are half dovetailed to the rails. Modern blocks support these.

The crest rail is tenoned to the stiles. Three banisters are set between the crest and rear rail; one over the rear center leg and one at each end next to the stiles. Two stay rails are tenoned to the banisters. The stiles are notched to accept the arms which are held in place by two screws each. The maple-veneered panels behind the turned arm supports are backed by banisters that are tenoned to the side rails and arms. A stay rail is set in the stile and banister at each side.

unupholstered frame shown on p. 252

56
Window Seat
1810–1820
New York
Mahogany; poplar, cherry
29⅜ x 36¼ x 16¼ in.
ACC. NO. 79.4

This window seat is a compact and beautifully carved example of New York's neoclassical style. Window seats came in two forms—with chair backs joined by rails, or smaller-scale, backless sofas. Examples of the former are shown in Montgomery 1966, no. 69 and Bishop 1972, no. 349. Because they were made to fit in windowed recesses, window seats were usually made at least in pairs. The Pierce-Nichols house in Salem still has a set of four, with a matching pair of small sofas. The mate to this New York piece is shown in Bishop 1972, no. 350.

The overall form of this window seat is that of a Grecian sofa. Designs for these had appeared in English price and design books by 1802, though the earliest American versions are traditionally dated after 1810. The design of the sides, with the scrolled crest and crossed banisters, is seen in the earliest documented pieces by Duncan Phyfe, which are dated 1807. Both the choice and high quality of the motifs are consistent with Phyfe's work and this piece may indeed be his.

The diminutive scale of this window seat produces a concentration of elements that accentuate both line and decoration. The delicacy of the carving on the front and crest rails belies the image of thunderbolts held by a bow. With every primary surface, either reeded or carved, this piece presents a highly refined example of an elegant form.

Provenance: Bernard and S. Dean Levy, Inc., New York

Construction and condition: This window seat is built around the mahogany seat frame. Both the legs and arms are tenoned to it. The side rails are mahogany and are tenoned to the front and rear rails just behind the floral squares of the front rail. Two poplar medial braces are half dovetailed to the frame. They are as deep as the rails and are dished on top and straight across the bottom. Vertically grained poplar blocks are set at the joints of the rails. A strip of cherry, rounded at the ends, is screwed to the top of the front rail. There is no corresponding strip on the rear or side rails. The brass nail pattern is based on evidence uncovered during reupholstery.

The arm sections are tenoned into the tops of the rails. The X-shaped splat is made of two pieces lapped together, with the ends tenoned to the arms. Both the crest and stay rails are tenoned to the arms as well.

Literature: The mate to this is shown in Bishop 1972, no. 350; Otto 1965, no. 67

unupholstered frame shown on p. 255

57
Settee
1805–1820
New York
Mahogany; ash
34⅝ x 57⅞ x 24¾ in.
ACC. NO. 82.2

Cross-stretchered seating furniture is ancient in its origins (see cat. no. 53) and so was ripe for adaptation by designers in the "antique" style. Starting with La Mesangere in 1800, soon followed by George Smith and Thomas Hope in 1806 and 1808, designs appeared for stools and chairs based on Roman curule chairs. Charges for chairs with "Grecian cross fronts" appear in the London chairmakers price book of 1808, showing their quick acceptance by the public. American interest in these designs was concentrated in New York, where chairs with cross stretchers at either the front or the side were available (Montgomery 1966, nos. 72, 72a). While ancient forms were limited to chairs and stools, New York artisans adapted the design for window seats and doubled the number of stretchers for sofas and couches. This example has all the finest elements of New York's neoclassical style, with its tapered reeding and beautifully carved tablets.

The mate to this settee is illustrated in Kane 1976, no. 230. The pair differ in execution from a suite of twelve chairs and a sofa (McClelland 1939, pls. 276, 280), made for Thomas Pearsall of New York, which have a strong tradition of Duncan Phyfe's craftsmanship. Sofas similar to the Pearsall group are illustrated in Hipkiss 1941, no. 124, Tracy 1981, no. 10, and McClelland 1939, no. 169; a window seat is shown in Cooper 1980, fig. 292 and a pair of Grecian couches are also known. The entire group uses smaller cross stretchers which overlap differently than those of cat. no. 57. Instead of carved paw feet they use cast brass paw feet. The majority of the sofas have cast brass lion heads at the crossing. This settee and its mate appear to be the work of another master of New York's neoclassical style.

Provenance: C.W. Lyon Antiques, Millbrook, New York; Robert Lee Gill Collection, New York; Israel Sack, Inc., New York

Construction and condition: The settee is built around the seat frame of mahogany, mortise-and-tenoned together, with a medial brace tenoned to the front and rear rails. The brace is ash and is curved top and bottom. The curule sections below the seat frame are made in three pieces each. The concave upper section is a single piece tenoned to the seat. Each of the legs are tenoned to the upper section. The castors are replacements. A turned mahogany stretcher connects the two curule sections.

The arms of the settee are constructed similarly to chair backs of the same design. The stiles are tenoned to the seat frame, and the carved crest rail and reeded stay rail are tenoned to them. Banisters parallel to the stiles are tenoned to the crest and stay rails through which the cane is woven.

The back is constructed in a way that is visually deceiving. The banisters of the back are actually part of the rear stiles, and the space between them is cut from the solid. The stay rail stops at each banister. The crest rail is supported by the mahogany medial brace and the curved pieces at each end between the crest and the banister. At one time the piece was upholstered.

Literature: Winchester 1963, 199; Garrett 1977, 996. The mate to this is illustrated in Kane 1976, no. 230.

58
Grecian Couch
1805–1820
New York
Mahogany; white pine
30⅝ x 61½ x 25⅛ in.
ACC. NO. 84.3

Any confusion over what to call this piece is not resolved by recourse to the original sources. Sheraton, in his 1803 *Cabinet Dictionary*, plate 49, referred to such a piece as a Grecian couch ("couch" being derived from the French *coucher*, to lie down), but in another plate showing a similar design he called it a "Grecian Squab." On a plate dated 1805 George Smith referred to the form as a "chaise lounge." In 1807 Thomas Hope called his design simply a couch and claimed the Roman triclinium as his inspiration. History has added injustice to inaccuracy: Jacques-Louis David immortalized Madame Recamier as much for his choice of furniture as for her beauty—and she was reclining on a backless sofa, not even a couch!

There is less confusion concerning the function of such furniture. The Grecian couch picked up the tradition of the eighteenth-century daybed, which had lost favor in the early classical revival. They were used primarily for reclining and were considered highly decorative. They were often made in mirror-image pairs to flank fireplaces, doorways, or to fill niches. Only five feet long, this example was probably made for a small niche and not a small person.

Besides its size, the most distinctive feature of this piece is its beautifully carved rosette. Grecian couches with a closed-scroll foot usually have a large turned roundel. The only other known example with a carved rosette (Nutting 1928–1933, 1:no. 1721) appears to be by a different hand.

Provenance: C.W. Lyon Antiques, Millbrook, New York; Norvin Green Collection; P-B, 2 December 1950, lot 660; Robert Lee Gill Collection, New York; Israel Sack, Inc., New York

Construction and condition: The couch is built around the seat frame which has mahogany front and rear rails. At each end, just outside the legs, poplar rails are tenoned to the mahogany rails. These joints are supported by large modern blocks. Three braces are dovetailed between the front and rear rails. The center one is ash and the other two are pine. They are as deep as the rails, dished on top, and straight across the bottom. A strip is screwed to the top of the front rail between the scrolls. The brass nails are tacked to it. There is no corresponding strip on the rear rail. (This technique is seen on cat. no. 56

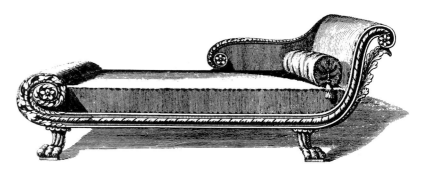

Sheraton, *Cabinet Dictionary* 1803, pl. 49

and KAF 81.2 [a New York neoclassical sofa not illustrated in this catalogue].) The strip is a replacement of the original that was lost during a previous upholstery. The mahogany legs are tenoned to the front and rear rails.

The scrolled ends are mahogany. They are tenoned to the top of the rails and are rabbeted to accept the upholstery. At the head, the scrolls are connected by five pine stretchers. The bottom stretcher is a replacement. The lower three are set horizontally and dadoed to the scrolls. The fourth stretcher is set vertically and tenoned in place. The fifth, at the top of the scroll, is shaped to the curve and tenoned. At the foot two stretchers are set horizontally below the rosette. Behind the rosette are five stretchers arranged like the blades of a paddle wheel. They are dadoed in place and the upper three are dished on top. A sixth stretcher is set behind the center of the rosette. All of the stretchers at the foot are pine.

The back is constructed as a parallelogram. The upper rail is mahogany and is tenoned to the head scroll, and at the other end a mahogany support is tenoned to it and to the rear rail. These have a raised and beaded edge that starts at the head scroll, runs across the upper rail, down the support, and continues up and over the foot scroll. At the head scroll a pine support is set diagonally between the upper rail and the rear rail. The support is shaped to conform to the scroll on one side and is straight on the other. A central pine support is set perpendicular to the rear and upper rail. Pine stay rails are set between the central support and each of the ends.

The back of the couch is finished. The space enclosed by the back is covered in upholstery nailed to a rabbet cut in the mahogany rails, head scroll, and end support. All the carving and reeding is cut from the solid.

Literature: Hinkley 1953, 301; Winchester 1963, 205; Garrett 1977, 998

unupholstered frame shown on p. 253

59
Grecian Couch
1810–1840
Baltimore
John 1777–1851 and/or Hugh Finlay 1781–1831
Walnut, cherry; white pine, poplar, cherry
31⅞ x 90¼ x 24⅛ in.
ACC. NO. 82.3

This piece perfectly exemplifies nineteenth-century Baltimore's love affair with painted furniture. It is not merely an attempt to imitate expensive materials in paint, but is a beautiful display of form and color. All the painted decoration is applied over walnut, not inferior soft woods. The gilt decorations, though derived from ormolu mounts, are applied in a painterly way, in sharp contrast to comparable New York examples (Fales 1972, figs. 248, 260) that attempt to realistically imitate with paint the effect of wood and metal.

The rosewood graining is interesting because it makes so little attempt at accuracy, concentrating instead on a vibrant display of color and pattern. The graining is laid out as if the entire piece were crossbanded. The gilt decorations have a base of gold leaf that is fleshed out in paint. Each decoration also has a black shadow painted in to add to the illusion of depth. This contrast between the gilded decoration and the darker graining creates a sense of movement. The decoration would be wasted were it not matched to an elegant form. The sinuous curve of the back and the vigorous scrolls of the head and foot show the cabinetmaker to be the equal of the decorator.

Every element of the form and decoration of this piece is consonant with a set made for the Wilson family of Baltimore, of which at least ten pieces survive (see Weidman 1984, no. 171 and Elder 1968, nos. 24–31). Family tradition held that this set was made by the Finlays. The Kaufman couch is most closely related to a sofa shown in Miller 1937, 1:no. 566, also from the Wilson set. Another closely related set was made for Hampton, the home of John Ridgely, north of Baltimore. The 1832 bill of sale from John Finlay for the Hampton set survives. The similarity of these two sets and of this Grecian couch to pieces in both, justifies an attribution to the Finlays.

The Finlays were the premier decorative painters in Baltimore from 1803 to 1840. The brothers, John and Hugh, worked together and independently over this period. Their most famous commission came in 1809 for the White House. The architect, Benjamin Henry Latrobe, designed a suite in the strict archaeological taste, and the drawings of it survive today. Unfortunately, the suite was lost when the British burned the White House in 1814.

Provenance: Dr. Lloyd Briggs Collection, Boston; Briggs estate sale at Skinner's Auction Galleries, Bolton, Massachusetts; C.G. Sloan and Company, Inc., Washington, sale 735, 3 October 1982, lot 1504

Construction and condition: The painted rails and scrolls are walnut and the legs are cherry. The rear rail and scrolls are rosewood grained but not decorated. The rosette of the head scroll is a replacement. The use of walnut as a base for painted surfaces was common in Baltimore. The legs are tenoned to the rails. The lower quarter of the right front leg has been rebuilt. At each end, just outside the legs, cherry rails are tenoned to the front and rear rails. There is a poplar medial brace, dished at a later date to accommodate springs. The front and rear rails have been rabbeted for a slip seat. This was lost and a replacement made based on examples shown in Weidman 1984, nos. 127 and 128. Screws through the frame secure the slip seat. The walnut scrolls are attached to the rails by lap joints, which are glued and screwed. Turned poplar cylinders are set between the volutes of the scrolls. Two cherry rails are also set between the head scrolls. The inner side of the head scroll and the outside of the foot scroll have thin poplar boards set horizontally and nailed to rabbets in the scrolls. The back is made of a single board of horizontally grained white pine. Inset in its lower edge are three walnut slip tenons that fit in corresponding mortises in the top of the rear rail. A screw through the back, at its highest point, secures the back to the scroll. The back is also screwed to the slip seat. A piece of walnut is set cross-grain into the volute of the back, for additional support at its weakest point. The center of the volute is hollowed. This and the evidence of the original tack line completing the circle of the volute was the basis for the present fabric rosette. The painted surfaces were cleaned and saturated with an acryloid resin, the minor losses were inpainted, and the surface coated with a clear lacquer.

unupholstered frame shown on p. 253

60
Pembroke Table
1795–1810
Baltimore
Attr. Levin Tarr group
Mahogany; yellow pine, oak
28⅝ x 43½ (open) x 33¼ in.
ACC. NO. 68.2

Baltimore's Federal furniture has long been known for its extensive use of pictorial inlays. These were usually produced by independent inlay-makers, or imported. This mass production and distribution has hampered efforts to identify the work of individual shops and craftsmen. Also, there are few documented examples on which to build attributions.

This table and cat. nos. 61 and 76 are part of a group of pieces that can now be distinguished from other Baltimore work and identified with a cabinetmaker. The group shows a pattern of inlays combined with construction techniques that is as distinctive as those of John Townsend. The consistency of decorations and construction techniques used on these tables allows the inclusion of sofas (cat. no. 54), chairs, and cellarettes (which cannot be analyzed for the same construction features). These pieces can be associated with the cabinetmaker Levin Tarr on the basis of a pier table which he signed and which was recorded by the MESDA field research program. Tarr's career is discussed more fully in the entry for cat. no. 61.

The stylistic features of the Levin Tarr group are these: the legs end in elongated spade feet, or have a band of contrasting wood separated from the leg by a thin cuff of inlaid banding; the legs have a string of four or five inlaid husks, always hung from a piece of rope-pattern inlay; the husks are in three parts, with the central petal the longest and all petals shaded; the husks are connected by inlaid dots; the plinth of the leg is inlaid with either a banded oval or a banded rectangle; the skirts have horizontally grained mahogany veneers set off by a frame of inlaid stringing; the lower edge of the frame is inlaid with patterned banding (usually dentil or rope) over dark-light stringing (this asymmetrical inlay is the most common, but symmetrical bands are sometimes used); the edges of the top and leaves are done in three ways—crossbanded and edged in satinwood, molded in a shallow cove, or scratch-beaded along the top and bottom edge. One of the most important aspects of the Levin Tarr group is that these features are seen in combination with each other. The construction techniques and wood-use described under *Construction and condition* for this table and cat. no. 61 are the standard for the Levin Tarr group.

This Pembroke table was acquired from descendants of Archibald Campbell, a prominent Baltimore merchant of the period. A card table (85.4, not illustrated in this catalogue but acquired from Campbell descendants) is also part of the Levin Tarr group. Two other Pembroke tables of the Levin Tarr group are known—Israel Sack photo no. 5748 and MESDA photo no. 5-11164.

Provenance: Descended from the family of Archibald Campbell of Maryland; Maria Campbell (Archibald's daughter) married Charles Ridgely of Hampton, Maryland, in 1810; Charles Ridgely died in 1819 and Maria Campbell Ridgely married George Winchester; Maria Campbell Winchester (their daughter) married Thomas Judge Murdock; Maria Campbell Murdock (their daughter) married Nicholas P. Bond; Hugh Lenox Bond, III (their son); Israel Sack, Inc., New York

Construction and condition: Each side of the frame has a yellow pine inner rail and oak fly rail. The inner rail is glued and nailed to the fly rail, which is tenoned to the legs. There is one fly leaf support on each side, cut on an angle, with a finger hold carved in the edge. They rotate on knuckle joints. A finger hole is also cut in the adjacent fly rail. The ends of the frame are each made of five layers of yellow pine, horizontally laminated, shaped on both sides, and tenoned to the legs. Each leg joint is supported by two-part vertically grained glue-blocks. A medial brace is set at an angle to the sides. It is dovetailed to the inner rails.

The top is held to the frame by a series of small glue-blocks set along each side and end and on both sides of the medial brace. It is also held by screws through the frame. The leaves rotate on rule joints and are held by three hinges each. The spade feet are applied.

Literature: I. Sack n.d.–1979, 1:280

61
Card Table
1795–1810
Baltimore
Attr. Levin Tarr group
Mahogany; yellow pine, oak
28¾ x 35⅜ x 34⅞ in.
ACC. NO. 72.9

Half-round was the most popular shape for a card table in Federal Baltimore. In fact all the known examples from the Levin Tarr group are half-round. The pier table signed by Tarr is also half-round. This card table offers two features not seen on the other Levin Tarr pieces in the catalogue (cat. nos. 54, 60, 76): it has ebonized feet and a twelve-point fan inset in the leaf. Three other card tables (BMA 1947, no. 5, Hewitt 1982, no. 51, and one shown in P-B 1944, Haskell sale, lot 405), while not mates to this one, employ all the embellishments seen here. Two other card tables from the Levin Tarr group are known, both with spade feet. One is also in the Kaufman Collection, but not illustrated here (85.4), and another is recorded at MESDA, photo no. 5-9666.

Levin Tarr was born in 1772 and was in Baltimore by 1794, where he married Rosetta Duplessis in December of that year. In June of 1800 he advertised that he was in partnership with Thomas Sherwood. He also appears in the accounts of a lumber merchant and inlay-maker around this time. This chronology follows the normal progression from apprentice to journeyman to shop owner. He continued to advertise until 1815 when his notices no longer appear. He died in 1821.

Tarr's documented work consists of two tables. One is a pier table recorded by MESDA, photo no. 5-9406. It is signed *Levin Tarr May 2, 1799* and has all the features associated with the Levin Tarr group. The other is a Pembroke table in the collection of MESDA, photo no. 5-2909. It is signed *Made by/Levin S. Tarr No. 28/Light Street Baltimore/January 10, 1806.* It has almost none of the features that mark the group.

This contrast in style over so short a period is explicable in light of Tarr's career. In 1799 Tarr was probably still working for someone as a journeyman. He would then have been following the dictates of that shop. In 1806 we know that he was on his own at the Light Street address and probably making his own decisions concerning ornament and construction. Unfortunately there is no documentation of Tarr's work situation between 1794 and 1799.

The discrepancy between the two documented examples prevents any clear attributions to Tarr. None of the pieces cited has ever been attributed to another shop nor have any family traditions survived connecting them to another crafts-

man. The consistency of both construction and decoration make the tables the easiest pieces to attribute. A group of sofas (see cat. no. 54), chairs (BMA 1947, no. 54), and cellarettes (BMA 1947, no. 38) have the same pattern of embellishment and merit attribution as well.

The Levin Tarr group is highly representative of Baltimore's early neoclassical taste; it is also a clearly defined and easily recognizable subgroup. Tarr's signature proves to be only a useful clue at this time in the search for the shop that produced these pieces.

Provenance: David Stockwell, Inc., Wilmington

Construction and condition: The curved section of the frame is made of four layers of yellow pine, horizontally laminated and shaped on both sides. The rear rail is yellow pine. It is dovetailed to the curved section. Vertically grained pine blocks support this joint. A yellow pine medial brace is dovetailed to the curved section and rear rail. The fly rail is oak. It is deeper than the frame and is attached by screws and a fillet block. Both rear legs rotate on knuckle joints and overlap the frame when closed. Poplar veneer is applied to the feet below the inlaid cuffs. These strips were originally ebonized. The stain was lost during a previous restoration and has been reapplied.

The top is secured by a series of glue-blocks along the curved section, medial brace, and rear rail. Screws through the frame also secure the top. There is one leaf-edge tenon for alignment. The front edge of the top and leaf were edged in crossbanding and stringing that is now lost.

62
Pembroke Table
1790–1800
Annapolis
John Shaw 1745–1829, fl. 1768–1816
Mahogany, oak; poplar, yellow pine
27¾ x 39 x 30¼ in.
ACC. NO. KAF 79.2

John Shaw is a cabinetmaker often better known for his labels than for the furniture he put them in. He was active in the cabinet trade nearly fifty years, was an ardent patriot and successful business man, yet our knowledge of his work covers mainly the years 1780–1800, and the narrow stylistic spectrum of the late rococo-early Federal.

Documentary records indicate that Shaw's trade was like that of most cabinetmakers of his day—repairing furniture, making coffins, building everyday furniture, and retailing dry goods. Despite this and the steady competition of wares first from London and then from Baltimore, his shop produced some masterpieces of design and craftsmanship including a desk and bookcase (Elder and Bartlett 1983, no. 40), a billiard table (Montgomery 1966, no. 428), and this Pembroke table.

The signature of Shaw's work is the cabinetmaker's attention to detail. The ovoid spade feet are cut from the solid, not applied. Twenty quatrefoils are inlaid in the table. The delicate stringing is formed into triple arches on both the legs and the plinths. The top has serpentine sides and ends with serpentine canted corners and is fully molded, an earlier feature more time-consuming to make than the Federal style oval top.

One may be tempted to see this marriage of a rococo top to a Federal base as a transitional form typical of Shaw's conservative taste. It is more likely, though, that Shaw relied upon plate 60 of Hepplewhite for inspiration. The plate shows a card table with serpentine top and rounded corners, with molding applied to the skirt and spade feet. Shaw also used this design for a number of card tables (Elder and Bartlett 1983, nos. 56–58). However one interprets the source, Shaw has taken a basic form, the Pembroke table, and through individual details created a rich and delicate expression of the cabinetmaker's craft.

Provenance: John Shaw's daughter Mary was born in 1784 and when Shaw died in 1829 he bequeathed to her two servants and the furnishings of her room. An inscription on the inside of a left drawer reads *Mary Shaw's Table.* Mary Shaw, then, was most probably the original owner of the table. Its history from the early nineteenth century until its appearance in the 1970s in the shop of an Ohio antique dealer is noted solely by a paper label on the drawer bottom with the inscription *Mrs. W.S. Wright.* SP-B, sale 4268, 23 June 1979, lot 1258; Israel Sack, Inc., New York

Construction and condition: The sides of the frame each have an oak inner rail and two oak leaf supports, with a strip of oak applied over the bottom edge. The leaf supports rotate on knuckle joints. They have an ogee profile and are molded along the inside edge of the profile. The torus molding is applied and extends the length of the frame. The back side is a false drawer front that matches the drawer side. The back side is made of mahogany shaped on one side only and tenoned to the legs. It is also veneered in mahogany. Satinwood cockbeading is set in the mahogany and there is a satinwood escutcheon. There are two rails to support the real drawer. The lower rail is oak veneered in mahogany and tenoned to the legs. The upper is mahogany dovetailed to the legs. Both are shaped on one side only. The drawer is also supported by yellow pine strips nailed to the inner rails. The drawer has poplar side, back, and bottom boards. The grain of the bottom is set side to side. The drawer front is mahogany shaped on both sides and veneered in mahogany. The keyhole escutcheon is ivory. Satinwood cock-beading the depth of the drawer front is applied to the top and bottom. Smaller strips are inset on the sides.

The table top is made of solid crotch mahogany, five-eighths of an inch thick. It is held by screws through the frame. The leaves rotate on rule joints and are held by three hinges each. The ovoid spade feet are cut from the solid. All four sides of each foot are inlaid with a satinwood quatrefoil; within each petal of each quatrefoil is an incised, pointed oval drop, filled with a black composition material.

Literature: Elder and Bartlett 1983, no. 26

Exhibitions: Baltimore, BMA 1983 (John Shaw, Cabinetmaker of Annapolis); Winston-Salem, North Carolina, MESDA 1978–1986

63
Card Table
1785–1805
Philadelphia
Satinwood; white pine, oak
29½ x 35⅝ x 35¾ in.
ACC. NO. 79.3

There is no wood as brilliant as satinwood; it shimmers and catches the light like no other. Most often it was used as an inlay or an accent panel, but here it is given its fullest expression. Satinwood alone, though, was not sufficient for this cabinetmaker, who chose even rarer curly satinwood for the top and skirt. Crotch mahogany is used at the base of the fan, for the central oval, and for the plinths of the legs. Ebony edges the top and leaf and is used as ribbing for the fan top and stringing on the legs. An Australian fancy wood similar to rosewood, so rare that it is only found as an inlay, is used in a crossbanded border on the top and the frames of the skirt. A triple band of patterned inlay borders the lower edge of the skirt.

This table is closely related in form, decoration, and materials to two work tables (Montgomery 1966, no. 426 and one in the collection of Yale University). Both work tables are satinwood, kidney shaped, use a fan pattern of decoration on the top, and have dark-wood inlay framing the skirt. The card table differs from the work tables in having tapered legs rather than turned ones.

The form of rounded ends and hollow center was often used for Philadelphia tables of the period. On Federal card tables the line of inlay along the lower edge usually forms a continuous line parallel to the top, which emphasizes the horizontal line of the skirt. This is seen on cat. nos. 61, 70, and 71. On this table the cabinetmaker has interrupted that line with a central panel which extends the full depth of the skirt, drawing the eye to the center of the concave front. The central oval is balanced by those on the plinths and a delicate interplay achieved between the dark frames outlined in light-dark stringing and the satinwood skirt. The top is a fan of sixteen panels tipped by black ovals that add depth to the shimmer and movement of the curly satinwood. The interior was originally lined with baize.

The emphasis of the Federal era on geometric forms, contrasts of light and dark wood, and clean lines are perfectly handled in this exquisite Philadelphia card table.

Provenance: SP-B, sale no. 4211, 3 February 1979, lot 1249; Israel Sack, Inc., New York

Construction and condition: The curved section of the frame is made of four layers of white pine, horizontally laminated and shaped on both sides. The rear rail is pine. It is dovetailed to the curved section. The fly rail is oak. The fly leg rotates on a knuckle joint and overlaps the frame when closed. The front legs are set in the frame. The top and leaf have a pine core with angled battens. The felt lining the interior is a replacement. The edge is covered in satinwood crossbanding. Screws through the frame secure the top. There are two leaf-edge tenons for alignment.

Literature: Tracy 1980, 367, fig. 5

Exhibition: New York, MMA 1980–1986

64
Card Table
1785–1810
New York
Mahogany; pine and ash
29⅛ x 37⅞ x 38¾ in.
ACC. NO. 74.4

The form of this piece with its baize-lined interior shows that the function is that of a card table, but the spectacular veneer work on the leaf suggests that it did not see many hands of whist. The leaf is a virtuoso display of craftsmanship and veneer. The design of the leaf starts with a lightly shaded, twelve-section fan. Radiating from the fan are six panels of crotch-grain mahogany. Stringing outlines the panels and echoes the design of the fan. Crotch-grain mahogany is created when the trunk splits to grow in two directions. The compression at that fork creates the fabulous patterns in the wood. These panels are noteworthy for their tight straight pattern and clear figure.

Both form and decoration mark this as a New York table. New Yorkers favored five- and six-legged card tables from the Colonial era onward. Though occasionally seen elsewhere, as in cat. no. 68, the form is most often found in New York. The tapering string of single-unit engraved bellflowers and lightly shaded paterae of the legs are seen in New York tables as well. The stringing inlaid in the skirt is U-shaped rather than a complete rectangle outlining the panel, another New York feature. The table is another successful interpretation of the Federal card table, effectively matching highly figured veneers with a contrasting pattern of inlaid decoration.

Provenance: Israel Sack, Inc., New York

Construction and condition: The curved section of the frame is made of five layers of white pine, horizontally laminated and shaped on both sides. The curved section is tenoned to the rear legs. The rear rail is pine, also tenoned to the rear legs. Vertically grained quarter-round pine blocks support the joint of the legs, frame, and rear rail. The fly rail is ash. It is deeper than the rear rail and is screwed to it. Both fly legs rotate on knuckle joints. The tops of the legs are flush with the rear legs. The front legs are attached by bridle joints. The top and leaf are constructed in typical New York fashion. The core is white pine, with angled battens tongued and grooved to it. The rear edge of the leaf is covered with a strip of mahogany but the rear edge of the top is not. The felt lining the interior is a replacement. The edge is covered in mahogany crossbanding. Screws through the frame secure the top. There are two leaf-edge tenons for alignment.

65

Card Table

1785–1810
New York
Mahogany; white pine, mahogany
29 x 36 x 17⅞ in.
ACC. NO. 75.7

New Yorkers, more than the patrons of any other region, favored highly veneered tops for their Federal card tables. These most often involved a single piece of figured veneer on the top and plainer wood or baize for the interior. This table, like cat. no. 64, shows one of the most elegant, and no doubt expensive, versions of the highly veneered card table.

The decoration of the top is based on its half-round shape. Divided by concentric rings of satinwood crossbanding intersected by rays of patterned stringing, the top is reminiscent of a sundial. A sense of movement is created by the tension between the bands and rays. The contrast between the outer band of mahogany and the satinwood center broadens the top and accentuates its half-round shape.

The decoration of the legs and skirt are variations on common New York inlay patterns. The inlaid bands of stringing set at the top of the legs, and the swags of husks, inlaid in the central panel of the skirt, are similar to examples seen on cat. no. 85. The pendant husks—often called bellflowers—connected by dotted oval stringing are seen on other New York tables (Montgomery 1966, no. 284 and Hewitt 1982, no. 38). These differ by using two types of husks and by not varying their size. A closely related table that varies only in having one less pendant husk on the legs is illustrated in I. Sack n.d.–1979, 1:69.

Provenance: C. W. Lyon Antiques, Millbrook, New York; Mrs. Richard I. Dupont Collection, Delaware

Construction and condition: The curved section of the frame is made of five layers of white pine, horizontally laminated and shaped on both sides. The rear rail is white pine. It is nailed to a rabbet in the curved section. This joint is supported by vertically grained wedge-shaped pine blocks. The fly rail is mahogany. The fly leg rotates on a knuckle joint and overlaps the frame when closed. The front legs are attached by bridle joints.

The top and leaf are constructed in typical New York fashion. They have white pine cores with angled battens and a strip of mahogany along the back edge. The interior is lined with baize edged in gold tooled leather. The edges are finished with mahogany crossbanding. Screws through the frame secure the top. There is one leaf-edge tenon for alignment.

66

Pembroke Table
1785–1805
New York
Mahogany; pine, poplar, cherry
27⅝ x 41½ x 33⅜ in.
ACC. NO. 77.1

With serpentine front and sides and wide ovolo corners, this New York Pembroke table is the boldest and most distinctive interpretation of this pattern known. Satinwood inlaid along the upper and lower edges highlights the shape of the top. The use of a fully serpentine top with ovolo corners is a carryover from the rococo style. It is seen in a more muted form in cat. no. 62.

A number of New York Pembroke tables are known that have serpentine sides and ovolo corners (A. Sack 1950, 253; Tracy 1981, no. 31). This is the only one seen so far with serpentine front, sides, and conforming frame. A card table (Hewitt 1982, no. 40) matches this in the outline of the top and all the decorations, though the Prince of Wales plumes inlaid in the plinths are somewhat different.

Inlaid Prince of Wales plumes in a number of styles have been found on pieces labeled by and/or strongly attributed to Michael Allison (Montgomery 1966, no. 452). The consistency of the entire decorative vocabulary of these pieces indicates more than a common inlay supplier. This version is the least common known. The inlay is set directly in the leg rather than in an oval or rectangle and is probably not the product of an inlay-maker but of a cabinet shop.

Provenance: Bernard and S. Dean Levy, Inc., New York

Construction and condition: Each side of the frame has a pine inner rail tenoned to the legs. Two cherry leaf supports are screwed to each rail. These leaf supports do not extend the length of the rail. Vertically grained mahogany blocks are set between them and the legs. The leaf supports rotate on knuckle joints, have an ogee profile, and are beveled on their bottom edges. The back side of the frame matches the drawer side in the illustration. It is made of three layers of pine horizontally laminated, shaped on both sides, and tenoned to the legs. Square, vertically grained pine blocks support these joints. The drawer has poplar sides, back, and bottom. The grain of the bottom is set side to side. The drawer front is made of three layers of pine with a thinner fourth layer of mahogany on top. These are horizontally laminated and shaped on both sides. The drawer is supported by, and overlaps, two cherry rails. The upper rail is dovetailed to the legs and the lower is tenoned. Upper and lower poplar strips are nailed to the inner rails to support the drawer as well. The top is held by screws through the frame. The leaves rotate on rule joints and are held by two hinges each.

67
Pembroke Table
1785–1805
Newport
John Townsend 1732–1809, fl. 1765–1805
Labeled: *Made by/John Townsend/Newport*
Mahogany; maple, chestnut, poplar
26¾ x 20⅛ x 33⅛ in. (closed)
ACC. NO. 74.1

John Townsend is an antiquarian's dream. He labeled his work. He had a distinctive style in both design and construction and was one of America's greatest craftsmen. He was also a rarity among successful craftsmen because after achieving financial success he remained a craftsman. Research indicates that he paid considerably more tax than any other cabinetmaker in the Goddard-Townsend clan (Moses 1984, 67). Success usually pulled a man away from the work bench and into the counting room, yet Townsend's earliest and latest pieces show the same superior construction and eye for detail (see cat. no. 12).

The design and construction of the drawer and surrounding frame highlight a facet of Townsend's craftsmanship. Pembroke tables typically have full-width drawers bounded by an upper and lower rail (see cat. nos. 15, 62). Here the drawer and its surrounding frame appear as a single unit. Townsend has taken a single board and cut the drawer front from the center, using the rest as a frame. The saw cut leaves the drawer front smaller than the opening. He corrects this with a beading applied to the frame. It is not applied to the drawer, as is commonly done, because the drawer would then have to be rabbeted to accept the beading. The drawer would then remain the same size and so would the gap. Applying the beading to the frame fills the gap. This, along with the stringing, creates the single-unit facade. The interior construction is not an idiosyncratic whim, but the logical result of Townsend's effort to create a unified design. Solutions in other regions are exemplified by cat no. 60, which uses no drawer, and cat. no. 66 where the drawer covers the entire facade.

John Townsend will always be more famous for his creations during the Colonial era. However, this modest interpretation of the Federal style shows that despite a change in fashion he remained a master of "the art and mystery" of his trade.

Provenance: Skinner Auction Galleries, Inc., Bolton, Massachusetts, 19 January 1974; Israel Sack, Inc., New York

Construction and condition: The sides of the frame have an inner rail and fly rail, both of maple. The inner rail is nailed to the fly rail, which is tenoned to the legs. Each of these joints is secured by two small pins. There is one fly leaf support on each side. These rotate on knuckle joints. They are cut at an angle, and finger holes are cut in the adjacent fly rail. The back side of the table matches the pictured drawer side, but is a false drawer front. The drawer end is described above. Both ends are tenoned to the legs. Square, vertically grained glue-blocks support these joints.

Three maple cross braces are dovetailed to the top of the inner rails. Screws through these where they join the inner rail secure the top. Two maple cross braces are dovetailed across the bottom to the inner rails. The drawer rides on L-shaped strips glued to the inner rails and supported by the lower cross braces. A strip of chestnut is notched and nailed to the front two upper cross braces. This prevents the drawer from tipping when opened.

The drawer has poplar sides and back. The front is mahogany. The bottom board is chestnut with the grain set front to back. It is nailed directly to the sides and back and to a rabbet in the drawer front.

The top is secured by screws through the upper cross braces and a series of seven chestnut blocks. These blocks are square in cross section and chamfered. Two are set at each side, two at the drawer end, and one, now missing, at the false-drawer end. The leaves rotate on a rule joint with two hinges each.

Literature: Moses 1984, figs. 2.12, 2.12a

68
Card Table
1785–1810
Newport
Mahogany; white pine, maple
28⅝ x 33½ x 17 in.
ACC. NO. 71.6

This table has many features in common with the documented work of John Townsend, but is probably by another Newport artisan. The flutes and cross-hatched pendants inlaid in the legs are also seen on two Pembroke tables in the Kaufman Collection, but not in this exhibition (nos. 68.1 and 72.7), both of which lack Townsend's distinctive construction techniques. The inlays of this table also differ from Townsend work in three ways. Here the central flute dips below the two side flutes, while on Townsend pieces the central flute is always higher. The banding of this table is set slightly above the lower edge and is made of light-dark-light wood stringing, whereas Townsend consistently uses a single line of light wood stringing set above the lower edge.

The cuffs of this table are set higher on the legs than they are on a Townsend table. Construction details differ from Townsend examples as well. Townsend favored double fly legs for his card tables (Montgomery 1966, no. 288) and this has only one. He also used a knuckle joint for his leaf supports and fly rails, and this table uses a type of finger joint.

Consideration of most cabinetmakers' work would find these differences to be acceptable variations. However, Townsend's work is so consistent that attributions can be given or withheld on the basis of small details. The differences also represent matters of choice, not quality. The inlays were probably produced by another craftsman and their arrangement decided by the cabinetmaker.

The origin of these distinctive Newport inlays probably lies in New York, where inlaid flutes are described in the 1802 price book. The cross-hatched pendants may be a stylized version of the string of overlapping husks used in New York (see cat. no. 39). The table also follows New York fashion in its use of six legs (see cat. no. 64). Interestingly, only one of the four rear legs swings. The cabinetmaker obviously was concerned with a balanced effect, while the client was concerned with cost. This arrangement can also be seen on other Newport tables (see Hewitt 1982, no. 28).

Provenance: Israel Sack, Inc., New York; Cornelius C. Moore Collection, Newport, Rhode Island; P-B, sale 3259, 30 October 1971, lot 95

Construction and condition: The curved part of the frame is made of three layers of white pine, horizontally laminated and shaped on both sides. The lower two layers are much thicker than the third. The curved section is tenoned to the rear legs. The rear rail is maple. It is nailed to the fly rail, which is also maple. The fly rail is tenoned to the rear legs. Vertically grained glue-blocks support the joint of the curved section, legs, and rear rails. Of the two inside rear legs only one moves. This fly leg is tenoned to the fly rail. The front legs are attached to the frame by bridle joints and secured by screws. The top is held by screws through the frame. There are two leaf-edge tenons for alignment.

69
Card Table
1798–1810
Newport
Attr. to Holmes Weaver 1769–1848
Mahogany; cherry
28½ x 34½ x 34¼ in.
ACC. NO. 80.7

Newport after the Revolution was no longer a major style center, though its cabinetmakers were no less skilled. The tables in cat. nos. 67 and 68 show that the city adapted to the new Federal style. Holmes Weaver, to whom this table is attributed, was born in 1769, which suggests that he probably did not become a journeyman before 1790. The *Newport Mercury* of 23 January 1798 announced the opening of Weaver's shop and on 19 February 1848 noted the death of Holmes Weaver, "Formerly clerk of the Supreme Court and a man respected by all who knew him."

Despite Weaver's long career there is little documented work, but a labeled Pembroke table (Hipkiss 1941, no. 67) gives a clear basis for the attribution of this table. The same pattern of inlaid urns, tassels, pendants, and stringing is found on both pieces. This card table and its mate (Hewitt 1982, no. 29) may have originally been part of a larger suite that included two Pembroke tables (Rodriguez-Roque 1984, no. 114 and Hipkiss 1941, no. 67).

The urn, tassel, and pendant inlays (like cat. nos. 42, 66, and 85, New York examples) rely on engraved details for effect. The style of execution indicates that they were an in-house product rather than an import or the work of a Newport inlay-maker. The diamond-shaped pendant is also seen on the spade feet of cat. no. 86 and may be a Rhode Island characteristic.

These tables represented an expensive commission, and Weaver responded with both quantity and quality of decoration. Each card table has four urns, twelve tassels, and ten pendants that, though set at floor level, have engraved tulips. Weaver has also been expansive in his use of stringing, with each pendant held by four lines, the tassels by bows, and the top outlined in a double line of inlay.

Provenance: Christie's, sale "Brooke," 24 June 1980, lot 691; Israel Sack, Inc., New York

Construction and condition: The curved part of the frame is made of five layers of cherry, horizontally laminated, roughly finished, and shaped on both sides. The four lower layers are of equal thickness, while the fifth is much thinner. There has been restoration work on the rear rail and fly legs. The rear rail is cherry. It is nailed to the curved section. Vertically grained, wedge-shaped blocks are glued and screwed at the joint. A cherry double fly rail is nailed flush to the rear rail. It has been sawn in half. One fly leg rotates on a finger joint and the other on a knuckle joint. The fly legs overlap the frame. The front legs are tenoned into the frame. One of these legs has been broken and pieced at the line of the inlaid bow. Screws through the frame secure the top. There are two leaf-edge tenons for alignment.

Literature: The mate to this table is shown in Hewitt 1982, no. 29

70
Card Table

1796–1805
Boston
John Seymour 1738–1818
Thomas Seymour 1771–1848
John Seymour & Son fl. 1796–1804
Labeled: *John Seymour & Son/Cabinet Makers/*
Creek Square, Boston
Mahogany; white pine, maple
28⅝ x 36 x 18 in.
ACC. NO. 75.8

A perfect harmony of design and materials is achieved in this labeled Federal, demilune card table. Classic dimensions are reinforced by choice of materials. The leaf has a knot, and the ovals emanating from it echo the curve of the top. The skirt is veneered in a single sheet of straight-grained mahogany that emphasizes both the continuous decoration across the skirt and also the demilune shape of the table. Inlaid bows, from which a line of husks descend, are centered over the legs. Thus the line of the leg is carried through the skirt without interruption of the design. The leaf edge is inlaid with a strip of curly maple, and the top is coved, which relieves the heaviness often seen in card-table tops.

Every facet of this table shows the Seymours' attention to detail. The inlaid bows are delicate and naturalistic and the knopped feet are crisp and tightly shaped. The husks, of which there are eighty-six, increase in size as they move to the center of the swags and increase in size down the skirt to the leg where they then decrease as they descend. The inlaid curly-maple strip tapers with the leg and is finished with a final husk that ties the entire design together. The legs are further shaped by a thin bead scratched into the face and sides. A string of dots and ovals, which starts in a corner of the top of the leaf rather than along the back edge, encircles the surface and adds a touch of movement.

Many pieces have been attributed to the Seymours, including cat. nos. 83 and 84, but only four labeled pieces are known. Two are tambour desks (Montgomery 1966, no. 184 and Stoneman 1959, 48) and two are card tables (I. Sack n.d.–1979, 7:1964 and this Boston piece). Some pieces can be documented by bills of sale (Hipkiss 1941, no. 42), but most attributions are based on a high level of quality in both form and execution. John Seymour and his family, including Thomas, arrived in Portland, Maine, in 1785 and moved to Boston in 1794. Their shop at Creek Square appears in city directories until 1804 when Thomas left to set up his own warehouse; John gave up his shop in 1813.

This table is not the Rosetta Stone of the Seymour style. Its distinctive features—the swags of graduated husks and knopped feet—cannot yet be considered exclusively Seymour, and the inlay on the top of the leaf is found on the leaf edge of a table labeled by another cabinetmaker. Rather, this piece shows the Seymours' ability to create a unique object from the basic vocabulary of Federal forms. Were there no other pieces labeled or attributed to them, the Seymours' reputation would stand with this piece alone.

Provenance: The table was found in an antique shop in Maine; Israel Sack, Inc., New York

Construction and condition: The curved part of the frame is made of five layers of pine, horizontally laminated and shaped on both sides. The top four layers are of equal thickness, while the fifth is much thinner. The rear rail is pine and is dovetailed to the curved section. The fly rail is maple, nailed flush to the rear rail. The fly leg rotates on a finger joint and overlaps the frame when closed. The top of this leg has been rebuilt. The front legs are attached to the frame by bridle joints. The feet are cut from the solid. Screws through the frame secure the top. The top and leaf are from different flitches with the leaf chosen for its rarer figure. There is a single leaf-edge tenon for alignment.

Literature: I. Sack n.d.–1979, 5:1272; Cooper 1980, fig. 20; Hewitt 1982, fig. 30

71
Card Table
1790–1810
Massachusetts
Mahogany; white pine, birch
29⅝ x 36 x 17½ in.
ACC. NO. 72.1

Price books of the day describe this piece as a square table with half-serpentine ends, serpentine front, and ovolo corners. This description no doubt reflects the craftsman's desire to leave no extra uncharged. However mundane the description, this fine table employs the dominant decorative schemes of New England tables inspired by Sheraton. These tables have mahogany tops, with three-bay facades of light wood panels set in mahogany frames with patterned inlay borders, and turned, reeded legs with bulbous feet. The countless variations of such legs may be beyond classification, but these show the style in its most streamlined form. They are powerfully simple, using the minimum number of elements to achieve the desired effect. The inset maple panels on the legs unite the sides and front in a continuous band of contrasting panels and frames. Without resorting to elaborate detailing the table succeeds by a judicious handling of line and decoration.

Provenance: Mrs. Giles Whiting Collection, New York; P-B, sale 3346, 16 April 1972, lot 751

Construction and condition: The frame is made entirely of pine. The side rails are shaped on one side only. The front rail is flat behind the concave sections and shaped behind the convex center. The rear rail is dovetailed to the sides. Vertically grained pine blocks support these joints. Large, vertically grained pine blocks are set at the joint of the side and front rails, obscuring it and the attachment of the front legs. The fly rail is birch. A fillet of pine is set between it and the rear rail. The fly leg rotates on a finger joint. There is a vertically grained glue-block at the joint of the fly leg and fly rail. The fly leg butts the frame. The top is held by screws through the frame. There are no leaf-edge tenons.

Literature: GSE 1929, no. 734; Montgomery and Kane 1976, no. 127

Exhibitions: New York, GSE, American Art Galleries 1929; New Haven, Connecticut, Yale University Art Gallery, and London, Victoria and Albert Museum 1976 (American Art: 1750–1800, Toward Independence)

72

Pair of Card Tables
1800–1815
Boston
Mahogany; white pine, birch
29¼ x 36⅞ x 18⅜ in.
ACC. NO. 83.9 a, b

This fine pair of Boston card tables shows the blending of influences in the late Federal period. The form of the tables reflects Thomas Sheraton's designs, while the lion head and inlaid Greek key point to the neoclassical motifs of Thomas Hope.

The aesthetic success of the Federal card table was based on its adaptability to various decorative schemes within a well-proportioned form. The serpentine sides and front with ovolo corners was the most popular form of turned-leg card table in New England. The lunette inlay in the leaf edge and the chamfered top are seen in a number of tables, including one example labeled by Adams and Todd of Boston (Fales 1976, no. 286). A related edge treatment is also seen in the labeled Seymour table, cat. no. 70.

The delicate turned legs of the early Federal period, seen in cat. nos. 71 and 79, have given way to fuller, more robust turnings. Skirts of crossbanded light wood panels and inlaid stringing are now figured mahogany set off by the black inlaid lines of a Greek key and a double-beaded molding along the bottom edge. The earlier baskets of fruit and leafage of the Salem examples (Montgomery 1966, no. 313) are now a stylized fern and the contented grin of a lion's head.

Just as the design of the tables represents a number of influences, so does their construction. The high quality of the carving, turnings, and inlay suggests a number of independent, specialized craftsmen rather than a single shop. The success of the tables is based on this complex trade that allowed the best elements to be assembled into a single piece.

Provenance: Berry Tracy, Inc., Goshen, New York

Construction and condition: The frame is made entirely of white pine. The side and front rails are shaped on one side only. The rear rail is dovetailed to the sides. Large, vertically grained mahogany blocks are set at the joint of the side and front rails. Each block is flanked by two vertically grained pine blocks. Two large screws through each mahogany block appear to hold the legs. The bead-edge molding is glued and nailed to the lower edge of the frame. There is a three-quarter-inch-thick pine fillet between the birch fly rail and rear rail. The fly leg rotates on a finger joint and butts the frame.

The tops and leaves are flitch-cut mahogany. The cabinetmaker apparently ran a little short, for one of the tops is roughly hewn on the bottom and pieced to thickness by a framing of one-half inch mahogany strips. There is one leaf-edge tenon for alignment.

73
Card Table
1810–1825
Philadelphia
Mahogany; cherry, oak
28¼ x 35 x 17⅝ in.
ACC. NO. 77.3

The lyre is one of the most recognizable motifs of the neoclassical period. It is documented in Philadelphia as early as 1794 in chairs ordered by William Bingham from Seddons in London (Montgomery 1966, no. 73). Despite their early appearance in Philadelphia and strong association with Phyfe klismos chairs, lyre-supported card, work, and sofa tables were the more common form of lyre decorated pieces, with examples ranging from Boston to Baltimore. Lyre supported tables do not appear in the 1811 Philadelphia price book, though they are fully detailed in the New York price book of 1817.

This table is one of the finest in a group of Philadelphia card and work tables. The group uses a pair of open lyre supports. Mahogany is the primary wood, with curly or bird's-eye maple panels in the skirt. Maple is overlaid on the bottom half of the lyre and in panels on the platform base. Curly maple is often inlaid in the top and leaf edges and a mahogany torus molding applied to the skirt. The skirts have ormolu mounts of pinwheels or cornucopias at the ends and often have a central mount, such as the one seen here. The lyres usually have three mounts, all pinwheels or two pinwheels and a cornucopia like those on the skirt (Cooper 1980, no. 301). The lyre strings are brass, and seven brass circles are set in the cross bar; five circles are often set at the bridge. The platform usually has a mount like the one used here or the one on the skirt. The volutes of the legs are marked by a turned button, often in ivory. The faces of the saber legs are veneered in crotch mahogany, with cast brass feet either paw shaped, as here, or with lions' heads flanked by tiny paws (Otto 1965, no. 179). This table is the only known example with carving and reeding on the lyres and legs. The popularity of the form can be seen at Cliveden, the Germantown home of the Chew family, which has a pair of card tables and a work table with lyre supports (Winchester 1963, 65 and Hendrickson 1983, 260).

The variety and completeness of the decoration enlivens the facade of the table beautifully. The figured maple contrasts with the mahogany, and the carving adds depth while softening the severity of the base. The ormolu and brass, handsome individually, highlight the form by their placement. This table, with its bold saber legs and gently curved lyre supports, owes its success to a blend of all the cabinetmaker's skills.

Provenance: Ronald A. DeSilva, Inc., New York

Construction and condition: The mahogany legs are dovetailed to an octagonal oak platform. These joints are supported by fitted metal strips, nailed in place. The platform is veneered on all four sides and on the top. The lyres are mahogany and are reeded along their edges. They are tenoned through the platform and through the cross brace of the frame. The cross brace is cherry and is screwed to the frame. The frame is cherry dovetailed together. The front rail is shaped on both sides. The torus molding is nailed and glued to the bottom of the frame. A thin cherry board is set in the frame on the right side to create a well. An oak cross bar is dovetailed to the top of the frame, slightly left of center. The top rotates on a wooden disk to which it is screwed. The disk is fitted in a hole cut in the oak cross bar. The top and leaf are mahogany. There is a single leaf-edge tenon for alignment.

74

Card Table
1805–1820
New York
Mahogany; white pine, mahogany
29 x 35⅞ x 18⅛ in.
ACC. NO. 78.8

From the beginning card tables have had a mechanical component to allow them to be set aside when not in use. Gate legs and concertina legs have been used, along with hidden drawers and double- and triple-leaf tops. The height of sophistication in card-table design in America was reached in New York in the early nineteenth century. Referred to as trick-leg tables today, they were called mechanical tables during the period. The leaf, when opened, is supported by two fly rails set against the rear rail. When these fly rails are extended the two rear legs rotate with them, an action controlled by metal rods through the pedestal (see *Construction and condition*). This design became so refined and the mechanical action so neat that on some models the skirt was eliminated altogether (Montgomery 1966, no. 315).

The elegance of this form is based upon simplicity. The card table is here transformed to a tripod stand, or console. The sweep of the legs, urn-shaped pedestal, and double-ellipse top add a dimension of movement and tension not seen in the geometric interplays of the early Federal form. In the execution one sees the finest elements of the neoclassical vocabulary—carved and reeded legs ending in brass paw feet, leaf-carved pedestal, and highly veneered top and leaf. The skirt is distinguished by its carved panels, turned drops, contrasting satinwood veneer, and an edge band of brass. Each of these embellishments is noted and priced in the 1810 New York price book (Montgomery 1966, no. 314). The numerous variations listed in the 1810 New York price book are reflected in surviving examples, which range from relatively plain all mahogany tables (A. Sack 1950, 286) to an all satinwood pair (Hipkiss 1941, no. 65). A very closely related example, differing mainly in the shape of the turned drops and the proportioning of the pedestal, is stamped by Michael Allison (McClelland 1936, pl. 187).

Provenance: Acquired from descendants of the Webster family of Englewood, New Jersey; H and R Sandor, Inc., New Hope, Pennsylvania

Construction and condition: The possibility of disassembling the leg mechanism and failing to reassemble the "trick" correctly firmly inhibited the author from an exploration of the inner workings of this table.

The front leg is affixed to the pedestal. The side legs are connected by iron braces to iron rods that pass through the pedestal and control leg rotation. The pedestal is carved all the way around. The rails and framing are entirely mahogany. The curved section of the skirt is made of two layers of white pine horizontally laminated and shaped on both sides. The carved squares are set in the skirt and the plinths and drops set beneath them. The central carved drapery plaque is applied. The brass edge is bent to shape and nailed to the skirt. The rear rail is tenoned to the curved section. A block is glued to the rear rail and the pedestal is tenoned to them. The fly rail is mahogany. It is attached to the rear rail and there are two leaf supports. These rotate on finger joints secured by iron pins. Two braces are set between the rear rail and skirt. They flank the pedestal and are set at about a forty-five degree angle to the rear rail. They are dovetailed to the rear rail and tenoned to the skirt. The rear rail, fly rail, and braces are deeper than the skirt in the area around the pedestal. They are stepped down to the depth of the skirt as they approach it.

The top is secured by screws through each end of the rear and fly rails, the ends of the braces, and through the skirt. The top and leaf are made in the typical New York manner, with a white pine core, angled pine battens, and strips of mahogany across the back edges. The top of the leaf is veneered in crotch-grain mahogany. The interior is veneered in a plainer straight-grain mahogany. The top is veneered on both sides. The edges are crossbanded in mahogany. Two off-center tenons have been shaved flat and the mortises filled, and replaced by a single one in the center.

75

Card Table

(one of a pair)
1805–1820
New York
Mahogany; white pine, mahogany
31 x 37⅜ x 20 in.
ACC. NO. 74.9 a, b

Card tables were regularly produced in pairs but rarely survived as such. Being identical objects, their division by inheritance was common. Of over twenty card tables in the Kaufman Collection, there are only two pairs and but a few with mates in other collections. This pair present a vibrant ensemble of repeated elements.

The tables have been attributed to the French émigré cabinetmaker Charles-Honoré Lannuier (1779–1819). The late Edward V. Jones argued that there is an identifiable difference between the work of Duncan Phyfe and Lannuier (Jones 1977, 4–14). Comparing similar forms he notes differences in proportioning and the type and execution of numerous elements. The attribution of these tables is based on the longer, more attenuated legs and extension of the leaf carving down the leg without any contrasting reeding. He noted Phyfe's adherence to a cast, or carved, paw foot where Lannuier is more variable. Lannuier turnings are said to be more fluid and robust where Phyfe was restrained and crisp. This analysis identifies a large group of New York neoclassical furniture that can be separated by these features. Wholesale attribution of these pieces to Lannuier or Phyfe is limited by the absence of either labeled or firmly documented examples among the pieces cited. The description of the Phyfe style perfectly describes a table stamped by Michael Allison (see cat. no. 74) as well. This approach identifies an aesthetic style, but denies the influence of the client and the possibility that a specialist craftsman may have supplied the same shops. This pair of tables is indeed the work of a master craftsman who matched the skills of his carver, turner, and veneer worker to an elegant design—but the name of the master remains uncertain.

Provenance: The pair of tables came from an estate in Irvington, New York. They were brought to the attention of Nancy McClelland after the publication of her book *Duncan Phyfe and the English Regency* (New York, 1939) and were acquired by Israel Sack. The pair was sold to Mrs. Paul Mellon by Sack and after her death reappeared at auction in the 1950s. They were repurchased by Israel Sack and sold to Mr. Richard Tishman. They were reacquired by Israel Sack and sold to Richard duPont who consigned them to auction in 1974; SP-B, sale 3638, 11 May 1974, lot 438; Israel Sack, Inc., New York

Construction and condition: The mahogany legs are dovetailed to the octagonal mahogany block. The four coved sides of the block are veneered in mahogany. The four turned and carved posts are tenoned to the block and to a cross brace in the skirt.

The curved sections of the skirt are made of two layers of pine and a thin top layer of mahogany, all horizontally laminated and shaped on both sides. The rear rail is mahogany. It is dovetailed to the curved section. A mahogany beading is applied to the bottom of the curved section, as are four turned drops. The cross brace is as deep as the skirt. It is made of two pieces of mahogany, horizontally laminated. It is double tenoned to the front of the skirt and the rear rail. On the right-hand side of the skirt a thin piece of mahogany, with grain set front to back, is set in a groove cut in the skirt, creating a well.

A large metal screw is attached to the top. It passes through the cross brace and is secured by a nut. The top rotates on this. The top and leaf are constructed in typical New York fashion. They have a white pine core with angled pine battens. The rear edges are covered with a strip of mahogany. The top of the leaves are veneered in crotch-grain mahogany, while the interiors are veneered in plain mahogany. The edges are crossbanded. There are three leaf-edge tenons for alignment.

Literature: A. Sack 1950, 287; I. Sack n.d.–1979, 2:325; Jones 1977, 4–14.

76
Sideboard Table
1795–1810
Baltimore
Attr. Levin Tarr group
Mahogany; oak, poplar
38¼ x 49⅝ x 23⅞ in.
ACC. NO. 78.1

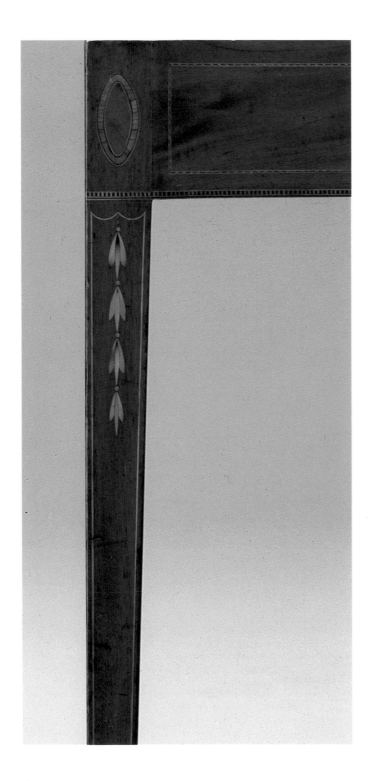

Tall, shallow, sideboard-length (five and a half feet and over) tables are today called huntboards. In the eighteenth and nineteenth century both design books and inventories referred to them as sideboard tables. Pier tables are any table higher than the dado and intended to be set between two windows. Traditionally they are approximately three feet wide (see cat. no. 77). This tall, shallow, four-foot-wide table, then, falls between descriptions and should probably be defined by its use. The marble top does not specify function, because though ideal for service, marble tops are often seen on pier tables. Only its Southern origin points to its use, for in the South both sideboard tables and cellarettes were very popular. This combination may find an explanation in Hepplewhite's *Guide* (1794, caption to pl. 37) in which he states that cellarettes are of general use where sideboards are without drawers. Two Baltimore Federal cellarettes (BMA 1947, no. 38 and Miller 1937, no. 1040), each with four tapered legs supporting an oval case, use the same pattern of inlays and could easily have been used ensuite with this table.

Two other sideboard tables (BMA 1947, no. 30 and one pictured in *Antiques*, January 1978, 128) have the same serpentine shape and show the same veneered facade and types of inlay seen here. Though the marble top means that the distinctive technique used to attach wood tops is missing, this table can still be considered part of the Levin Tarr group (see cat. nos. 60 and 61).

Provenance: Acquired from descendants of the Winchester and Selby families of the Eastern Shore of Maryland; Bernard and S. Dean Levy, Inc., New York

Construction and condition: The rear rail is oak and the side rails oak veneered in mahogany. The front rail is of five layers of poplar, horizontally laminated and shaped on both sides. Each of the rear leg joints are supported by two vertically grained quarter-round glue-blocks. The front leg joints are each supported by a single vertically grained quarter-round glue-block with a fillet along the front rail.

77

Pier Table

1801–1802
Baltimore
Eglomisé panels by Samuel Kennedy
Mahogany; pine, poplar
39½ x 40½ x 19 in.
ACC. NO. KAF 78.4

This elaborate pier table, with five inlaid *églomisé* panels and decorative bellflowers, expresses two distinctive elements of the Federal aesthetic in Baltimore. *Eglomisé* panels occurred on mirrors and glazed doors in Boston and New York, while in Baltimore they were inlaid in tables and case pieces (see Weidman 1984, nos. 148, 149; Tracy 1970, no. 16, and Montgomery 1966, no. 188).

The Baltimore bellflower, with its elongated central petal, is doubly represented in contrasting panels of dark bellflowers on a satinwood ground and satinwood bellflowers on a mahogany ground. The pier table was an adaptable form that allowed for elaboration at will. A six-legged version at Winterthur (Montgomery 1966, no. 351) lacks the *églomisé* panels and substitutes tassels for the bellflowers in the satinwood panel.

The *églomisé* panels, a great rarity in themselves, are signed *Kennedy* in the lower right-hand corner of the central panel and across the belt of one of the female figures. In 1801 Samuel Kennedy advertised in the *American and Daily Advertisor of Baltimore* that he had removed from Philadelphia to No. 2 North Gay Street, an area where a number of fancy furniture manufacturers had their shops. Among his services he listed gold letters on glass. In an advertisement dated 27 January 1802 in the *Alexandria Advertiser*, Kennedy spoke of himself as "of Baltimore, late from Philadelphia" and that he would be in town for a few days and would take orders for a number of services, including "gold letters or ornaments on glass." He was last listed in the 1803 city directory and was advertising in Philadelphia again in 1819.

Provenance: By family tradition this piece was purchased by Col. Robert Beverley (1822–1901) of Blandfield in Essex County, Virginia, from J. Augustine Washington, who inherited Mt. Vernon. From Col. Robert Beverley the table descended to Robert Beverley, Jr. (1858–1928) and then to Fannie Scott Beverley Osburn, born in 1886; Lindsey Grigsby Antiques, Richmond, Virginia; Israel Sack, Inc., New York

Construction and condition: The frame has white pine front and rear rails tenoned to the legs. Each of the sides has a white pine rail tenoned to the rear leg. A fillet is applied to these rails behind the *églomisé* panels. The ovolo corners are made of three layers of poplar, horizontally laminated and shaped on both sides. They are glued and screwed to the fillets on the side rails and to the front legs. Vertically grained triangular pine blocks support all the leg joints and the joints of the ovolo sections.

The legs have been pieced below the cuffs. The inset crotch-mahogany panel in the right ovolo section is a replacement. The outer petals of the bellflowers in the satinwood panels were originally dyed red to contrast with the green central petals. The *églomisé* panels are inlaid in the skirt and secured by frames of satinwood banding.

The mahogany top is held by screws through the frame. It is crossbanded along its front and top edges. The upper edge of the top has been beveled. This has removed the inlaid edge which remains only along the rear edge.

Exhibition: Winston-Salem, North Carolina, MESDA 1978–1986

78
Nest of Tables
1790–1810
Boston
Maple
29¼ x 17⅞ x 12⅞ in.
ACC. NO. 73.7

American taste for painted decoration and an increased use of design books are both seen in this delicate and well-proportioned nest of tables. The tables are copied from plate 75 of Sheraton's 1803 *Cabinet Dictionary* where he shows a "Quartetto Table." The American craftsman has copied the overall form, including the eccentric shaping of the battens. He has proportioned the columns differently through stressing balance instead of Sheraton's ascending series of rings. Sheraton's design suggests a veneered and inlaid top. Another nest of tables in the Kaufman Collection (73.15, not shown here) is in mahogany. Simpler overall, with crotch-mahogany veneer tops, the largest top is a checkerboard of mahogany and crotch satinwood with flanking bird's-eye maple panels, a lunette inlaid border, and rope edging.

Curly maple is the perfect complement to the painted decoration. Its rippling grain adds depth and movement to the columns and base, and its yellow-gold color highlights the leafage, fruit, and shells of the painted tops and battens.

The painted decoration on the tops and sides of this set relates to the known work of John Ritto Penniman. The great demilune commode in the Karolik Collection (Hipkiss 1941, no. 42) was decorated by Penniman, as noted in a bill from John Seymour in 1809 to Elizabeth Derby West. Both the commode and the tables were inherited by Martha Codman Karolik, a descendant of the Derby family. No firmer connection has yet been established, but Seymour or Penniman, or both, are the most likely candidates as maker and/or decorator of these tables.

Provenance: The tables descended in the family of Elias Hasket Derby of Salem to Martha Codman Karolik and after her death were sold by her husband, Maxim Karolik; Israel Sack, Inc., New York; Lansdell K. Christie Collection, Syosset, New York; P-B, sale 3422, 21 October 1972, lot 27

Construction and condition: The tables are made entirely of maple and the painted decoration is applied directly to the wood. The tables are constructed as two frames joined by the tops and curved stretchers attached to the base of the columns. The frames are made of the turned columns tenoned to shaped bases and battens. On the three largest tables rabbets are cut in

the upper inside edges of the battens to accommodate the tops of the next table. The first and third tables differ from numbers two and four in the design of the painted decoration and condition of the finish.

Literature: I. Sack n.d.–1979, 1:98; Biddle 1963, no. 86; Stoneman 1965, no. 67; Fairbanks et al. 1975, nos. 281–284

Exhibitions: New York, MMA 1963 (American Art from American Collections); Boston, MFA 1975 (Paul Revere's Boston, 1735–1818)

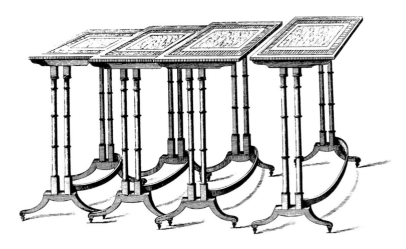

Sheraton, *Cabinet Dictionary* 1803, pl. 75

194

79
Gaming Table

1795–1810
Boston
Mahogany; pine, mahogany
30⅜ x 29⅞ x 19¾ in.
ACC. NO. 73.14

The gaming table was a great rarity in Federal America, unlike the card table which was found in abundance. This elegant table is not based on any design plates, though both Sheraton and Smith published designs for gaming tables in the Regency style. Sheraton, in plate 59 of his 1803 *Cabinet Dictionary*, called it an occasional table and Smith in 1808, plate 78, called his a backgammon work table. The other known American gaming tables also predate these designs, including a Baltimore Federal Pembroke gaming table (Comstock 1962, no. 579). Two New York tables are known—one stamped *H Lannuier* (McClelland 1936, 173) and the other shown in Israel Sack (n.d.–1979, 5:1247). An example similar in form to the Lannuier example, but thought to be from Virginia, is shown in the MESDA Guide, page 83. One is attributed to Salem makers (Warren 1975, no. 156). All these tables except the MESDA example have a checkerboard top covering an open well for backgammon. The checkerboard tops can be turned so that the table has a flat surface and plain top. This table has the practical feature of drawers at each end, which swing out on pins and can hold the chessmen and checkers.

The table has been attributed to the Seymours because of the high quality of the design and the similarity of the turnings to other pieces attributed to them (see cat. no. 55). Yet while cat. nos. 70, 83, and 84 can be firmly attributed to the Seymours, their authorship of this gem remains speculative.

The simplicity of form allows one to concentrate on each element. The turnings are crisp and the reeding finely tapered; the beautiful veneers of the skirt lighten the table and the molded edge softens the profile of the top. The effect is refined without being overwrought and the elegance is direct and simple, all of which make it one of the finest pieces of New England Federal furniture.

Provenance: This table first appeared at an auction in New Hampshire; Dedham Antique Shop, Dedham, Massachusetts; Israel Sack, Inc., New York

Construction and condition: The oval frame is made of vertically set rails on the long sides and horizontally set rails at the drawer ends. The long side rails are pine and the lower ones are mahogany. They are shaped on one side only and tenoned to the legs. Beneath the checkerboard playing surface is a well for backgammon. The bottom board is birch covered in tooled leather. It is supported by glue-blocks set along the curved sides and by strips at the ends. Mahogany boards behind the drawers make up the sides of the well. In the center is a divider set in grooves in the sides and veneered.

The drawers are wedge shaped and rotate on metal pins set in the rails. The sides, front, and back are mahogany. The drawer front is shaped on both sides. The drawer bottom is pine, with the grain set side to side.

The top is made in three pieces. The two ends are set over the drawers and are secured by screws through the horizontal rails. The center section has mahogany cross-grain tongues that slide in matching grooves in the ends. The checkerboard surface is also tooled leather. The chessmen and checkers are thought to be original.

Literature: Fairbanks et al. 1975, no. 287; Fairbanks and Bates 1981, 248; A. Sack 1985, 288

Exhibition: Boston, MFA 1975 (Paul Revere's Boston, 1735–1818)

80
Work Table

1795–1810
Boston
Mahogany; mahogany, white pine
30⅞ x 20 x 15¾ in.
ACC. NO. 82.6

The value placed on an activity can be seen by the quality of objects designed for it. The great Newport tea table (cat. no. 12) testifies to the importance of tea-drinking in the eighteenth century. This exquisite work table, or pouch table as Sheraton referred to it, shows the importance of ladies' needlework. The fabric bag is missing, but a sliding tray on the right (not visible in the photograph) informs us of its function (see cat. no. 82 for a sewing table with a pouch). The table had an additional use, as the interior of the upper drawer has pen and ink compartments and was originally fitted with an adjustable writing board.

Beyond these functional features this delicate table is beautifully decorated. The top has a central panel of burl outlined by satinwood crossbanding, which, in turn, is framed by strips of beefwood. The joints of these bands are delineated by lines of dark-light stringing. Rectangular panels of crotch satinwood embellish the frame, drawers, and plinths of the legs, which are also delineated by stringing. The use of two panels on each side lightens the frame more than a single sheet of veneer would. The desire to characterize the delicacy of this piece as a reflection of a feminine user might be checked by a comparison with cat. no. 79, a gaming table just as delicate, but without specific use by either sex.

A small group of tables, closely related to this one, are known (e.g., Fairbanks et al. 1975, no. 258, Montgomery and Kane 1976, no. 134, and Israel Sack n.d.–1979, 6:1610 and 1666). They are all attributable to Boston, and claims for Seymour authorship have been made. No two tables in this group are exactly alike, but they all share the same type and combination of decorative elements. This table differs from the others in having turned and inlaid legs instead of turned and reeded ones. Instead of an engaged column, the plinths of the legs are contained within the frame.

Provenance: Millicent Grant Belknap Collection, New York; Berry Tracy, Inc., Goshen, New York

Construction and condition: The sides and back are mahogany and are tenoned to the legs. The front has three mahogany rails. The top rail is dovetailed to the legs and the lower two are tenoned. The drawers are supported by white pine strips nailed to white pine drawer guides set between the legs and glued to the sides. White pine strips are glued to the sides behind the top rail to prevent the drawer from tipping when opened. The top is a single board of mahogany, now attached by a series of metal clips and screws that replace the original screws and glue-blocks.

The drawers are made entirely of mahogany. The top of the sides and back are molded to a double-beaded edge. The grain of each drawer bottom is set side to side. The top drawer was fitted with an adjustable writing surface. The lower drawer has a single row of partitions just behind the drawer front.

Behind the bottom rail is the sliding frame for the sewing pouch. The frame is of mahogany, its outer edges grooved. Tenons are set in the inside of the right side legs to support the frame. To support the sliding frame grooves for cross-grain tenons are cut in the back of the bottom rail and in a strip along the bottom of the backboard, and a strip is nailed to the side.

81
Table with Dressing Glass

1800–1815
Salem
Mahogany; white pine, poplar, cherry
62¼ x 36¼ x 18½ in.
ACC. NO. 82.5

This mahogany dressing table with matching dressing glass is a rare form. Many such combinations were made in pine, painted and/or draped with fabric (Montgomery 1966, no. 476, Jobe and Kaye 1984, no. 71). A few exist in mahogany with an attached box but no mirror (Randall 1965, no. 48). The preference for paint and fabric made these pieces fashionable but did not assist their survival as treasured heirlooms.

This table with glass was made in Salem. The use of serpentine sides and front, with reeded legs on canted corners for tables, was a popular form throughout New England (see cat. nos. 71, 72), and the mahogany crossbanding with sapwood highlights is characteristic of Massachusetts. The reeded legs with leaf carving on the plinths and the molding of roundly serrated rings are distinctly Salem. The piece has been attributed to both Samuel McIntyre and William Hook. At a time when everything Salem was McIntyre, this piece was caught in that net. The Hook attribution is based on five pieces Hook made as a wedding present for his sister in 1809 (Randall 1965, no. 70). While this piece fits within the group, there is enough variation among the pieces to suggest that Hook was buying legs and moldings from others; each piece, however, uses mahogany drawer sides and pine bottoms. The drawers on this piece have cherry sides with poplar bottoms. This alone does not exclude Hook, but a number of other Salem craftsmen, including Nathaniel Appleton and Nehemiah Adams along with the unknown turners, carvers, and molding makers who supplied them, were capable of this fine piece.

There is a wonderful architectural quality to this table and glass. The progression from the three-bay facades of the table, to the two drawers, to the single mirror is well handled. The scale of table to box to mirror gives each a sense of mass within the lightness of the overall form. Repetition of line and decoration unite the separate forms into a unit.

Provenance: George Arons Antiques, Connecticut; John Walton Antiques, New York; Joe Kindig, Jr., Antiques, York, Pennsylvania; Berry Tracy, Inc., Goshen, New York

Construction and condition: The table frame is made entirely of white pine. The front and side rails are shaped on one side only. The rear rail is dovetailed to the side rails. The rear legs are tenoned to the side rails. Large, vertically grained pine blocks are set at the joints of the side and front rails. Screws through these blocks appear to hold the legs. A mahogany bead molding is glued and nailed to the bottom edge of the frame. The top of the table is pine, veneered in mahogany, with quarter-round serrated beading set along the edges.

The dressing box has pine sides shaped on one side only. These are dovetailed to the top and bottom boards. The top board is pine and the bottom is pine faced with mahogany. The central partition is pine; it extends the depth of the box and is tenoned through the bottom board. The pine backboard is set side to side. The rear feet are tenoned to the sides and the front feet are applied to the case. The feet are fitted with iron pins which fit in corresponding holes in the top of the table.

The upper drawers are supported by pine rails shaped on one side only and pine strips nailed to the sides. The lower drawers ride on the bottom boards. The drawers have cherry sides and backs. The bottom boards are poplar set side to side. The drawer fronts are pine shaped on both sides. They are veneered in mahogany with applied cock-beading. The brasses are replacements and originally were wooden or ivory knobs.

The standards are mahogany and are tenoned to the box. Screws through the standard secure the mahogany scrolls. The mirror frame is mahogany and is dovetailed together with applied mahogany crossbanding. The backboard is chestnut, and the mirror is a replacement.

A paper label on the bottom of the box reads *F.E. Daiger/ 106 N. Howard/Furniture Upholstery Bedding.*

82
Work Table
1810–1825
Boston
Rosewood; mahogany, white pine
29¼ x 20⅜ x 16¾ in.
ACC. NO. 74.14

Rosewood began to make inroads in the popularity of mahogany early in the nineteenth century. The rich subdued pattern of its red and black grain gave neoclassical and Empire designers a new palette with which to work. Its darker hues proved a perfect ground for brass inlay, ormolu mounts, and gilded figures, which are so fully illustrated by this Boston sewing table.

The restrained, plainer forms favored in the Empire period are evident in the simple canted corners of the case, bulb and block stretcher, and stylized lyre. The inlaid brass stringing and applied brass banding, while highlighting these elements, are similarly subdued. The placement of the mounts are echoes of ancient construction techniques.

The severity of the form belies the fact that an all-rosewood exterior, brass and ormolu embellishments, and an all-mahogany interior combined the most expensive options available. Two similar work tables are known—one in the Grand Rapids Museum (see *Antiques,* January 1979, 131) and the other in a private collection. Canted-corner work tables were popular in New England from the Federal era on. The all-rosewood exterior and beaded brass molding are typical of Boston (see Fairbanks and Bates 1981, 276, 279). A much less sophisticated version of the lyre support and legs is seen in a sewing table labeled by Rufus Pierce of Boston (Talbott 1976, 1010).

Provenance: Mrs. George A. Robbins, Philadelphia; Samuel T. Freeman, Auctioneers, Philadelphia; U.S. Antiques, Peter Hill, Washington

Construction and condition: The sides of the case are trapezoidally shaped blocks of mahogany. The backboard is white pine. Two mahogany rails at the front support the upper drawer. Mahogany strips nailed to the sides support both drawers. There is no front rail for the lower drawer as it would prevent the use of a sewing bag. The top is mahogany, veneered in rosewood and glued to the case.

The upper drawer is constructed entirely of mahogany, fitted with partitions. The grain of the bottom board is set side to side. The lower drawer is also mahogany but it has no bottom board. Instead strips are fitted to the inside, creating a ledge upon which the frame for the sewing bag rests. The sewing bag is a replacement based on antique designs.

Each of the lyres are made of two pieces of vertically grained rosewood tenoned to the case and to the legs at a line above the stretcher. The sides of each lyre are connected by a rosewood crossbar. Each pair of legs is made of two pieces of horizontally grained rosewood joined by a slip tenon. The stretcher is tenoned to the legs. The brass feet are screwed to turnings doweled to the legs. All the decorations, from the lyre strings to the inlay, are brass.

83
Tambour Desk
1795–1810
Boston
John Seymour 1738–1818
Thomas Seymour 1771–1848
John Seymour & Son fl. 1796–1804
Mahogany; white pine
41¾ x 37⅝ x 28¼ in.
ACC. NO. 73.1

The full-size tambour desk is one of the few distinctly American, and specifically Boston, designs of the Federal era. It is based on much smaller and more delicate English and French writing tables. (An American version is pictured in McClelland 1939, 87.) The smaller pieces are often referred to as ladies' writing tables, but there is little reason to carry the term over to the larger desk. The best of these tambour desks are either labeled or attributed to John and Thomas Seymour, and this desk is no exception. In form and construction it matches the labeled two-drawer tambour desk (Montgomery 1966, no. 184). The interior, with mahogany drawers, ring-pulls, blue-green pigeonholes, and shaped brackets, also matches. The major difference is in the handling of the tambours. The labeled desk has molded slats inlaid with swags of husks. This desk, however, follows the other labeled desk, a three-drawer version in satinwood (Stoneman 1959, 48–51) with highly figured flat tambour slats.

The Bilston enamel ring-pulls depict each of the four seasons. They are the major curvilinear element in the form and its strongest visual statement. Long considered a strictly Boston feature, they have recently been found on a library bookcase attributed to Baltimore (*Antiques*, October 1985, inside cover).

The form of the desk is restrained and simple as is the interior, with a row of valanced pigeonholes over a row of four drawers over two drawers. The interior of the pigeonholes is painted robin's-egg blue. The brackets smooth the transition from the leg to the case. The molding along the lower edge helps to frame the case. The lower edge of the writing surface is chamfered, avoiding the heaviness of two hard edges. The thinner top of the tambour reflects the smaller scale of the tambour section in relation to the case. This control of form creates a three-dimensional frame in which each of the planes is colored by the veneers, inlays, and brasses. The inlaid pilasters, strings of husks, enameled brasses, crotch mahogany of the drawers, and curly maple of the tambour create a wonderful interplay of pattern and color.

Provenance: Israel Sack, Inc., New York; Mr. and Mrs. Andrew Varick Stout Collection, New York; P-B, sale 3467, 27 January 1973, lot 943

Construction and condition: The lower case has mahogany sides and a white pine back, all tenoned to the legs. The drawer dividers are mahogany; the top partition is dovetailed to the legs and the lower two are tenoned. The writing surface supports are mahogany with mahogany facings. The top is white pine, with applied battens of white pine at each end and in the middle. The top is edged in a chamfered mahogany molding, tongue and grooved to the pine. The sides and front strip butt each other and are not mitered. The front half of the top is a writing surface of modern felt framed in mahogany veneer. The back is unfinished, with mahogany also framed in mahogany veneer and covered with felt. The mahogany molding below the tambour is glued to the leaf section.

The drawers have white pine sides, backs, and bottoms. The grain of the bottoms runs side to side. The drawer fronts are mahogany veneered in mahogany. Cock-beading is set in the drawer fronts. The drawers are supported by white pine runners nailed and glued to white pine strips set against the sides between the legs.

The tambour section is a white pine box dovetailed together. The sides are veneered in mahogany. The top has a false top of mahogany glued to it. The backboard is a piece of horizontally grained white pine. The entire inside surface is painted blue. The interior is made of white pine edged in mahogany. The pigeonhole valances are mahogany supported by pine blocks. The pigeonhole drawers have oak sides and backs, with white pine bottoms and mahogany fronts.

The tambours ride in grooves cut in the mahogany applied to the front of the box. They slide into a cavity between the sides and the pigeonholes, behind the pilasters. The central pilaster encloses a locking mechanism for the tambours. This keyhole is hidden by the closed writing surface.

Literature: McClelland 1939, pl. 197; Stoneman 1959, no. 11; Montgomery and Kane 1976, no. 128

Exhibitions: New Haven, Connecticut, Yale University Art Gallery, and London, Victoria and Albert Museum 1976 (American Art: 1750–1800, Toward Independence)

84

Tambour Desk
1795–1810
Boston
John Seymour 1738–1818
Thomas Seymour 1771–1848
John Seymour & Son fl. 1796–1804
Mahogany; white pine
65½ x 37½ x 27½ in.
ACC. NO. 73.6

The limited number of pieces on which to base a Seymour attribution has already been noted (cat. no. 70). This desk, besides its obvious stylistic affinity to the labeled examples, shares a number of construction features and has additionally a noteworthy family history. It descended in the family of Benjamin Proctor who, in 1799, was a partner of Thomas Seymour in the purchase of land from a Diana Ring of Boston. The combination of these facts argues strongly for an attribution to the Seymours. A unique feature of the desk is the oval portrait bust of a man on the back of the lower case, accompanied by some undeciphered writing.

Two other pedimented tambour desks are known (Stoneman 1959, figs. 34, 37). The theory has been advanced that the pediments were an option that could be exercised at any time, as these pediments are not fixed to the tambour sections. They rest on the mahogany top and are framed by shallow moldings lightly tacked in place. As often happened, finials and cartouches, removable parts, were often permanently removed. The survival of only two or three pediments may not reflect their initial popularity. Pediments were not the only design variation available—a number of tambour desks with bookcase tops are known (Montgomery 1966, no. 186, Stoneman 1959, fig. 50, and Stoneman 1965, no. 13).

The front of the pediment is hinged and locked, covering a plain storage area. Practicality, however, is not its primary function, which is to balance and lighten the mass of the three-drawer case. This is born out by the pedimented desk with only two drawers (Stoneman 1959, 37), whose pediment is narrower and lower than cat. no. 84. The finely patterned inlay of the legs, the husks, and alternating tambour slats of mahogany and maple delicately embellish this well-proportioned form.

Provenance: Descended in the family of Benjamin and Eliza Proctor of Boston; Mrs. Alfred Bacon of Danvers, Massachusetts (Mrs. Proctor's granddaughter); Mrs. Helen Wentworth (Mrs. Bacon's daughter); Mrs. Herbert Traut (Mrs. Wentworth's daughter); Harry Arons Antiques, Ansonia, Connect-

icut; Vernon Stoneman, Belmont, Massachusetts; Lansdell K. Christie Collection, Syosset, New York; P-B, sale 3422, 21 October 1972, lot 89; Israel Sack, Inc., New York

Construction and condition: The lower case has mahogany sides and a white pine back, all tenoned to the legs. The drawer partitions are mahogany. The writing surface supports are mahogany with mahogany facings. The top is white pine with attached pine battens. A strip at the rear of the top is a replacement. The front half of the top is a writing surface covered in modern felt framed in mahogany veneer. The rear half is unfinished pine, with mahogany moldings at each side to enclose the tambour section. A chamfered mahogany molding edges the top. The leaf section is mahogany covered in felt. The mahogany molding below the tambour is glued to the leaf section.

The drawers have white pine sides, backs, and bottoms. The grain of the bottoms runs side to side. The backboards are thicker than the sides. The fronts are walnut veneered in mahogany. Cock-beading is set in the drawer fronts. The brasses are replacements. The drawers ride on white pine runners nailed to white pine strips glued to the side between the legs.

The tambour section has mahogany sides dovetailed to white pine top and bottom boards. There is a false top of mahogany nailed and glued to the top. The back is made of vertically grained white pine boards nailed in place. The interior is white pine painted blue and edged in mahogany. The valances are mahogany. The pigeonhole drawers have white pine sides, backs, and bottoms with mahogany fronts.

The tambours ride in grooves cut in the mahogany applied to the front of the section. They slide into a cavity between the sides and the pigeonholes, behind the pilasters. The central pilaster contains a locking mechanism for the tambours. This keyhole is hidden by the closed writing surface.

The pediment rests on the tambour section enclosed by strips of mahogany molding tacked in place. It is topped by a mahogany plinth and urn which has had its base and tip replaced. The pediment has a white pine back dovetailed to mahogany sides. The hinged fall front is a frame of mahogany veneer on mahogany. Its inside edge is rounded. The bottom board is white pine nailed to the sides. The curved top is made of mahogany boards nailed at the back and front. The inside of the pediment is covered in blue paper.

Literature: Stoneman 1959, no. 30; Fairbanks et al. 1975, no. 286; Fairbanks and Bates 1981, 231

Exhibitions: New York, MMA 1965–1972; Boston, MFA 1975 (Paul Revere's Boston, 1735–1818)

85
Sideboard

1793–1795
New York
Labeled: *Mills & Deming/no. 374 Queen Street, two above the Friends Meeting./New York/Makes and sells all kinds of Cabinet Furni——/and Chairs after the most modern fashions/. . . on reasonable terms.* [Handwritten under Queen is the word *Pearl.* Queen was changed to Pearl Street in 1794.]
William Mills and Simeon Deming fl. 1793–1798
Mahogany; white pine, poplar, cherry, maple, ash, chestnut
40¾ x 74¾ x 32¼ in.
ACC. NO. 75.3

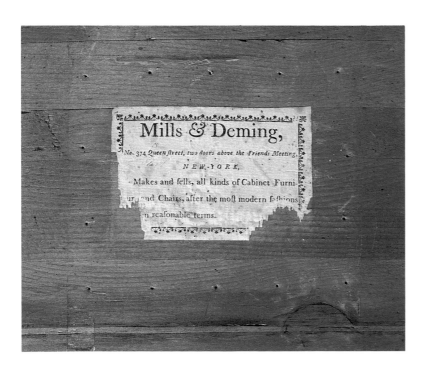

The sideboard was a relatively new form in the early Republic but it quickly found its fullest expression in this piece. All the elements of the New York form are found here as well as a number of customized details that reflect the makers' talents and the client's—Oliver Wolcott (1726–1797)—pocketbook. The price books of the period specify in detail the costs of inlaid ornament; the extent, scale, and proportion leave little doubt that most of the ornament was customized for this piece alone.

The New York sideboard is characterized here by concave ends coming to a sharp line on the canted center legs. The bowed central drawer projects over two slightly recessed bowed doors flanked by concave panels. In general, sideboards throughout the Republic favored a continuous, softly curved facade. Here the case thrusts forward, with each section clearly separated by the canted leg of undecorated mahogany. The projecting central drawer is separated from the recessed cupboard doors, and the flanking panels are marked by a slightly raised, crossbanded strip.

The legs are inlaid with a tapering line of husks and dots interlaced with fine satinwood stringing. They are also chamfered on the back. They are plain in the case, while the ornament picks up again in a series of dark-light vertical bands in the frieze, a typical New York feature.

The entire facade of the case is veneered in vertical panels of crotch mahogany, book-matched on the doors. The drapery work hangs from a central urn and winds around an inlaid tieback. It is shaded to indicate folds and engraved along its border, as are the tassels strung below. The central drawer has swags of dyed husks that dip below the brass ring-pulls. The two cupboard doors unite these elements with husks interlaced with the drapery. The door and drawer fronts are further framed by crossbanding outlined with stringing. A quarter-round fan is set in each corner.

The top, which is crossbanded and edged with satinwood lines, and the white-black-white border at the bottom of the case are the only continuous lines across the case. The contrast of the satinwood, curly maple, and dyed-wood inlays against the mahogany are matched by the clear definition of each section balanced against the mass of the case.

While New York continued to produce sideboards well into the nineteenth century, none surpassed this example.

Provenance: Governor Oliver Wolcott (1726–1797), signer of the Declaration of Independence from Connecticut, Litchfield, Connecticut; Oliver Wolcott, Jr. (1760–1833), Governor of Connecticut; Dr. John Stoughton Wolcott; Jason Whiting, Litchfield, Connecticut, purchased sideboard from sale of effects of Oliver Wolcott, Jr., 1843; Miss Edith Whiting, granddaughter of Jason Whiting; Israel Sack, Inc., New York;

Mr. and Mrs. Walter Robb Collection, Buffalo, New York; Israel Sack, Inc., New York

Construction and condition: The sideboard has two-board mahogany sides and a white pine back, all tenoned to the mahogany legs. At the front none of the rails extend the length of the case, but are set between the legs. The white pine bottom board runs the length of the case and is nailed in place. The upper rails are ash, shaped on both sides and double tenoned to the legs. The lower rails are cherry. The two end rails are shaped on both sides and the center rail on one side only. The center legs are made in two parts. The mahogany part is pentagonal in cross section. It is glued to a piece of maple that extends from the top to just below the bottom rails of the case. It is rectangular in cross section. All the rails are tenoned into this part. White pine boards are set behind the center legs. They extend the height and depth of the case and are tenoned through the back. Pine strips are nailed to these to support the drawer. All the leg joints in the case are supported by vertically grained glue-blocks. The top has a pine frame to which has been glued a thin piece of mahogany. The edges are cross-banded to hide the joint. The top is secured by screws and glue-blocks.

The drawer has poplar sides, back, and bottom boards. The bottom boards are set side to side. The drawer front is made of four layers of white pine horizontally laminated and shaped on both sides. The brasses are replacements. The area behind each door is open storage. The two end doors are made of seventeen layers of white pine horizontally laminated, shaped on both sides, and secured by vertical chestnut battens. The center doors are constructed in the same fashion, but with only fourteen layers. The label is pasted to the inside of the right side door.

Literature: Walcott 1928, 516–517; Downs and Ralston 1934, no. 118; A. Sack 1950, 220; Gaines 1967, 375; Tracy 1970, no. 4; I. Sack n.d.–1979, 5:1204–1205, 6:44; Tracy 1980, 364; Fairbanks and Bates 1981, 237; Martin 1985, 42–43

Exhibitions: New York, MMA 1934 (A Loan Exhibition of New York State Furniture and Contemporary Accessories), 1970 (Nineteenth Century America), 1980

86
Sideboard
1803
Providence
Mahogany, cherry; white pine, chestnut, poplar
39⅞ x 66 x 23¾ in.
ACC. NO. KAF 82.1

Dating furniture is one of the most difficult (and least accurate) pursuits in the field. This wonderfully exuberant piece saves any possible embarrassment because it has engraved in an inlaid oval on the top the letters *J.B. 1803* and two oval silver mounts engraved *JB and TB April 20, 1803* on the doors.

The maker was more modest about his identity. The use of white pine and chestnut, the engraved bellflowers, and the black-white quarter fans all point to Rhode Island and more specifically to Providence. After the Revolution Providence supplanted Newport as the major urban area of Rhode Island. But even more important was the rise of New York City as the financial and artistic center of the region. Providence and Newport craftsmen became the interpreters of styles set in New York and Boston instead of the creators of styles.

The piece is in many ways a provincial masterpiece. The urban masterpieces of Federal furniture are built around the choice veneers and inlays available to the urban craftsman. This Providence sideboard represents the finest product of the skills and resources available to the local craftsman. The design of the sideboard and arrangement of the inlays show a cabinetmaker with an excellent eye for scale and proportion. The construction of the central section with its "trick drawer" and coopered door (see *Construction and condition*) show a further refinement. The corners of the top are inlaid with quarter fans and the sides of the case and legs with bellflowers. The spade feet are inlaid with black-white diamonds, an ensemble that indicates a wealthy client and a responsive cabinetmaker.

The difference between this piece and cat. no. 85 lies in the adage that a craftsman is only as good as his tools, and in this case materials. Where Mills and Deming could call upon large lumber yards for the finest in fancy mahogany veneers, the maker here has used plainer straight-grain mahogany, and even mixes cherry in as a primary wood. The inlay rather than being from a specialist's shop—or even imported—is probably an in-house product.

Provenance: Acquired from descendants of the Rhodes and Corbin families. The engraved *B* in the ovals is thought to stand for the Bucklin family. Elizabeth Bucklin married James Rhodes in 1848; Israel Sack, Inc., New York

Construction and condition: The mahogany sides and white pine back are tenoned to the mahogany legs. All the front rails are cherry. None of the rails extend beyond the next leg. All are shaped on one side only and tenoned to the legs. The bottom of the case is made of three boards, all nailed in place. Behind the doors is a poplar board and at each end is one of chestnut. White pine boards are set behind the center legs, extending to the back where they are through tenoned. The drawers are supported by pine strips nailed to these boards behind the rails. At each end drawer guides are set between the legs, and strips are nailed to these to support the drawers.

The doors are cherry veneered in mahogany. They are shaped on both sides and coopered. The silver mounts have threaded shafts which pass through the door and are held by nuts. The upper drawer is a visual trick. The drawer actually extends only slightly below the midline of the brasses. The next part of the "drawer" is actually the rail. Beneath that is a sliding tray. It is made with a pine center tongue and grooved to a pine batten and at the front to a piece of cherry. The tray is covered with a patterned black oilcloth. Together the drawer, rail, and tray present a drawer of equal size to the two flanking drawers. None of the top row of drawers has a lock, and each is fitted and covered in green velvet.

The drawers have white pine sides, backs, and fronts; and chestnut bottoms set side to side. The drawer fronts are shaped on both sides and made of two layers of white pine vertically laminated. The dovetails are thick and well spaced.

Only two sides of the back legs and only three sides of the center legs have the spade foot. The top is mahogany and is held by screws to the case.

An interesting fragment was hidden by an early twentieth-century repair. The interior behind the doors was faced with finished poplar boards wedged in place. When removed they revealed the interior covered in an early nineteenth-century wallpaper. The corners have been scraped, indicating an attempt to remove it. Failing this, the poplar boards seem to have been installed for a more presentable face, happily also preserving the wallpaper.

Literature: Monohan 1965, 573; I. Sack n.d.–1979, 7:1940

Exhibition: New York, MMA 1982–1985

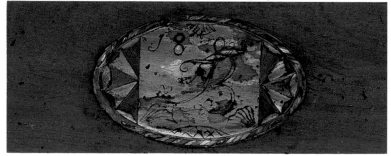

87
Tambour Writing Table
1795–1810
Philadelphia
Mahogany; poplar, white pine
57⅝ x 36⅛ x 37⅝ in.
ACC. NO. KAF 79.4

Tambour writing tables were introduced after the Revolution and offered an alternative to the four-drawer, slant-front desks of the Colonial period. Here the drawer just above the arch is fitted with boxes and partitions, making it a dressing as well as writing table.

This desk offers one of the fullest realizations of Federal Philadelphia's restrained geometric style. Visually the desk is divided into three sections, both horizontally and vertically. The recessed arch in the lower case, between the cabinets and the ogival domes, creates space within the overall form. This manipulation of mass, reinforced by the arrangement of the veneer and inlay, was the dominant concern of Philadelphia cabinetmakers and patrons in the early Federal period.

Plate 13 of Shearer's illustrations for *The London Book of Prices 1788* (1962) shows a simple, large, bell-shaped cabinet above the tambour desk. The specifications note that this part of the design may be altered or omitted. The cabinet section seen here may be drawn from plate 50, dated 1792, of Sheraton's *Drawing Book*. His "Lady's Cabinet and Writing Table" has cabinets above a simpler writing table with fall front. (Sheraton thought tambours to be flimsy.) Interestingly, a more complete interpretation of this design, also from Philadelphia (GSE 1929, no. 718), uses the same interlaced ovals in its fall board as those seen in the recessed panel of this Kaufman piece. Another tambour writing table (*Antiques*, December 1941, 344) nearly duplicates this one in form and decoration, but has no upper section. There is one with cabinets (*Antiques*, June 1985, 1199) that is signed by Joseph Beale of Philadelphia, but the desk shown here does not reflect his hand. These are hints at the variety of tambours produced in Philadelphia around 1800. The popularity of the desk, however, seems to have been limited to this time, as few examples incorporating later designs or decorative elements are known.

Provenance: This piece was acquired from descendants of the Etting family of Philadelphia living in England; Bernard and S. Dean Levy, Inc., New York

Construction and condition: The piece is built in three sections—the lower case, tambour desk, and upper case.

The lower case has mahogany sides and white pine back-board, all tenoned to the legs. At the front the vertical drawer partitions run the length of the case and are set in the back-board. A poplar board is set at the top of the case separating it from the desk section. The inlaid band along the lower edge of the case extends both the length of the sides and of the vertical partitions. Each of the spandrels is made of two pieces of poplar mitered together. The cuffs of the legs are replaced. The drawers have poplar sides, backs, and bottoms. The drawer fronts are white pine with a mahogany strip at the top. The diamond-shaped ivory escutcheons are additions. The center drawer is partitioned and fitted with mahogany boxes. Five of the boxes have mahogany lids with inlaid stringing and ivory knobs. Two are shallow open boxes with shaped dividers.

The tambour desk section has mahogany sides with a white pine top and back. The front rail is mahogany. There is a sliding mahogany-framed writing-board with a tilting, leather-covered surface. The tambours are backed in linen and slide in grooves cut in the side. The interior drawers have poplar sides, backs, and bottoms. The drawer fronts are mahogany with satinwood veneer and ebony knobs. The bottom row of drawers is attached to the writing board. Pen drawers are at the ends; the others are false fronts.

The upper case is made in four sections: the two end cabinets, a central drawer, and a back panel. Each piece was constructed separately, then fitted to each other and to the desk. The cabinets are made entirely of mahogany. The doors have mitered battens set at the top and bottom. On the interior the cabinets have two drawers under a central vertical divider. The construction of these drawers matches that of the interior desk drawers except that the front is inlaid with an ebony oblong and an ivory knob. The ogival domes are solid mahogany with the end-grain faces veneered. The center drawer has poplar side, back, and bottom boards. The front is mahogany veneered in satinwood. The ivory knobs are replacements; remnants of the original ebony shafts remain. The drawer is fitted in a mahogany box that is fitted to the cabinets and the back panel is mahogany and is screwed to the cabinets.

Exhibition: Winston-Salem, North Carolina, MESDA 1980–1986

88
Tambour Desk and Bookcase
1790–1800
Philadelphia
Mahogany; poplar, pine
104¼ x 45 x 35½ in.
ACC. NO. 81.4

Both Hepplewhite and Shearer published designs for a "tambour writing table," and it is Shearer who seems to have been the inspiration for this piece. In plate 13 (Shearer 1962) he shows a writing table with a horizontal tambour over a row of three drawers, over two drawers flanking a central kneehole, all on tapered legs. Plate 1 shows a library bookcase with glazed doors and cornice very similar to the ones used here. Hepplewhite shows a tambour writing table and bookcase where the desk is similar, but there is no cornice and the mullions are very different.

A small group of Philadelphia tambour-secretaries are known, of which this is the most ambitious. The most famous one was purchased in 1797 by George Washington from John Aitken of Philadelphia for $145 (Fede 1966, 67; another is illustrated in Miller 1937, 1:no. 825). Two have appeared at auction—one at the Reifsnyder sale in 1929, lot 695, and the other at Phillips, New York, 20 October 1983, lot 717. A number of Philadelphia tambour desks topped by flanking cabinets also exist, including cat. no. 87 and one signed by Joseph Beale (*Antiques*, June 1985, 1199).

This desk and bookcase is the tallest of the group, and the cabinetmaker has altered a number of elements to maintain the proper scale and proportion. All the additional height is in the bookcase. To accommodate this, the oval at the top of the mullions has been added to the pattern shown in Shearer. The central panel of the pediment has been changed from the high arch in Shearer and on the Washington example to a lower mahogany rectangle framing a satinwood oval. This has created a pattern of ovals—the half oval of the kneehole, the oval of the mullions, and the oval of the pediment. The cabinetmaker has increased the height but minimized the effect by emphasizing the horizontal elements within the form. In this highly vertical piece he has achieved a balance between his client's desire for ample storage space and his own aesthetic sensibilities.

Provenance: Purchased from descendants of the Ferris family of Philadelphia; David Stockwell, Inc., Wilmington, Delaware; Boscobel Restorations, Inc., Garrison, New York; Berry Tracy, Inc., Goshen, New York

Construction and condition: This piece can be dismantled into three sections—the cornice, the bookcase, and the desk. The cornice is built up from a dovetailed pine frame. A mahogany torus molding is applied to the lower edge. The cornice moldings have pine cores and mahogany faces. The pediment is backed by new poplar blocks throughout. The panels between the plinths are solid mahogany, but the plinths are veneered.

The bookcase has mahogany sides dovetailed to poplar top and bottom boards. The back is framed in poplar with four poplar panels. It is screwed to the case. The doors are mahogany, crossbanded in mahogany veneer. The rails of the door are tenoned through the stiles. The shelves are poplar with a mahogany facing. Serrated strips with adjustable crossbars are nailed to the sides to support the shelves.

The desk is made of two parts—the tambour and the drawer sections. The tambour case has mahogany sides dovetailed to a poplar back. At the front, a thick mahogany rail is set into the sides. There is a sliding mahogany writing-board with an adjustable writing surface covered in leather. The tambours are glued to a canvas backing and slide in grooves cut into the sides. The interior drawers have poplar backs tenoned to the legs. In the front the uppermost drawer partition is cherry and the lower two are mahogany. The vertical partitions are pine and extend the length of the case; they are tenoned through the poplar back. The bellflowers in the legs are later additions. The drawer supports are nailed to the sides. The drawers are also poplar and have mahogany fronts veneered in mahogany. The grain of the bottom boards runs front to back. The tambour and drawer sections are glued together at the front and sides.

Exhibition: Garrison, New York, Boscobel Restorations 1962–1981

89
Clothes Press
1785–1805
Charleston
Mahogany; white pine, red cedar
90½ x 53⅝ x 25⅞ in.
ACC. NO. 83.4

"The clothes press or wardrobe is an article of furniture that seems to be associated with the South and especially Charleston," wrote E. Milby Burton in his pioneering book *Charleston Furniture, 1700–1825* (1955, 46). That assessment has not changed in thirty years. This example will certainly enhance Charleston's reputation as the manufacturing center of the finest clothes presses in the early Republic.

This wardrobe presents a serpentine facade seven and a half feet high. While serpentine chests of drawers are common, a two-part all-serpentine case piece is a rarity. The form may be drawn from Chippendale, plate 130, where he shows a fully serpentine clothes press with canted corners and bracket feet. A Baltimore Federal chest-on-cabinet (Weidman 1984, no. 75) of near identical dimensions also presents a fully serpentine facade. It has five large drawers over two smaller doors.

The technical achievement of these doors (see *Construction and condition*) gave the cabinetmaker an uninterrupted plane on which to work. The choice of veneers is exemplary. The grain of the door panels rises from the bottom, narrowing as it carries the eye toward the center of the cornice. The book-matched veneer strips of wavy-grain mahogany that frame the door show the same care. The extensive inlay on the bracket feet lighten them, and the bellflowers at the top of the canted corners serve as highlights. The alternating inlays of floral sprigs in ovals and blocks of vertical bands embellish the cornice without the use of carving or heavy moldings and obviate the need for a pediment.

All the most distinctive elements of Federal Charleston's decorative vocabulary are seen in this piece. Here are the narrow canted corners of the base and plain bracket feet with a simple ogival curve. This type of foot is not a carryover from the Colonial period, but appears primarily on pieces in the Federal style. The distinctive inlays are bellflowers of the engraved, single-unit variety. On the side of the frieze these are hung horizontally. Another highly regional feature is the leaf motif set at the miter joints of the door framing.

Provenance: Sylvia Tearston Antiques of New York purchased this piece in 1962 from the estate of Edward Jenks. A letter from his mother, Mrs. Eloise Jenks, stated that Edward had inherited the piece from his great-aunt, Mrs. Roland Lin-coln of Boston. She is described by Mrs. Jenks as a collector of antiques early in the century. The piece was sold to George Subkoff in the early 1980s; Berry Tracy, Inc., Goshen, New York

Construction and condition: The piece is constructed entirely of mahogany, white pine, and red cedar. This is typical of Charleston after the Revolution, when imported white pine replaced native cypress as the main secondary wood.

The cornice is a separate unit. The upper case is dovetailed together, with mahogany sides and top and bottom boards of pine. The pine back is framed with two vertically grained panels and is nailed to rabbets in the sides. A medial brace is dovetailed to the sides at the middle hinge. There are four open-faced drawers in pine with serpentine mahogany fronts inlaid with stringing. The drawer bottoms extend beyond the drawer sides into grooves in the case, eliminating the need for drawer supports. This technique is also seen on a clothes press signed *John Elliott 1799*, in the collection of Historic Annapolis Inc. One drawer rides on the medial brace and does not use this technique. Its mahogany front is lipped to conceal the medial brace.

The doors are masterpieces of construction. First, the mahogany frames were mortise-and-tenoned and shaped on both sides. Next, coopered panels made of five to six staves were set in each frame to follow the curve of the case, and then the entire face was veneered. Because the frame and coopered panels are lighter than any other construction they reduce warpage and shrink less, preventing splits in the face veneer. The doors are lipped for better closure and have three hinges each.

The lower case is dovetailed together with a pine bottom board. At the top a pine rear rail and mahogany front rail are dovetailed to the sides. A strip is set between them on each side to keep the drawer level as it is pulled out. The mahogany top is screwed to the rails and a waist molding for the upper case is glued to the top. The back, like that of the upper case, is framed with two panels and nailed to rabbets in the sides.

The canted corner is made from an additional strip glued to the side. Full-panel pine dust boards are set in grooves in the sides. The rails are half-dovetailed to the canted corners. Guide strips are set at the joint of the dust boards and sides. sides.

The drawers have cedar frames with pine bottoms, and the fronts are cedar veneered with mahogany. Cock-beading extending the full thickness of the drawers has been planed flush. The top drawer interior has been altered with new sides, and bottoms that once had partitions. The brasses are replacements. The feet are supported by quarter-round vertically grained blocks flanked by horizontal blocks.

90
Writing Table with Bookcase
1815–1830
Philadelphia
Mahogany; white pine, poplar
73⅝ x 43⅛ x 20⅝ in.
ACC. NO. 83.8

This beautifully proportioned and decorated writing table (its drawer is fitted with an adjustable writing slide and pen and ink compartments) with bookcase is one of a small group of Philadelphia case pieces with boulle-work decoration. Boulle work is a technique whereby panels of brass and ebony are cut in marquetry style to produce intricate designs of brass in ebony and vice-versa. It was popularized by the French cabinetmaker Charles André Boulle (1642–1732) at the court of Louis XV. Pieces from this group include a sideboard with matching knife boxes and cellarette (PMA 1976, no. 221), a winged secretary made for the Gratz family, and a *secretaire à abattant* from the Kuhn family. These pieces have long been associated with the shop of Joseph Barry (1757–1839), based on an 1824 newspaper advertisement for "2 Rich sideboards Buhl [sic] work and richly carved" (PMA 1976, 266). All the boulle work of this group is cut from the same patterns and may have been imported (see cat. no. 50). Elements other than the boulle-work panels, including the ball feet, the shape of columns, and interior details show these to be the work of a single shop. The labeled Barry pier table (Tracy 1970, no. 34) shows that he was capable of such quality and the open carved guilloches of the pier table appear as inlay in the winged secretary and as blind carving on the sideboard.

Here, as in cat. no. 50, the form is austere. There are no large moldings or carvings. The emphasis is entirely on the architectural elements. The moldings are all simple coves. The rich decoration of boulle work, ormolu, and crotch-mahogany veneer are all contained within these architectural elements, emphasizing them without disturbing the lines of the piece. This interplay of simple form and rich decoration no doubt satisfied the owner's desire for a certain opulence within the restrained vocabulary of Empire forms.

Provenance: This piece was purchased at the estate sale of Miss Elsie V. McClintic of Richmond, Virginia, in March of 1983, before it was consigned to Christie's; Christie's, sale 5370, 2 June 1983, lot 345; Berry Tracy, Inc., Goshen, New York

Construction and condition: The ball feet are ebonized mahogany. The base has a poplar frame with pine top and is veneered and crossbanded in mahogany. The front columns are mahogany veneered in crotch mahogany between the base and capital. The rear pilasters are plain mahogany. The drawer is fitted with an adjustable writing surface and pen slots. The drawer sides are mahogany and the bottom is pine. The boulle-work panel is flanked by mahogany strips. Evidence indicates that these strips were originally ebonized to match the boulle panel, and they have been redone accordingly. Both are veneered on the mahogany drawer front.

The upper case is screwed to a coved waist molding attached to the base. The upper case has mahogany sides dovetailed to pine top and bottom boards. The back has a pine frame with two vertically grained pine panels and is screwed to the sides. The adjustable shelves are pine, with mahogany facing strips. The doors are mahogany veneered on mahogany. The molding surrounding the glass is brass. Inside each door, above and below the glass, are rows of brass knobs through which the curtains are strung. The rounded wooden strip between the doors is an addition that replaces the original brass strip.

The cornice is a separate unit screwed to the top. It is mahogany veneer over pine. The pediment is closed, with mahogany boards nailed in place.

91

Secretaire à abattant

1815–1830

Philadelphia

Mahogany; white pine, poplar

65½ x 36¼ x 21⅞ in.

ACC. NO. 83.7

Continental forms that found their way to these shores were usually transshipped through English designers (sec. cat. no. 46). The *secretaire a àbattant* is a Continental form that was adopted without any English modification. It never caught on in England and its popularity here was limited to the urban centers of Boston, Philadelphia, and New York. The earliest known record of one in Philadelphia is the combination *secretaire-organ* imported from Germany in 1804 by Simon Chaudron for Stephen Girard. The form did not become popular till about 1815 and had lost favor by the 1830s.

"French" was used as a descriptive adjective by American and English craftsmen at least from the time of Chippendale. The *secretaire à abattant* is often referred to in contemporary accounts as a French *secretaire*. Designs for the *secretaire* were not limited to France. The tabernacle top and contrasting burl wood panels are features derived from German, not French, sources. These Germanic examples were limited to Philadelphia.

This one is closely related to four others (Fairbanks and Bates 1981, 274, Christie's, sale 5890, 25 May 1985, lot 183, and two in private collections). None are exactly alike in decoration, but each is constructed in exactly the same way. A number of construction features, especially the back, are typical of German furniture of the period. This strongly argues that they were produced by a German-trained artisan utilizing German designs. Two other tabernacle-top secretaries have been published (Tracy 1963, no. 19 and Fitzgerald 1982, fig. VI-41). Though similar, they do not appear to be the same hand.

The influence of French culture on early nineteenth-century Philadelphia has long been noted. This specialized form points to a German influence as well on high-style designs.

Provenance: Ramon Osuna Collection, Washington; Christie's, sale 5370, 2 June 1983, lot 189; Berry Tracy, Inc., Goshen, New York

Construction and condition: The case of this piece, though visually divided in two parts, is actually one. The sides are mahogany dovetailed to white pine top and bottom boards. The back is three vertically grained boards held by nails. The pine center board is thicker than the two poplar ones and is lapped over them.

The doors of the lower section have mahogany frames and fielded panels veneered in mahogany. The center of each panel is inset with burl. The bases of the pilasters are missing. Behind the doors are four drawers of equal size set two over two. The lower drawers ride on the bottom of the case, the upper drawers on pine rails veneered in mahogany. The drawers have poplar sides, backs, and bottoms. The grain of the bottoms is set side to side. The drawer fronts are white pine veneered in mahogany, with button and bail handles.

The upper section has a fall front hinged with lead counterweights set behind the columns. Its inside surface is a modern baize framed by mahogany veneer. The interior is a separate box that slides into the case and rests on two pine boards set behind the mid-molding. It is made of pine and poplar dovetailed together with a backboard nailed on. The interior drawers are all mahogany, with the fronts veneered in maple and with brass knobs. One is partitioned with a pen holder. The columns flanking the fall front are mahogany veneered in crotch mahogany.

The case rests on a poplar and pine frame mortise-and-tenoned together and veneered in crotch mahogany. The rear rail is thinner than the other three. The brass paw feet are replacements.

The pediment starts with a white pine frame mortise-and-tenoned together and veneered in crotch mahogany. The large cove molding is made of four layers of horizontally laminated white pine veneered in horizontally grained mahogany. The tabernacle is a box made of white pine and poplar dovetailed together; it is veneered in crotch mahogany with a poplar back nailed in place. Its triangular pediment is made of two layers of white pine horizontally laminated, veneered in mahogany, and edged with a mahogany and brass molding. The tabernacle drawer has mahogany sides with poplar back and bottom boards. The grain of the bottom board is set side to side. The drawer front is mahogany veneered in mahogany. The semicircular insert is mahogany veneered in a burl wood. It is set in a rabbet and held by brads.

Literature: The piece is discussed more fully in Venable 1986

92
Pair of Knife Boxes
1785–1805
American
Mahogany veneers; *white pine
15⅞ x 9¾ x 15⅜ in.
ACC. NO. KAF 78.1 a, b

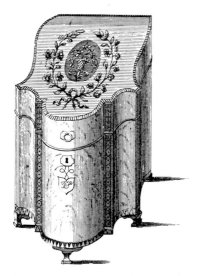

Sheraton, *Drawing Book* 1794, pl. 20

Today many a cabinetmaker is kept busy converting the drawers of antique sideboards to "silver drawers," and in a few years he will be busy again repairing them. The knife box, or case, as it was originally called, was the eighteenth century's answer to cutlery display and storage. Hepplewhite states in his caption to plate 38 that the universal utility of this piece renders a particular description not necessary, but does say they may be placed at each end of a sideboard, or on pedestals. This pair draws upon plate 20 of Sheraton's 1794 *Drawing-Book*. He also says that little need be said respecting these, but, happily, goes on to comment that these cases are not made in regular cabinet shops and even mentions a specialist by name. In fact, these shops exported such a large number to America that we can document only a few Federal pieces (see Weidman 1984, nos. 34, 35 and Fales 1965, no. 20). No cabinetmaker or family history is associated with these, but microanalysis of the secondary wood shows white pine throughout, supporting an American attribution. The popularity of white pine as a secondary wood and the probable importation of the pictorial inlays limits any regional attribution. A closely related pair (Jensen 1978, 1092) have a history of descent in the Faulkner family of New York.

The bold shape of the front, the lavish use of inlay, and the silver hardware mark this pair as among the finest of known American knife boxes.

Provenance: Charles Weida Collection, Greenwich, Connecticut; Israel Sack, Inc., New York

Construction and condition: The boxes are white pine veneered in mahogany. The bases are veneered on the exterior only. The lids are veneered on both sides except for the molded face which is covered inside with a red wash. The molded face is shaped on both sides of the base and lids. A series of pine dividers set parallel to the face are below the partitioned insert. The bottom boards of the boxes are white pine set side to side. The insert, the bead edge applied to the bottom, and the feet are solid mahogany. Each of the ogee bracket feet are cut from the solid with no supporting blocks. The escutcheon and ring-pulls are silver.

Literature: I. Sack n.d.–1979, 5:1185

Exhibition: Houston, Texas, Bayou Bend 1978–1985

93
Dressing Glass
1790–1810
Boston
Mahogany; white pine
29½ x 20⅞ x 13⅝ in.
ACC. NO. 80.1

This dressing glass is closely related to a more ornate version made for Elizabeth Derby West, daughter of Elias Hasket Derby (Hipkiss 1941, no. 136). The looking glass, standards, and veneers differ, but the correspondence in the form and construction of the box is so close that there is little doubt they were made in the same shop. Both pieces have been attributed to Samuel McIntyre on the belief that he made much of the Derby family furniture. More recent evidence shows that Elizabeth Derby West had extensive dealings with Boston area craftsmen including John Doggett, the leading looking-glass manufacturer of Roxbury. Given the complexity of the cabinet trade at that time, each element of this small piece could represent the work of a different independent craftsman.

The Derby family example is undeniably more ornate, but a comparison of the two highlights the basic elegance of the form. The elliptically shaped box, with its fully curved skirt, is on its own a flawless example of Federal cabinetry. The looking glass and carved standards are beautifully matched, with the tightly handled and strongly vertical curves of the frame echoed and supported by those of the standards. Each element expresses a different aspect of the Federal aesthetic. The box uses a simple geometric form emphasized by highly figured veneers and inlay. The lion's head brasses, carved drapery standards, and shield-shaped frame were all classically inspired motifs. The extent of decoration seen here shows this piece to be no poor relation of the Derby dressing glass.

Provenance: Israel Sack, Inc., New York; Harry Carlson Collection, Cincinnati; Mrs. Ruth Howard Collection, Cincinnati; SP-B, sale 4338, January 1980, lot 1483; Israel Sack, Inc., New York

Construction and condition: The case is built around three blocks. Each block is made of three layers of white pine horizontally laminated and shaped on one side only. The grain of the side blocks is set front to back and the rear block is set side to side. These blocks are sandwiched between two pieces of pine the shape of the case. The grain of these is set side to side. Together these form the drawer openings. The case is veneered all the way round in crotch-grain mahogany.

The upper drawer is supported by a pine rail and pine strips nailed to the side blocks. The lower drawer rides on the bottom board. The drawers have white pine sides, backs, and bottoms. The grain of the bottom board is set side to side. The drawer fronts are pine with a strip of mahogany along the top. They are shaped on both sides.

The skirt and feet extend the circumference of the case. They are made of six pieces of pine shaped on both sides, relieved along their inner edges, and veneered in mahogany. The standards are single pieces of mahogany tenoned and glued, with a crossbanded mahogany facing. The backboard is a single piece of rough-sawn pine.

94
Looking Glass
1785–1810
New York
Mahogany; *white pine
71 x 27½ in.
ACC. NO. KAF 80.5

This looking glass is based on one of the most durable designs of the eighteenth century. The original version dates from the early Georgian period when such a piece was referred to as a "tabernacle glass." The form was derived from designs for overmantels and doorways. Its neoclassical incarnation was limited in popularity to the greater New York area. Within this group there is little variance in the form or choice of decorations. There is, however, great variety in execution, indicating the work of a number of shops. Only one labeled example is known. It is in the collection of Sleepy Hollow Restorations and bears a stenciled inscription: *From Del Vecchio Looking Glass & Picture Frame Manufacturers, New York.* Members of this family were in business in New York throughout the first half of the nineteenth century.

The beading surrounding the oval shell inlays and running along the inside of the scroll pediment is a rarely seen feature. It may be derived from a group of mirrors associated with William Wilmerding of New York, one of which is documented by a bill of sale from 1794 (Comstock 1962, no. 499). These mirrors are in the late rococo style, similar in form to this one. One of the distinguishing features is a beaded oval set in the tympanum. Whether Wilmerding produced or merely retailed these is unknown, but New Yorkers' preference for them is clear.

Provenance: Israel Sack, Inc., New York

Construction and condition: The rectangular frame surrounding the mirror provides the structural basis for the looking glass. It is white pine, mortise-and-tenoned together. A mahogany bead applied to the outside edge extends the depth of the frame. The face of the frame is veneered in mahogany, and a gilded molding is applied to the inside edge. The pendant, scroll ears, and pediment are mahogany veneered with mahogany. Battens are applied to the pendant and pediment. The leafage along the sides is made of composition applied over wire. The urn is gilded pine, with wire and composition ornament.

The backboards for the mirror are rough-sawn white pine. The grain is set horizontally and the pieces are ship lapped.

Literature: I. Sack n.d.–1979, 7:1808

Exhibition: Norfolk, Virginia, Chrysler Museum 1980–1986

95
Looking Glass
1790–1810
New York
White pine
60 x 23
ACC. NO. 74.8

The adaptation of this Georgian style frame to the newer classical taste is taken a step beyond that seen in cat. no. 94 with the inclusion of the *églomisé* panel. This feature is the least common and most desirable refinement of the form (see also Comstock 1962, no. 500; Montgomery 1966, nos. 214, 215, Tracy 1981, no. 75; and I. Sack n.d.–1979, 5:1228).

This glass is shorter than cat. no. 94 by about a foot. Despite this, it exhibits a stronger vertical emphasis and delicacy. The maker of cat. no. 94 has attempted to diminish its dominance by the design of the frame. The scrolls of that pediment have a short arch and do not rise to the center but turn down. The rosettes marking the scrolls' terminations are large in comparison. The urn is broad and flat. The short pendant strings of leafwork attempt to divide the glass. All these considerations serve to minimize the verticality of the glass.

This example takes the opposite tack in every way. The inclusion of the *églomisé* panel shortens the rectangular frame by adding a horizontally oriented element. Every other detail, however, is used to assert the vertical line. The frame is outlined by two gilded bands that highlight the frame's real size. The pendant leafage extends further down the frame, beyond the *églomisé*, to stress the vertical line. The scrolls of the pediment have a high arch and rise toward the center. The rosettes interfere less with the line of the scroll. The narrower urn adds to the tall effect.

An important point to note about these pieces is that the glass was often the dominant factor in the design equation. Frames were built around the glass which was cut to fit a space. While looking glasses and frames were a stock item, the size and quality of these looking glasses indicate that they were custom made.

Provenance: Israel Sack, Inc., New York; SP-B, sale 3638, 10–11 May 1974, lot 440

Construction and condition: The rectangular frame surrounding the mirror provides a structural basis for the looking glass. The frame has white pine rails mitered together and reinforced by two splines at each joint. The frame is veneered in mahogany and has applied gilded molding. The mirror is separated from the *églomisé* panel by a wooden strip faced with a gilded molding. The pendant is a horizontally grained white-pine board veneered in mahogany. It is edge-glued to the frame with two pine blocks along the joint and a pine batten for support. The scrolled ears are vertically grained white pine veneered in mahogany and supported by a single pine block each. The pediment is constructed like the pendant. The urn is made of gilded white pine, wire, and composition. The urn is attached by a strip nailed to both it and the pediment. Each of the gilded scrolls is made of two pieces of white pine vertically laminated and glued to the veneered pediment. The leafage along the sides are iron wire and composition. The backboard is horizontally grained white pine.

96
Looking Glass
1790–1815
New York
White pine
62 x 28⅝ x 9 (approx.)
ACC. NO. 81.7

Verre églomisé, the technique of embellishing the back of a glass panel with painted and gilded decoration was known from antiquity. The practice was revived in France around the mid-eighteenth century. It was used extensively during the Federal period in New York mirrors, as seen in this example. *Eglomisé* panels were also used in Boston and Baltimore.

New York *églomisé* panels generally are more freehand and abstract than Boston or Baltimore examples. The central tablet of this mirror is built around a pair of entwined cornucopias set in a pointed oval framed by freehand designs. Another mirror of this same design (GSE 1929, no. 701), but with a different-sized glass, has *églomisé* panels set above the columns—an uncommon feature (see also Biddle 1963, no. 93). The use of decoration atop the frame is a New York feature, as are the large-eared urn finials, wire floral sprigs, and triangular plinth.

This mirror descended in the family of Governor and Mrs. Joseph C. Yates of Albany, New York. A painted settee, two painted side chairs, a bed, and an overmantel looking glass (Montgomery 1966, nos. 4, 63, 64, 235) have this same provenance. The overmantel glass and the Kaufman mirror share a number of features specific to New York, but do not appear to be by the same hand.

Provenance: Descended in the family of Governor and Mrs. Joseph C. Yates of Albany, New York; Jane Josepha DeLancey Neill; Edward Montandevert Neil; Anna DeLancey Neill Grinnell; Harry Arons Antiques, Ansonia, Connecticut; Israel Sack, Inc., New York; Cornelius C. Moore Collection, Newport, Rhode Island; Providence College, Rhode Island; Christie's, sale 5079, 19 September 1981, lot 542; Israel Sack, Inc., New York

Construction and condition: A pine frame nailed together provides the structural basis for the looking glass. The frame has two stiles at each side behind the columns. The rails are at the bottom and on a line behind the row of gilded balls. All the visible elements are purely decorative and are supported by this frame. The triangular *églomisé* panel above the cornice is a replacement. The eagle is supported by a shaft that runs behind the panel.

97

Convex Mirror
1810–1825
New York
*White pine
57 x 35 x 10 in. (approx.)
ACC. NO. 83.10

A new style of looking glass, the convex mirror, was introduced in America around 1800. The first examples were probably imported because the form was advertised before it appeared in design books (Weidman 1984, no. 105). The term mirror, or convex mirror, was defined by Sheraton in his 1803 *Cabinet Dictionary*: "A circular convex glass in a gilt frame, silvered on the concave side. . . ." This type of glass is often referred to today as a girandole glass, a much older term referring to any wall-mounted lighting fixture. Many designs, however, did have mirror backs and so the term could be used here. The earliest versions of convex mirrors were Adamesque in their ornamentation. Plates in George Smith's *Designs for Household Furniture* (1808) show the form quickly adopted the neoclassical and Empire embellishments seen in the Kaufman piece. The style of decoration, the white pine frame, and composition ornaments strongly point to a New York attribution.

This glass is distinguished by a profusion of delicately executed ornaments. They are applied over the entire circumference of the frame, rather than the usual cluster at the top and bottom. This gives the mirror a balanced and organic look. The handling of the quiver and bow under the eagle shows the craftsman's effort to maintain this balance. The quiver and bow design is weighted to the left. This is balanced by the eagle's head and tail which point to the right.

The tableau this piece presents is happily devoid of any ideographic explanation, leaving one free to explore its purely visual delights.

Provenance: George Subkoff Antiques, New York; Edward Vason Jones Collection, Albany, Georgia; Israel Sack, Inc., New York

Construction and condition: The mirror is constructed of white pine. The circular frame around the mirror is made of layers of pine laid in brickwork fashion to form the circle. The ornament applied to the inner surface is composition. The eagle, quiver and bow, and leafage are applied to a shaft attached to the frame. The bow-tied leafwork is also applied to a shaft attached to the frame. The seahorses and flowers are attached to the frame by metal pins. The candle arms are wire covered in composition and are screwed to the frame. The candle sockets are turned wood.

Literature: Cooper 1980, pl. 298

Exhibition: Washington, National Gallery of Art 1980 (In Praise of America)

98

Pair of Wall Brackets
(one of two pairs)
1790–1810
Philadelphia
*Poplar, *white pine
18¾ x 16¾ x 8⅛ in (a and b)
17⅝ x 16¾ x 8⅛ in (c and d)
ACC. NO. 72.8 a–d

Sheraton, *Cabinet Dictionary* 1803, pl. 20

This set consists of two pairs. They differ in that one set has two pendant husks and the other set has but one. In each pair the eagles face in the same direction. One of the one-husk pair is a later copy. Sheraton's *Cabinet Dictionary* (1803, pl. 20) shows a design similar to these. He refers to them as clock brackets. Hepplewhite (1794, captions pls. 90, 91) says that brackets are suitable for clocks and busts, and that larger ones can accommodate lights. Brackets such as these were produced by carvers and looking-glass manufacturers. Many carvers were also gilders and one man could easily have made them. The New York convex mirror (cat. no. 97), the Massachusetts girandole clock case (cat. no. 101), and these brackets all drew upon the same design sources and were produced by the same type of craftsmen. Each has the same three basic design elements of carved leafage and an eagle around a decorated circle or semicircle for the brackets. Looking glasses, clocks, and brackets were imported from colonial times; microanalysis of the wood shows that these are made of poplar and white pine, indicating they were produced here.

Provenance: Robert Kennedy Wurts, Philadelphia, Pennsylvania; C.W. Lyon Antiques, Millbrook, New York; Lansdell K. Christie Collection, Syosset, New York; P-B, sale 3422, 21 October 1972, lot 17

Construction and condition: Both pairs of brackets are constructed in the same fashion. Each is made in three sections. The semicircular top is fashioned from a single piece of poplar. The balls are wood and are attached by pins. A modern slotted metal bar is screwed to the rear edge, allowing the bracket to be hung from the wall. A pine shaft extends down from the top; the eagle is screwed to this and the foliage is glued. The back and top are covered with ochre paint.

Literature: Hornor 1935, pls. 443, 445; PMA 1976, no. 128

Exhibition: Philadelphia, PMA 1976 (Philadelphia: Three Centuries of American Art)

99

Sconces

1795–1835
American
*White pine, iron
24¾ in.
ACC. NO. 80.208 a, b

Decorated and mounted lighting fixtures, with or without mirror backs, were commonly referred to throughout the eighteenth and nineteenth centuries as girandoles. Designs for them appear in Chippendale, Hepplewhite, and Sheraton. Other examples were imported, and both carvers and looking-glass makers advertised their availability for purchase. The term has become associated with convex mirrors (cat. no. 97) and with clocks of a similar form (cat. no. 101). This new usage has crowded out the old so that the simpler term, sconces, that used to refer only to mounted candle arms, is now the accepted term.

The presence of eagles alone does not confirm the American origin of these, but the use of white pine does. It was the preferred wood for gilded and painted carvings throughout the colonies and states. It was even imported into Charleston in the 1760s for the specific use of the carver in the construction of the State House.

The production of these sconces was a relatively simple matter, with each of the elements carved separately and then affixed to the central shaft. For those people who worried that they might be too fragile, Thomas Sheraton had a word. He noted in his *Drawing Book* (1802, pl. 55) that persons unacquainted with the manufacturing of these stands may apprehend them to be light and easily broken, an objection that vanishes when it is considered that the scrolls are made of strong wire and the ornaments cemented to them.

Provenance: William Grey (Lieutenant Governor under Elbridge Gerry), Massachusetts; The Gardiner Family, Salem, Massachusetts; Teina Baumstone Antiques, New York; Col. Edgar William and Mrs. Bernice Chrysler Garbisch, Pokety Farm, Maryland; SP-B, sale H-2, 23–25 May 1980, lot 1007

Construction and condition: The sconces are constructed around a central shaft of white pine. Each of the carved elements and iron arms are screwed to it. The wooden elements are white pine, gessoed and gilded. The arms are iron bent to shape, covered in a molded composition material, and gilded. The candle sockets are brass. The backs of the sconces are covered with ochre paint.

100
Tall Clock
1790–1800
Boston
Works by Simon Willard 1753–1848, fl. 1775–1830
Mahogany; pine, chestnut
104½ x 22¾ x 10⅝ in.
ACC. NO. 81.6

There is no more famous name in American preindustrial clockmaking than Willard. The work of the brothers, Simon and Aaron, was highly esteemed in their own day and has been ever since. Simon patented the popular "banjo" clock in 1802 and the rarer "lighthouse" clock in 1820. This Kaufman tall clock has eight-day brass works with rack-and-snail strike and the anchor recoil escapement typical of Willard clocks. There are two eccentric dials for seconds and days of the month. *Simon Willard* is painted below the days dial. Willard often used dials imported from England, and this one is similar to known English examples (see Montgomery 1966, no. 148 and Randall 1965, no. 204).

Our interest here is with the case that houses Simon Willard's clock. The case is stylistically part of the "Roxbury" group, so called because Willard had his shop there, as did a number of allied craftsmen. The elements of the form are simple cases, with tall waists and cove moldings at the hood and base. They have domed hoods and a cove molding cornice. The pediments have pierced fretwork between fluted plinths topped by ball and spire finials. The bases rest on ogee-bracket feet, a holdover from the rococo period, but seen on Federal clocks throughout the early Republic.

The decorations seen on this case are among the most extensive in the Roxbury group. The crotch mahogany panels, the light-and-dark wood crossbanding, quarter-fan inlay, and rope stringing are skillfully arranged, showing the hand of a master cabinetmaker. There are two notable features. The first are the cast brass Corinthian capitals of the waist and hood. These are complemented by brass reeding set in the fluted columns. The other is the pierced fretwork set in the frieze of the hood, set over fabric that covers holes drilled through the hood to allow a clearer sounding of the hours. Fretwork panels over fabric are also set in windows in the sides of the hood.

Provenance: Richard Opfer Auctioneers, Timonium, Maryland; Israel Sack, Inc., New York

Construction and condition: The clock case is built around the white pine backboard that runs from the top of the feet to the top of the hood. It is as wide as the waist, and pieces are glued to it at the hood and base to accommodate their greater width. The mahogany sides of the waist and base are butt-joined to the backboard. Vertically grained quarter-round pine blocks are glued the length of the joints.

The front of the base is a piece of horizontally grained pine. The bottom board is pine, with the grain set side to side. The moldings are applied to the base. Pine blocks applied to the bottom support the molding extending below the base. The feet have been reattached. They are secured by screws through them and vertically grained glue-blocks behind them.

The large cove moldings at the top and bottom of the waist have triangular pine cores and mahogany facings. The front edges of the cove molding at the top of the waist have been beveled. The waist is made of a mahogany frame with flanking quarter columns. Large, vertically grained blocks behind the quarter columns join the frame to the sides. The door is made of a single board of chestnut veneered in mahogany and edged with a molding. The works rest on horizontally grained pine blocks set between the backboard and blocks that extend up from the quarter columns.

The hood, which rests on the cove moldings at the top of the waist, starts with a U-shaped mahogany frame faced with mahogany moldings. The sides of the hood are vertically grained pieces of mahogany tenoned to the frame. The upper part of the hood is made of pine. Horizontally grained blocks of pine are glued to the sides. At the rear an arch-shaped pine board is dovetailed to the pine blocks. There is another pine block at the front, which has a number of holes drilled through to allow the striking to be heard clearly. The fretwork and arched cornice molding are set over this piece. The columns are set in it also and in the U-shaped mahogany frame. The clock face is set behind another frame of thin pieces of mahogany of the same shape as the door. The glazed door is mahogany veneered on mahogany. The fretwork is a replacement, based on a similar example pictured in Nutting (1928–1933, 2:no. 3287). The top of the hood is covered in thin strips of pine set front to back and nailed in place.

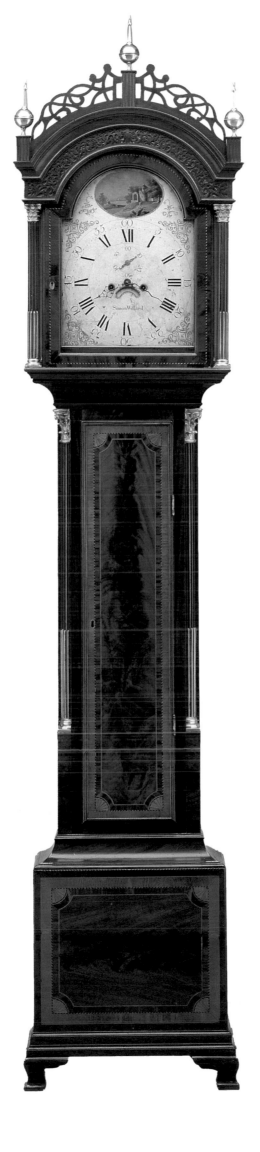

101
Girandole Clock
1811–1821
Massachusetts
Works by Lemuel Curtis 1790–1857, fl. 1811–1832
Mahogany veneers; white pine
45 x 12 in.
ACC. NO. 78.7

Lemuel Curtis produced this masterpiece at a time when clocks were still an expensive and prized possession. The "girandole" clock is so named because of its similarity to the mirrors (see cat. no. 97) of that name. They used eight-day works like those of the Willards' banjo clocks. Their greatness lies in their beautifully decorated cases. These cases start with a richly carved and gilded acanthus-leaf bracket. This supports the convex, reverse-painted glass surrounded by gilded balls. The waist has a bowed painted glass with *L. Curtis* emblazoned above the outstretched wings of an eagle. The curve of the pierced brass standards attenuates the transition between the base and the dial, which the straight taper of the waist cannot do. The dial, which has a convex face and glass, is surrounded by gilded balls and topped by an eagle. The girandole glasses have a variety of scenes depicting mythological, religious, and military events. This one shows Commander Oliver Hazard Perry's victory on Lake Erie in 1813. The entire front is gilt and glass, and the sides are mahogany.

Clockmaking and the associated trades of ornamental painting and gilding were practiced by men related through birth, marriage, apprenticeship—and sometimes all three. Lemuel Curtis was the son of a clockmaker. His father, Samuel, married Sarah Partridge, whose four sisters all married clockmakers, including Aaron Willard. Lemuel's three brothers started out in the ornamental painting business. Benjamin, who painted glasses as well as military banners, and Charles, who later became a portrait painter, both worked at one time with Lemuel. Samuel, the eldest, achieved great financial success as a supplier of painted clock faces, mirrors, and looking glasses.

Lemuel Curtis, though, was a man whose artistic accomplishments far outran his financial success. He probably was apprenticed to one of the Willards. He set up shop in Concord, Massachusetts, in 1811 and received a patent in 1816, for which the exact design is not known. The girandoles, of which less than thirty are known, were produced during this time. By 1821 he had moved to Burlington, Vermont, and was in partnership with Joseph N. Dunning. Their business prospered for a while but failed in 1832. Curtis then tried his hand as a dry goods merchant but again failed and finally declared bankruptcy in 1842. He and his family soon after moved to New York City where he died in 1857.

Lemuel Curtis' girandole clocks are the highest achievement of American clockmaking in the neoclassical and Empire period. Their works were modern and the cases both artistically unique and superbly executed. As Curtis' later career shows, they represent the last flowering of the group of craftsmen, painters, and clockmakers before mechanization made individual shops an anachronism.

Provenance: An old label inside the clock is inscribed with the following: *Property of Charles Francis Corbett, Son of John D. and (Emmy) Corbett*; Israel Sack, Inc., New York; Mrs. Richard Mellon Collection, Ligonier, Pennsylvania; Israel Sack, Inc., New York

Construction and condition: The author was unwilling to remove the face to examine the works and construction behind it.

The case consists of a pine backboard extending the length of the case. This board has a half-round molded edge. The circular box is made of two pieces of wood shaped on both sides and veneered with a single sheet of mahogany. This wood core is covered with an ochre-colored paint. A sheet-metal plate in the box separates the weight from the pendulum. The wooden door is gilded and painted on the inside.

The waist is made of a single piece of pine on each side, veneered in mahogany. The gilded waist door has a wooden frame and is painted on the inside. The dial is enameled iron and is screwed to a wooden frame. This, like the box, is veneered with a single piece of mahogany. The door of the clock face is brass. Both this door and that of the box are held by spring latches set in the sides.

Literature: I. Sack n.d.–1979, 2:539; Tracy 1970, no. 61; Carlisle 1978, 97, fig. 10

Exhibition: New York, MMA 1970 (Nineteenth Century America)

Bibliography and Abbreviated Titles

BMA 1947
Baltimore Furniture: The Work of Baltimore and Annapolis Cabinetmakers from 1760 to 1810 [exh. cat., The Baltimore Museum of Art] (Baltimore, 1947).

Beckerdite 1985
Luke Beckerdite, "Philadelphia Carving Shops, Part II, Bernard and Jugiez," *The Magazine Antiques* (September 1985), 498–514.

Biddle 1963
James Biddle, *American Art from the American Collections: Decorative Arts, Paintings, and Prints of the Colonial and Federal Periods from Collections in an Exhibition* [exh. cat., The Metropolitan Museum of Art] (New York, 1963).

Bishop 1972
Robert Bishop, *Centuries and Styles of the American Chair, 1640–1970* (New York, 1972).

Burton 1955
E. Milby Burton, *Charleston Furniture, 1700–1825* (Charleston, South Carolina, The Charleston Museum, 1955).

Carlisle 1978
Lillian Baker Carlisle, "New Biographical Findings on Curtis and Dunning, Girandole Clockmakers," *American Art Journal* (May 1978), 90–109.

Carpenter 1954
Ralph E. Carpenter, Jr., *The Arts and Crafts of Newport, Rhode Island, 1640–1820* (Newport, Preservation Society of Newport County, 1954).

Carson 1979
Marion S. Carson, "'The Duncan Phyfe Shops' by John Rubens Smith, Artist and Drawing Master," *The American Art Journal* (October 1979), 69–78.

Chippendale's *Director* 1754 and 1762
Thomas Chippendale, *The Gentleman and Cabinet-Maker's Director,* 1st and 3d eds. (London, 1754, 1762), reprint (New York, 1966).

Comstock 1962
Helen Comstock, *American Furniture, Seventeenth, Eighteenth, and Nineteenth Century Styles* (New York, 1962).

Cooper 1980
Wendy A. Cooper, *In Praise of America: American Decorative Arts, 1650–1830/Fifty Years of Discovery Since the 1929 Girl Scouts Loan Exhibition* (New York, 1980).

Cornelius 1922
Charles Over Cornelius, *Furniture Masterpieces of Duncan Phyfe* (Garden City, New York, 1922).

Davidson and Stillinger 1985
Marshall B. Davidson and Elizabeth Stillinger, *The American Wing at the Metropolitan Museum of Art* (New York, 1985).

Decatur 1941
Stephen Decatur, "George Washington and His Presidential Furniture," *The American Collector* (February 1941), 8–11.

Dorman 1980
Charles Dorman, "Philadelphia Furniture 'of the Best Sort,'" *Treasures of Independence: Independence National Historic Park and Its Collections,* ed. John C. Milley (New York, 1980), 121–149.

Downs 1952
Joseph Downs, *American Furniture in the Henry Francis du Pont Winterthur Museum, Queen Anne and Chippendale Periods* (New York, 1952).

Downs and Ralston 1934
Joseph Downs and Ruth Ralston, *A Loan Exhibition of New York State Furniture and Contemporary Accessories* [exh. cat., The Metropolitan Museum of Art] (New York, 1934).

Elder 1968
William Voss Elder, III, *Maryland Queen Anne and Chippendale Furniture of the Eighteenth Century* [exh. cat., The Baltimore Museum of Art] (Baltimore, 1968).

Elder and Bartlett 1983
William Voss Elder, III and Lu Bartlett, *John Shaw, Cabinetmaker of Annapolis* [exh. cat., The Baltimore Museum of Art] (Baltimore, 1983).

Fairbanks and Bates 1981
Jonathan L. Fairbanks and Elizabeth Bidwell Bates, *American Furniture, 1620 to the Present* (New York, 1981).

Fairbanks et al. 1975
Jonathan Fairbanks, Wendy A. Cooper et al., *Paul Revere's Boston, 1735–1818* [exh. cat., Museum of Fine Arts] (Boston, 1975).

Fales 1965
Dean A. Fales, Jr., *Essex County Furniture, Documented Treasures from Local Collections.* [exh. cat., Essex Institute] (Salem, Massachusetts 1965).

Fales 1972
Dean A. Fales, Jr., *American Painted Furniture, 1660–1880* (New York, 1972).

Fales 1976
Dean A. Fales, Jr., *The Furniture of Historic Deerfield* (New York, 1976).

Fede 1966
Helen M. Fede, *Washington Furniture at Mount Vernon,* Mount Vernon Ladies' Association of the Union (Mount Vernon, 1966).

Fitzgerald 1982
Oscar P. Fitzgerald, *Three Centuries of American Furniture* (Englewood Cliffs, New Jersey, 1982).

Flayderman sale
Colonial Furniture Silver and Decorations. The Collection of the Late Philip Flayderman, New York [auct. cat., The American Art Association] (New York, 1930).

Gaines 1967
Edith Gaines, "The Robb Collection of American Furniture, Part I," *The Magazine Antiques* (September 1967), 322–328.

Gaines 1968
Edith Gaines, "The Robb Collection of American Furniture, Part II," *The Magazine Antiques* (April 1968), 484–489.

Garrett 1977
Elisabeth Donaghy Garrett, "Living with Antiques: The Manhattan Apartment of Mr. and Mrs. Robert Lee Gill," *The Magazine Antiques* (May 1977), 990–1001.

Greenlaw 1974
Barry A. Greenlaw, *New England Furniture at Williamsburg* (Williamsburg, Virginia, The Colonial Williamsburg Foundation, 1974).

GSE 1929
Loan Exhibition of Eighteenth and Nineteenth Century Furniture and Glass. . . . For the Benefit of the National Council of Girl Scouts, Inc. [exh. cat., American Art Galleries] (New York, 1929).

Gusler 1979
Wallace B. Gusler, *Furniture of Williamsburg and Eastern Virginia, 1710–1790* (Richmond, Virginia Museum, 1979).

Hall 1840
John Hall, *The Cabinet Maker's Assistant* (Baltimore, 1840), reprint (New York, 1944).

Heckscher 1985
Morrison Heckscher, *American Furniture in the Metropolitan Museum of Art* (New York, 1985).

Hendrickson 1983
Hope Hoppage Hendrickson, "Cliveden," *The Magazine Antiques* (August 1983), 259–263.

Hepplewhite 1794
George Hepplewhite, *The Cabinet-Maker and Upholsterer's Guide,* 3d ed. (London, 1794), reprint (New York, 1969).

Hewitt 1982
Benjamin A. Hewitt, Patricia E. Kane, and Gerald W. R. Ward, *The Work of Many Hands: Card Tables in Federal America, 1790–1820* [exh. cat., Yale University Art Gallery] (New Haven, Connecticut, 1982).

Hinkley 1953
F. Lewis Hinkley, *A Directory of Antique Furniture* (New York, 1953).

Hipkiss 1941
Edwin J. Hipkiss, *Eighteenth-Century American Arts: The M. and M. Karolik Collection of Paintings, Drawings, Engravings, Furniture, Silver, Needlework and Incidental Objects Gathered to Illustrate the Achievements of American Artists and Craftsmen of the Period from 1720 to 1820* [coll. cat., Museum of Fine Arts, Boston] (Cambridge, 1941).

Holloway 1937
Edward Stratton Holloway, *The Practical Book of American Furniture and Decoration,* rev. ed. (Philadelphia, 1937).

Hope 1807
Thomas Hope, *Household Furniture and Interior Decoration* (London, 1807), reprint (New York, 1971).

Hornor 1935
William Macpherson Hornor, Jr., *Blue Book Philadelphia Furniture, William Penn to George Washington* (Philadelphia, 1935), reprint (Washington, 1977).

Hummel 1976
Charles F. Hummel, *A Winterthur Guide to American Chippendale Furniture: Middle Atlantic and Southern Colonies* (New York, 1976).

Jensen 1978
James P. Jensen, "Eighteenth and Early Nineteenth Century American Furniture at the Honolulu Academy of Arts," *The Magazine Antiques* (May 1978), 1086–1097.

Jobe and Kaye 1984
Brock Jobe and Myrna Kaye, *New England Furniture. The Colonial Era: Selections from the Society for the Preservation of New England Antiquities* (Boston, 1984).

Jones 1977
Karen M. Jones, "American Furniture in the Milwaukee Art Center," *The Magazine Antiques* (May 1977), 974–984.

Kane 1976
Patricia E. Kane, *300 Years of American Seating Furniture: Chairs and Beds from the Mabel Brandy Garvan and Other Collections at Yale University* (Boston, 1976).

Kindig 1978
Joseph K. Kindig, III, *The Philadelphia Chair, 1685–1785* [exh. cat., Historical Society of York County] (York, Pennsylvania 1978).

Kirk 1972
John T. Kirk, *American Chairs: Queen Anne and Chippendale* (New York, 1972).

Kirk 1982
John T. Kirk, *American Furniture and the British Tradition to 1830* (New York, 1982).

Levy and Levy 1984
Bernard and S. Dean Levy, *Opulence and Splendor. The New York Chair 1690–1830* [exh. cat., Bernard and S. Dean Levy] (New York, 1984).

Levy and Levy 1986
Bernard and S. Dean Levy, *Catalogue*, vol. 5 (New York, 1986).

Lockwood 1901
Luke Vincent Lockwood, *Colonial Furniture in America*, 2 vols. (New York, 1901, rev. eds. 1913, 1926, and 1951).

Loughlin 1978
David Loughlin, *The Case of Major Fanshawe's Chairs* (New York, 1978).

Lovell 1974
Margaretta M. Lovell, "Boston Block Front Furniture," in *Boston Furniture of the Eighteenth Century*, ed. W. M. Whitehill (Boston, Colonial Society of Massachusetts, 1974), 77–137.

Manwaring 1765
Robert Manwaring, *The Cabinet and Chair Maker's Real Friend and Companion* (London, 1765).

Martin 1985
Rebecca Martin, "Past Masters," *American Heritage* (February–March 1985), 36–47.

McClelland 1939
Nancy McClelland, *Duncan Phyfe and the English Regency, 1795–1830* (New York, 1939), reprint (New York, 1980).

MESDA Guide
Frank L. Horton, *The Museum of Early Southern Decorative Arts: A Collection of Southern Furniture, Paintings, Ceramics, Textiles, and Metalware* (Winston-Salem, North Carolina, Old Salem, Inc., 1979).

Miller 1937
Edgar G. Miller, Jr., *American Antique Furniture: A Book for Amateurs*, 2 vols. (Baltimore, 1937).

Miller 1956
V. Isabelle Miller, *Furniture by New York Cabinetmakers, 1650 to 1860* [exh. cat., Museum of the City of New York] (New York, 1956).

Monohan 1965
Eleanor Monohan, "Providence Cabinetmakers of the Eighteenth and Nineteenth Centuries," *The Magazine Antiques* (May 1965), 573–579.

Montgomery 1966
Charles F. Montgomery, *American Furniture: The Federal Period in the Henry Francis duPont Winterthur Museum* (New York, 1966).

Montgomery and Kane 1976
Charles F. Montgomery and Patricia E. Kane, eds., *American Art: 1750–1800, Towards Independence* [exh. cat., Yale University Art Gallery] (Boston, 1976).

Moses 1984
Michael Moses, *Master Craftsmen of Newport, the Townsends and Goddards* (Tenafly, New Jersey, 1984).

New York Price Book
The New York Book of Prices for Manufacturing Cabinet and Chair Work (New York, 1817).

Nutting 1928–1933
Wallace Nutting, *Furniture Treasury (Mostly of American Origin), All Periods of American Furniture with Some Foreign Examples in America, also American Hardware and Household Utensils*, 3 vols. (Framingham, Massachusetts, Old America Company, 1928–1933).

Ott 1965
Joseph K. Ott et al., *The John Brown House Loan Exhibition of Rhode Island Furniture, Including Some Notable Portraits, Chinese Export Porcelain and Other Items* [exh. cat., The Rhode Island Historical Society] (Providence, 1965).

Ott 1973
Joseph K. Ott, "John Innes Clark and His Family, Beautiful People in Providence," *Rhode Island History* 32, no. 4 (November 1973), 123-132.

Otto 1965
Celia Jackson Otto, *American Furniture of the Nineteenth Century* (New York, 1965).

Pearce 1962
Lorraine Waxman Pearce, *The White House—An Historic Guide* (Washington, 1962).

P-B 1955
Art Treasures Exhibition [exh. cat., Parke-Bernet Galleries] (New York, 1955).

Philadelphia Price Book
The Journeyman Cabinet and Chair Maker's Pennsylvania Book of Prices (Philadelphia, 1811, 1818, 1828).

PMA 1976
Philadelphia: Three Centuries of American Art [exh. cat., Philadelphia Museum of Art] (Philadelphia, 1976).

Randall 1965
Richard H. Randall, Jr., *American Furniture in the Museum of Fine Arts, Boston* (Boston, Museum of Fine Arts, 1965).

Randall 1966
Richard H. Randall, Jr., "The Finest American Senior Warden's Chair," *Connoisseur* 112 (April 1966), 286–287.

Randall 1974
Richard H. Randall, Jr., "William Randall, Boston Japanner," *The Magazine Antiques* (May 1974), 1127–1131.

Reifsnyder sale
Colonial Furniture: The Superb Collection of the Late Howard Reifsnyder [auct. cat., American Art Association] (New York, 1929).

Rice 1962
Norman S. Rice, *New York Furniture Before 1840 in the Collection of the Albany Institute of History and Art* [exh. cat., Albany Institute of History and Art] (Albany, New York, 1962).

Rodriguez - Roque 1984
Oswaldo Rodriguez - Roque, *American Furniture at Chipstone* (Madison, 1984).

Rollins 1984
Alexandra W. Rollins, "Furniture in the Collection of the Dietrich American Foundation," *The Magazine Antiques* (May 1984), 1100–1119.

A. Sack 1950
Albert Sack, *Fine Points of Furniture, Early American* (New York, 1950).

A. Sack 1985
Albert Sack, "Unique Masterpieces of American Furniture," *Art and Auction* (October 1985), 184–191.

I. Sack n.d.–1979
Israel Sack, *American Antiques from the Israel Sack Collection*, 7 vols. (Washington, n.d.–1979).

I. Sack 1984
Israel Sack, *Opportunities in American Antiques*, brochure no. 40.

Shearer 1788
Thomas Shearer, *The Cabinet-Maker's London Book of Prices* (London, 1788), rev. ed. *Shearer Furniture Designs from the Cabinet-Maker's . . .*, pref. and notes by Ralph Fastnedge (London, 1962).

Sheraton *Drawing Book* 1802
Thomas Sheraton, *The Cabinet-Maker and Upholsterer's Drawing-Book*, 3d rev. ed. (London, 1802), reprint, intro. Joseph Aronson (New York, 1972).

Sheraton *Cabinet Dictionary* 1803
Thomas Sheraton, *Cabinet Dictionary* (London, 1803), reprint, eds. Wilfred P. Cole and Charles F. Montgomery, 2 vols. (New York, 1970).

Sheraton *Encyclopedia* 1804–1806
Thomas Sheraton, *The Cabinet-Maker, Upholsterer and General Artist's Encyclopedia* (London, 1804–1806).

Sheraton *Household Furniture* 1812
Thomas Sheraton, *Designs for Household Furniture* (London, 1812).

Smith 1808
George Smith, *Collection of Designs for Household Furniture and Interior Decoration* (London, 1808), reprint, eds. Charles F. Montgomery and Benno M. Forman (New York, 1970).

Smith 1971
Robert C. Smith, "Finial Busts on Eighteenth-Century Philadelphia Furniture," *The Magazine Antiques* (December 1971), 900–905.

Smith 1973
Robert C. Smith, "A Philadelphia Desk and Bookcase from Chippendale's *Director*," *The Magazine Antiques* (January 1973), 129–135.

Snyder 1975
John J. Snyder, ed., *Philadelphia Furniture and Its Makers* (New York, 1975).

Stoneman 1959
Vernon C. Stoneman, *John and Thomas Seymour, Cabinet-Makers in Boston, 1794–1816* (Boston, 1959).

Stoneman 1965
Vernon C. Stoneman, *A Supplement to John and Thomas Seymour, Cabinet-Makers in Boston, 1794–1816* (Boston, 1965).

Swan 1931
Mabel M. Swan, "Where Elias Hasket Derby Bought His Furniture," *The Magazine Antiques* (November 1931), 280–282.

Swan 1937
Mabel M. Swan, "The Furniture of His Excellency John Hancock," *The Magazine Antiques* (March 1937), 119–121.

Talbott 1976
Page Talbott, "Boston Empire Furniture. Part II," *The Magazine Antiques* (May 1976), 1004–1013.

Tracy 1963
Berry B. Tracy and William H. Gerdts, *Classical America, 1815–1845* [exh. cat., The Newark Museum Association] (Newark, New Jersey, 1963).

Tracy 1970
Berry B. Tracy, Marilynn Johnson, et al., *19th Century America: Furniture and Other Decorative Arts. An Exhibition in Celebration of the Hundredth Anniversary of the Metropolitan Museum of Art* [exh. cat., The Metropolitan Museum of Art] (New York, 1970).

Tracy 1980
Berry B. Tracy, "Federal Furniture, Major Acquisitions and Special Loans," *Apollo* (May 1980), 362–369.

Tracy 1981
Berry B. Tracy, *Federal Furniture and Decorative Arts at Boscobel* (New York, 1981).

Venable 1986
Charles L. Venable, "Philadelphia Biedermeier: Germanic Craftsmen and Design in Philadelphia, 1820–1850" (Master's thesis, University of Delaware, 1986).

Vincent 1974
Gilbert T. Vincent, "The Bombé Furniture of Boston," in *Boston Furniture of the Eighteenth Century*, ed. W. M. Whitehill (Boston, Colonial Society of Massachusetts, 1974).

Wainwright 1964
Nicholas B. Wainwright, *Colonial Grandeur in Philadelphia* (Philadelphia, 1964).

Walcott 1928
William Stuart Walcott Jr., "Ten Important American Sideboards," *The Magazine Antiques* (December 1928), 516–517.

Warren 1975
David B. Warren, *Bayou Bend: American Furniture, Paintings and Silver from the Bayou Bend Collection* (Houston, The Museum of Fine Arts, 1975).

Weil 1979
Martin E. Weil, "A Cabinetmaker's Price Book," in *American Furniture and Its Makers. Winterthur Portfolio 13*, ed. Ian M. Quinby (Chicago, 1979), 175–192.

Weidman 1984
Gregory R. Weidman, *Furniture in Maryland 1740–1940* (Baltimore, 1984).

Whitehill 1974
Walter Muir Whitehill, ed., *Boston Furniture of the Eighteenth Century* (Boston, Colonial Society of Massachusetts, 1974).

Winchester 1959
Alice Winchester, *The Antiques Treasury of Furniture and Other Arts at Winterthur, Williamsburg, Sturbridge, Ford Museum, Cooperstown, Deerfield, Shelburne* (New York, 1959).

Winchester 1963
Alice Winchester, *Living with Antiques* (New York, 1963).

Woodhouse 1975
Samuel W. Woodhouse, Jr., "Benjamin Randolph of Philadelphia," in *Philadelphia Furniture and Its Makers*, ed. John H. Snyder, Jr. (New York, 1975), 33–43.

Zimmerman 1979
Philip D. Zimmerman, "A Methodological Study in the Identification of Some Important Philadelphia Furniture," in *American Furniture and Its Makers, Winterthur Portfolio 13*, ed. Ian M. Quinby (Chicago, 1979), 193–208.

Abbreviated Titles

Antiques	*The Magazine Antiques*
BMA	Baltimore Museum of Art
GSE	Loan Exhibition of Eighteenth and Nineteenth Century Furniture and Glass. . . . For the Benefit of the National Council of Girl Scouts, Inc. New York, 1929
KAF	Kaufman Americana Foundation
MESDA	Museum of Early Southern Decorative Arts
MFA	Museum of Fine Arts, Boston
MMA	The Metropolitan Museum of Art
P-B	Parke-Bernet
PMA	Philadelphia Museum of Art
SP-B	Sotheby Parke-Bernet
SPNEA	Society for the Preservation of New England Antiquities
*	woods analyzed by microanalysis

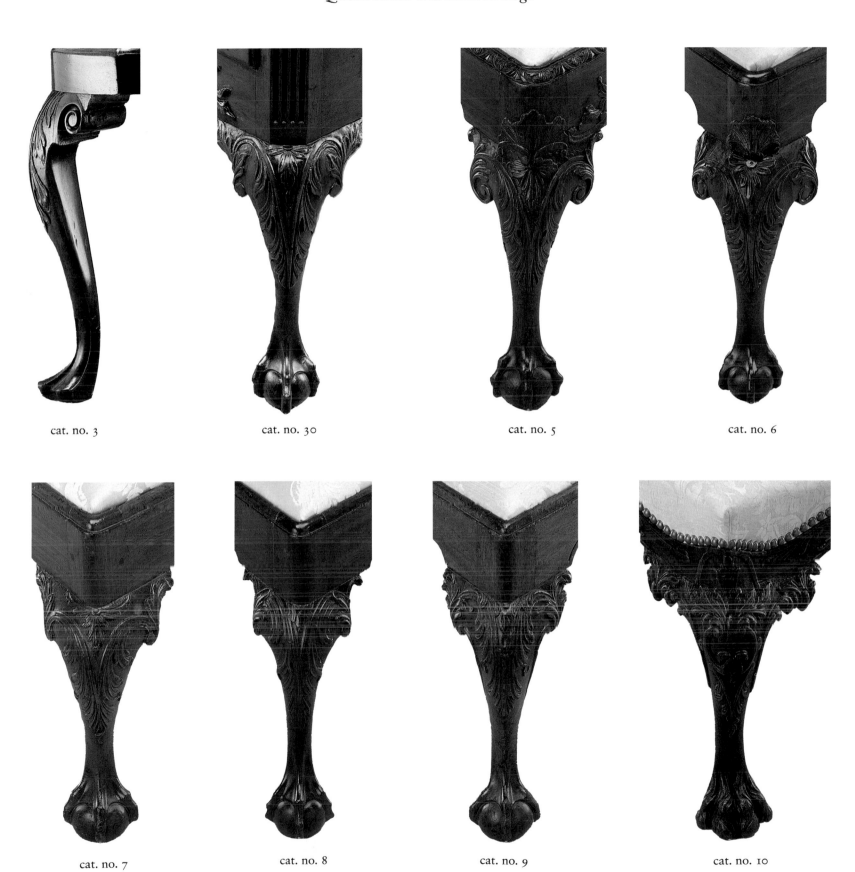

cat. no. 3

cat. no. 30

cat. no. 5

cat. no. 6

cat. no. 7

cat. no. 8

cat. no. 9

cat. no. 10

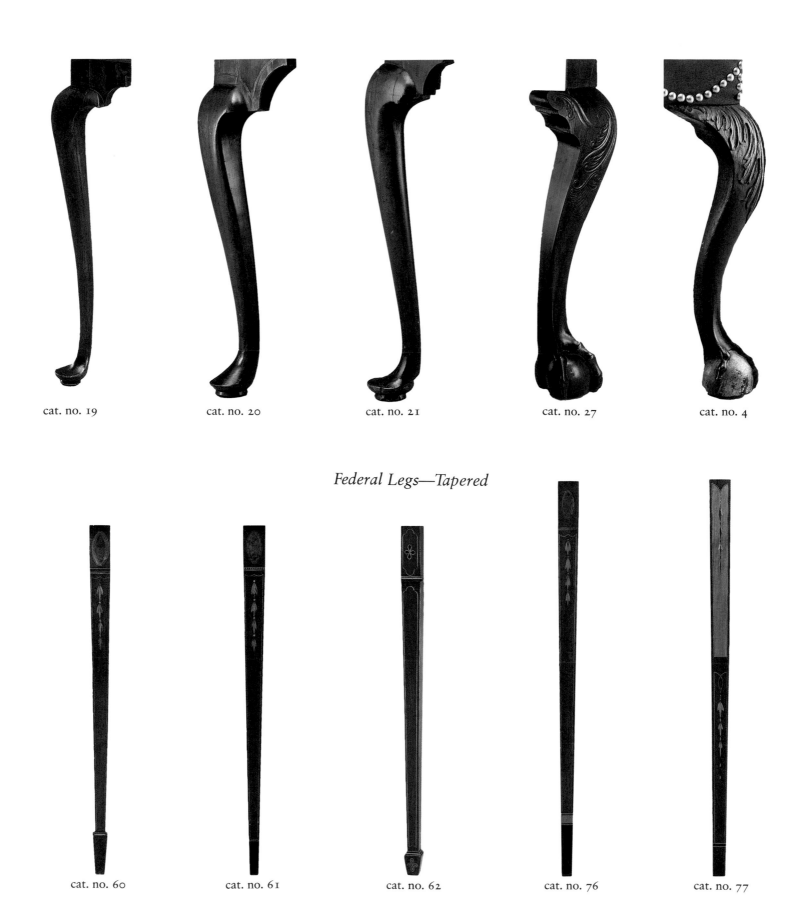

cat. no. 19   cat. no. 20   cat. no. 21   cat. no. 27   cat. no. 4

Federal Legs—Tapered

cat. no. 60   cat. no. 61   cat. no. 62   cat. no. 76   cat. no. 77

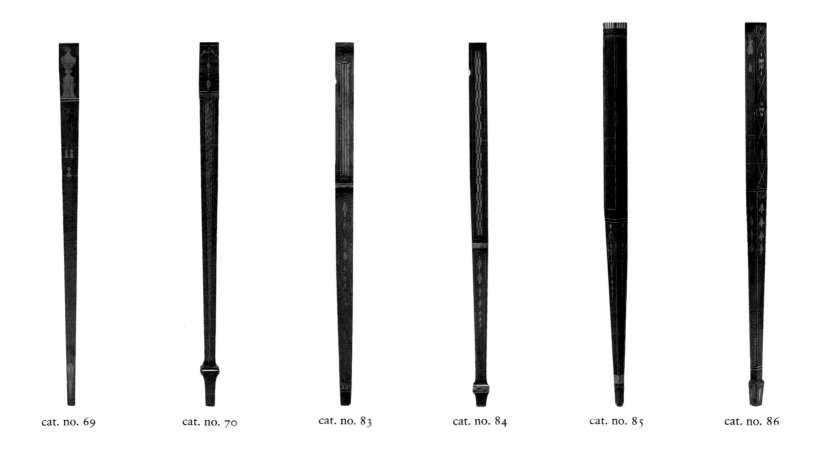

cat. no. 69   cat. no. 70   cat. no. 83   cat. no. 84   cat. no. 85   cat. no. 86

Federal Legs—Turned

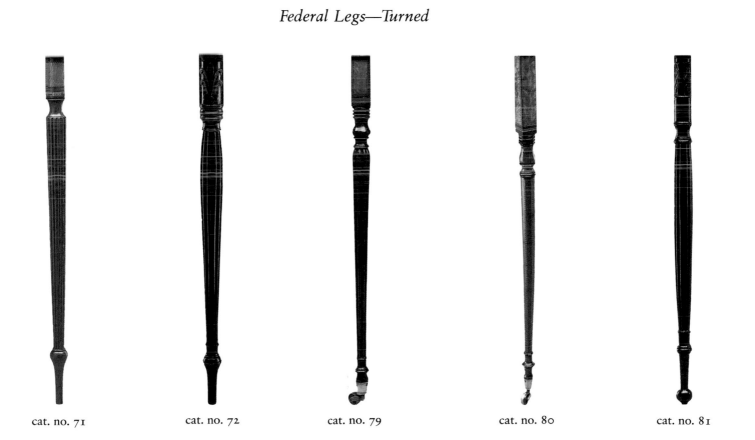

cat. no. 71   cat. no. 72   cat. no. 79   cat. no. 80   cat. no. 81

Unupholstered Frames

cat. no. 54

cat. no. 55

252

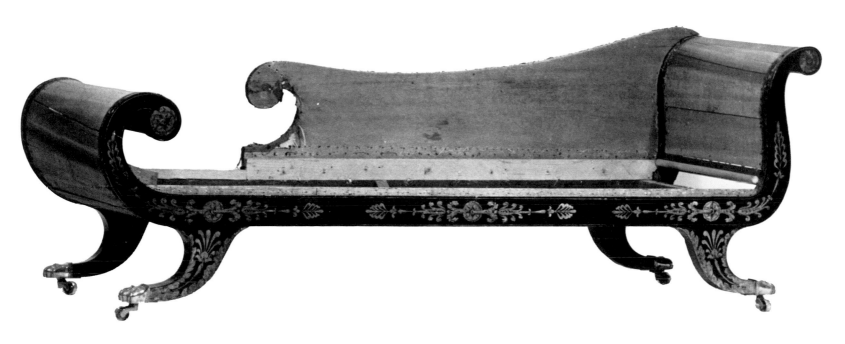

cat. no. 58

cat. no. 57

cat. no. 43

cat. no. 52

Glossary

flyleg

flyrail

inner rail

plinth

stationary leg

rule joint

leaf

fly leaf support

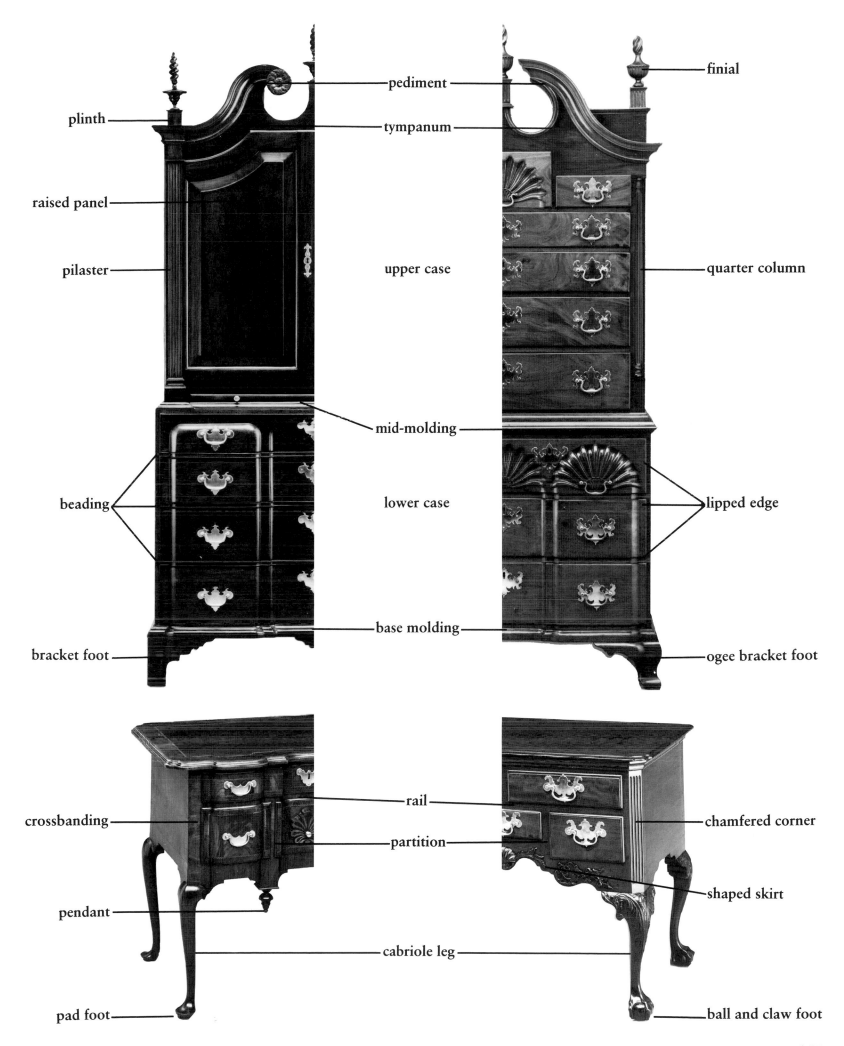

plinth

pediment

finial

raised panel

tympanum

pilaster

upper case

quarter column

mid-molding

beading

lower case

lipped edge

base molding

bracket foot

ogee bracket foot

crossbanding

rail

chamfered corner

partition

pendant

shaped skirt

cabriole leg

pad foot

ball and claw foot

257

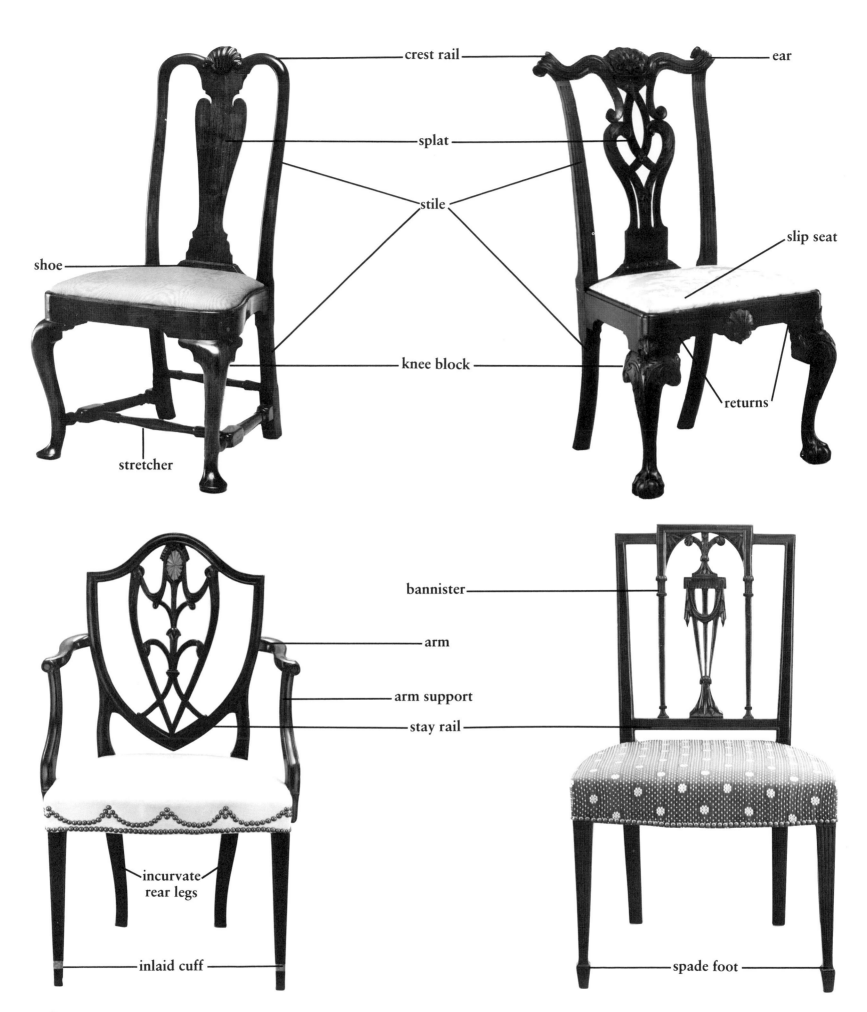

crest rail

ear

splat

stile

slip seat

shoe

knee block

returns

stretcher

bannister

arm

arm support

stay rail

incurvate
rear legs

inlaid cuff

spade foot

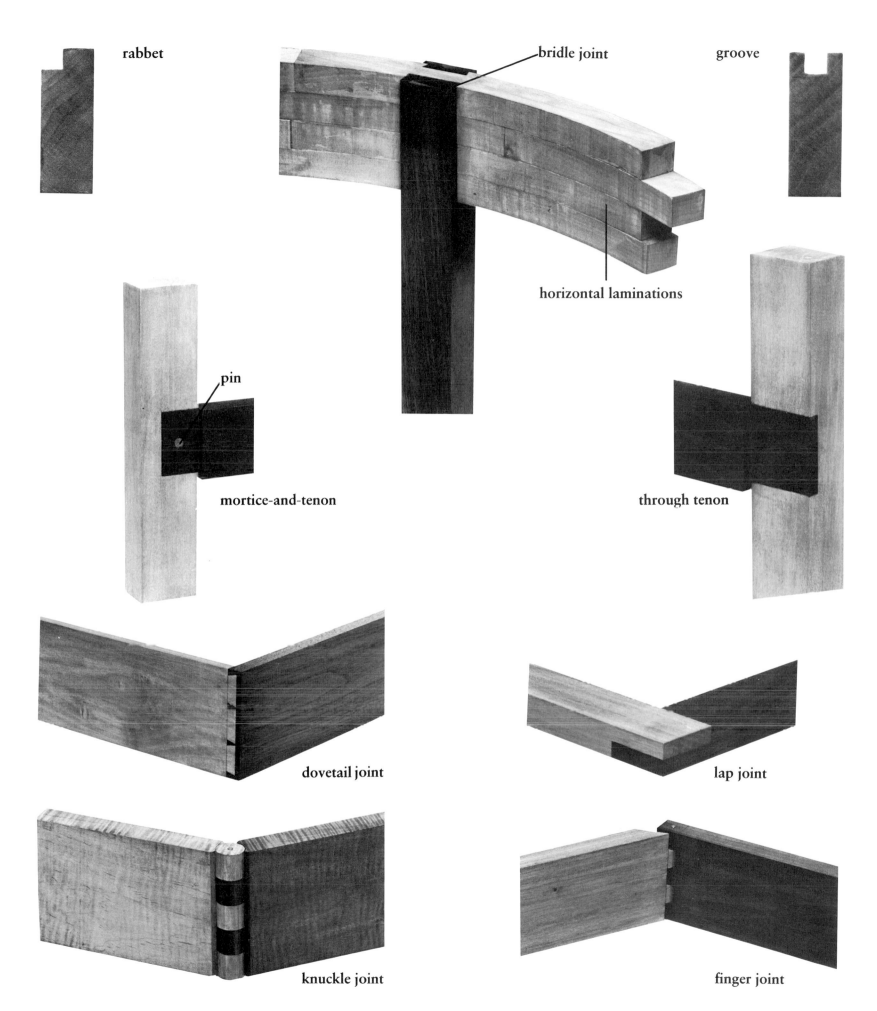

rabbet

bridle joint

groove

horizontal laminations

pin

mortice-and-tenon

through tenon

dovetail joint

lap joint

knuckle joint

finger joint